Present Perfect

Praise for *Present Perfect: The Essential Guide to Gift Giving*

"My reading *Present Perfect* is the best thing that ever happened to my wife!"
—Gregory Hansen

"*Present Perfect* is a must-have for gift givers everywhere."
—Barbara Bigelow

"*Present Perfect* is eye opening...from now on, people will only laugh at my gifts if I want them to!"
—Greg Wheeler

"A real treat...I'm sure I'll have as much fun giving gifts as I've had reading this book."
—Eleanor Umdenstock

"They say it's better to give than to receive. The Athays explain how to better give, and how to have fun doing it!"
—Alyce Croasdale

"*Present Perfect* makes a perfect present."
—The Authors

"Hallelujah! After 13 years in the making, the book is finally finished."
—Sherri's Mother

Present Perfect
The Essential Guide to Gift Giving

by Sherri & Larry Athay
Present Perfect Gift Consultants

Mobius Press • Hyde Park, UT • First Edition

Mobius Press
P.O. Box 8
Hyde Park, UT 84318-0008

Although exhaustive efforts have been made to ensure the accuracy of the information contained in this book, the authors and publisher assume no responsibility for errors, inaccuracies, omissions, or any other inconsistency herein. Furthermore, we are not responsible for injury caused by use or misuse of this product. Do not drive or operate heavy machinery while reading this book. Contents under pressure—do not puncture or incinerate. Highly flammable—keep away from open flame. No food or drink allowed beyond this point. Do not remove back cover—hazardous electrical shock may occur. Void where prohibited by law or otherwise restricted. No lifeguard on duty—swim at your own risk.

Copyright © 1996 by Sherri L. and Lawrence D. Athay

All rights reserved. No part of this book may be used or reproduced by any means, including photocopying and information storage and retrieval systems, without written permission of the publisher.

Graphics by Dean Stanton for Image Club

This book is available at quantity discounts when purchased in bulk.

First printing February 1996

Manufactured in the United States of America

ISBN 0-9650617-0-1

To gift givers everywhere

Contents

Contents ix
Acknowledgments xiii
Why This Book? xv
Preface xvii
How to Use This Book xix

Part One

Defining Perfect Presents 5
Characteristics of the Perfect Gift 7
So, Are You a Gifted Giver? 11
Creating a Personalized Gift Bio 18
Coming Out of the Gift Closet 21

Part Two

—A—

Anniversary Presents 27
Apartment Dwellers 30
Arts Lovers 32
Aviators 34

—B—

Baby Shower Presents 36
Backpackers and Hikers 38
Bar/Bat Mitzvah Presents 40
Birders 41
Birthday Presents 43
Boaters 47
Bookworms 49
Bowlers 52
Business Gifts 53

—C—

Campers 59
Car Buffs 61
Cats and the People That Love Them 63
Charitable and Philanthropic Gifts 64
Children—Infants 66

Children—Ages One to Two 67
Children—Ages Three to Four 68
Children—Ages Five to Eight 70
Children—Ages Nine to Twelve 71
Children's Magazines, Gifts of 73
Chocoholics 76
Christmas Presents 78
Clergymen 85
Collectors 86
Computer Buffs 88
Consumable Gifts 90
Cooks 91
Couch Potatoes 94
Country Western Fans 95
Cyclists 97

—D—

Dancers 98
Desk Dwellers 100
Dogs and the People That Love Them 101

—E—

Easter Presents 103
Employee Gifts 104
Environmentalists 108
Expectant Parents 110

—F—

Families 112
Farewell Presents 115
Father's Day Presents 116
Fishermen 121
Fitness Buffs 123
Flowers and Plants, Gifts of 125
Food or Candy, Gifts of 129
Friendship Gifts 131

—G—

Gardeners 133
Genealogists 135
Gift Baskets 136
Gift Certificates 139

Golfers 140
Graduation Presents 142
Grandparents 144

—H—

Hanukkah Presents 146
Have Everything, Those That 147
Heirloom Gifts 150
Home Office Dwellers 151
Homeowners 152
Horses and the People That Love Them 154
Hospitalized or Ill Persons 156
Hosts and Hostesses 158
Housewarming Presents 160
Humorous and Whimsical Gifts 162

—I—

Inexpensive Gifts 163
International Giving 168

—L—

Last-minute Gifts 170

—M—

Men 173
Military Persons and Veterans 177
Money, Gifts of 179
Mother's Day Presents 183
Music Lovers 186

—N—

New Neighbors 188
New Year's Presents 189
Nurses 191
Nursing Home Residents 193

—O—

Outdoor Cooks 195

—P—

Party Favors 196

Photographers 198
Photographs, Gifts of 199
Physical Disabilities, People with 200

—R—

Retirement Presents/Retirees 202
Romantic Presents 203
Runners and Walkers 207

—S—

Self, Gifts of 208
Seniors 212
Snow Sporters 215
Sports Fans 216
St. Patrick's Day Presents 220
Star Gazers 221
Students 223

—T—

Teachers 225
Teens 227
Tennis Buffs 230
Travelers 232

—V—

Valentine's Day Presents 237

—W—

Water Sports Enthusiasts 240
Wedding Presents 241
Wedding Shower Theme Gifts 247
Wedding Registries 249
Wedding Attendants, Presents to 251
White Elephant Gifts 252
Women 254
Workplace Gift Exchanges 258

Appendix

Personalized Gift Bio Forms 265

Acknowledgments

For conceptual, professional, and moral support we feel a deep sense of gratitude

- to Ellen Russell for the birthday party invitation that was the genesis for this book and related projects;

- to Tom McNiven, president of Discovery Research Group, for his extremely generous and meaningful contribution of the nationwide gift-preferences poll referenced throughout this book;

- to the countless people that have shared gift-giving anecdotes, participated in our workshops, and responded to our surveys, for their candor and insightful input;

- to our dear friends and family for their love and encouragement over the years, especially Kathryn and Kent Colton, Karan and David Duncan, Victoria Radford, our brothers and sisters, and our parents;

- to our children, three of our most precious gifts, for assuming extra responsibilities during our countless hours of research, writing, and design;

- to Julie Wheeler and Gregory Hansen for their invaluable personal and professional assistance in bringing the book to fruition;

- to Christine B. Needham, editor, Special Sections Advantage, Los Angeles Times Syndicate, for her interest and support;

- to our editor, Kristen Black, for her editorial suggestions and careful attention to detail; and

- to Tom Kupka, Layne Robison, Mike Cooper, and others at Banta-Information Services Group for their courteous and professional handling of all printing details.

Why This Book?

Why a guide to gift giving?

    a.   Virtually everyone gives gifts.

    b.   Almost everyone would like to know how to be a better gift giver and how to make gift giving easier and more fun.

    c.   Each season brings a multitude of gift-giving dilemmas.

    (d.)   All of the above.

Virtually everyone gives gifts—homemakers, construction workers, sports heroes, grandparents, business men and women, students, public officials, diplomats. And, while most people enjoy doing so, fewer than 35 percent of those we polled feel they are creative gift givers.

We have surveyed and interviewed hundreds of individuals on the subject of gift giving. The data reveal that women and men (surprise!?) want a single source of information on this subject. Over 95 percent of the respondents in one particular study said they would benefit from such a book as *Present Perfect*.

Each season brings a multitude of gift-giving dilemmas. Sprinkled between the holidays are weddings, baby showers, anniversaries, birthdays, bar mitzvahs, graduations, retirements, promotions, and other occasions. This book is a resource that will be used all year round.

Preface

The search for a single gift over a decade ago launched the most extensive research project of our lives. Larry informed Sherri that we had been invited to a birthday party for one of the managers at his office...and would she please help select an appropriate gift for her. *Why not? After all, there must be a publication somewhere,* Sherri thought, *with sound advice on gift-giving etiquette and mile-long lists of proper gifts for people I've never met.*

It was the futile search for such a primer that compelled us to "write the book" on gift giving. We introduce this book to you, not as ones who were born with the perfect present in hand, but as two who have lived and breathed the subject of gift giving for the past 13 years. We've learned a good deal in this time and hope you'll be inspired and amused as you read this book. We look forward to hearing from you. (See page 277 for information on how to get in touch with us).

—Sherri & Larry Athay
Hyde Park, Utah

How to Use This Book

This book is written *to* givers, but it is primarily *about* recipients. Hence we've organized our findings in a framework designed to help givers focus on the wants, interests, passions, and desires of recipients—with special care given to the relationship and other circumstances attending specific gift presentations. We hope you'll find this book highly informative, fun to read, fast and easy to use, and invaluable for all your gift-giving situations.

Part One shares what we've learned over the years about the basics of gift giving. Included are a definition of the "perfect present," an exercise for assessing your strengths and weaknesses as a giver, the seven characteristics common to the best gifts, suggestions for creating a personalized gift bio, and tips for creating and maintaining a gift closet.

Part Two is filled with thousands of gift ideas, conveniently arranged alphabetically by interests, occasions, holidays, circumstances, and gift categories (i.e., Arts Lovers, Baby Shower Presents, Cooks, Father's Day Presents, Gardeners, Hospitalized or Ill Persons, Gifts of Money). Cross references tell you where to look for even more gift ideas. Because the book is intended to be used as a reference guide, rather than read cover to cover, some gift ideas are mentioned in more than one section.

Toll-free numbers are listed for many of the vendors mentioned in the book. When 800 numbers are not available, area codes, phone numbers, addresses, and—in some cases—fax numbers are given. We would like to hear from you concerning your experiences with vendors referenced in the book. Most of them have been highly recommended to us. Although we cannot accept responsibility for their actions, we would like to know how you are treated by them. Information about how to contact us appears on page 277.

Throughout the book, room has been left on each page to add your own thoughts or gift ideas. In addition, illustrations and sidebars of several flavors spice the overall content. While they may not directly relate to the adjacent text, we hope they'll inform and amuse. Regular sidebar categories include:

- **Present Danger!** For obvious reasons, there are some gifts that should never be given—a scale to the wife who no longer fits into her wedding dress, cheese to a person who lives in Wisconsin, a "little something" to your secretary from the lingerie catalog. On second thought, considering the number of such gifts that are received, maybe the reasons are not so obvious—so we've pointed out a few of them in "Present Danger!" sidebars.

- **It's a Wrap!** Gift wrapping can be a revelation or a diversion, an invitation or an obstacle. Special touches in wrapping and embellishing presents reflect the thought and care you put into your selections. Make your gift presentations more memorable by incorporating the easy, innovative, and just-plain-fun ideas listed in "It's a Wrap!" sidebars.

- **Consider This.** Zeroing in on the perfect gift requires sensitivity, thoughtfulness, and an understanding of the recipient's needs, interests, and wants. In conjunction with the Personalized Gift Bio described on page 18, "Consider This" sidebars will help you make perfect gift choices for any recipient—for any occasion.

- **Best/Worst.** Everywhere we go, we ask people, "What is one of the best gifts you have ever received?" and "What is one of the worst gifts you have ever received?" The answers range from heartwarming to inspiring and from humorous to disastrous. Several of the answers appear in "Best/Worst" sidebars. In some cases, the names have been changed to protect the innocent (and the guilty).

- **Celebrate!** Ever see something that strikes you as just the right gift and then realize it's months before the next gift-giving occasion? Or maybe you're just a spontaneous kind of guy. "Celebrate!" sidebars feature obscure, whimsical, and under-celebrated occasions which make great excuses for gift giving (not that you need an excuse). Make up your own reasons to celebrate, or peruse *Chase's Annual Events* and other reference books for such events as Bachelor's Day, Eat What You Want Day, Aardvark Week, or International Drum Month.

- **Shopping Tips.** Some people are born to shop. Others consider shopping an inevitable burden to be borne. Mall marauders and couch potatoes alike will find no-nonsense tactics for beating the crowds, the frenzy, and the frustration of tracking down the perfect gift in "Shopping Tips" sidebars.

- **What Gives?** Do you have a great gift idea or anecdote you would be willing to share? Are there any interest groups for which you would like to see gifts listed in future editions of *Present Perfect*? We have scattered "What Gives?" sidebars throughout the book to encourage reader feedback. We hope you'll let us know what's on your mind. See page 277 for details about how to get in touch with us.

Results of a nationwide gift-preferences poll conducted for us by Discovery Research Group in Salt Lake City, Utah are highlighted throughout *Present Perfect*. Eight hundred men and women across the country rated gifts from 16 categories on a scale of 1 to 5 (1 being the least preferred, 5 being the most preferred). The following chart shows a ranking, by gender, of the overall scores. Additional "Survey Scoops!" can be found in the sections about *Bookworms, Father's Day Presents, Flowers and Plants, Men, Money, Sports Fans, Travelers,* and *Women.*

what do we WANT?

Preferences for gifts by gender, on a scale of 1 being least preferred and 5 being most preferred.

MEN

rank	gift	total
1	Money	4.24
2	Travel	3.81
3	Audio/Video	3.56
4	Tools	3.35
5	Sports equipment	3.30
6	Clothing	3.19
7	Books	3.03
8	Home accessories	2.75
9	Photographs	2.71
10	Kitchen gadgets and appliances	2.50
11	Jewelry	2.46
12	Magazine subscriptions	2.42
13	Games	2.37
14	Fragrance	2.34
15	Food or candy	2.21
16	Flowers and plants	2.17

WOMEN

rank	gift	total
1	Money	4.17
2	Travel	3.79
3	Clothing	3.64
4	Jewelry	3.41
5	Flowers and plants	3.37
6	Books	3.31
7	Photographs	3.28
8	Home accessories	3.20
9	Audio/Video	2.98
10	Fragrance	2.97
11	Kitchen gadgets and appliances	2.96
12	Food or candy	2.34
13	Magazine subscriptions	2.15
14	Games	2.14
15	Sports equipment	2.08
16	Tools	1.87

Source: Discovery Research Group/Present Perfect Survey

Present Perfect

Part One

Defining Perfect Presents

Characteristics of the Perfect Gift

So, Are You a Gifted Giver?

Creating a Personalized Gift Bio

Coming Out of the Gift Closet

Defining Perfect Presents

The perfect present. That seemingly elusive, know-it-when-we-see-it, nothing-else-will-do, guaranteed-to-please embodiment of our sentiment. What single object or gesture can convey the sum of our emotion? And, what transforms an item or gesture into the perfect present—the present to accompany and enhance the verbal expression of our feelings?

Think back on the most memorable gifts you've received. Why do these particular gifts stand out? Perhaps they revealed how intimately you were known by the giver. Maybe they expressed an understanding of what would bring you pleasure, stir an emotion, or evoke a sentiment. Such gifts cultivate, enhance, or nurture relationships between the giver and the recipient. This point is eloquently illustrated in a letter written to us by Bruce Christensen when he was president of the Public Broadcasting System (PBS).

> Among the most memorable gifts I've received are a Mont Blanc diplomat fountain pen and a photograph. Both were presents from the same person. The cost of each gift was about the same, but their value as a reminder of a deep and treasured friendship has increased as the years have passed.
>
> Much of my life's work has been spent writing. Every note, letter, check, or memo written with the pen reminds me of friendship. My pen is an instrument of expression for me, while speaking to me. It was, indeed, an ideal gift.
>
> The photograph is an Ansel Adams print titled "Moon Rises Over the Hernandez." Purchased and given many years ago when such prints could be had for a modest price, it was a token of shared professional goals and aspirations between two friends

---

Best/Worst

Best: A jewelry box made by my husband

Worst: Knick-knacks

RANDIE C.

Defining Perfect Presents

> ### Right in Our Backyard
>
> "When we lived in Thailand, our house was next to a canal which was used as a Thai highway. Underneath a nearby bridge lived a large family. One Christmas, we took our children to visit the family and to distribute food, clothing, and other gifts. Our children were wide-eyed to think that anyone could live in such conditions—especially only a few feet from our own house. The Thai children were wide-eyed that foreigners would actually visit their home—an area partitioned off by wood and cloth—and bring them gifts. It was a memorable experience."
>
> —Ruth R.

struggling to succeed. It was the focus of many, many conversations about the lighting, the detail, and wonderment at the extraordinary talent that captured that photograph. A matched print hangs in my friend's office. Mine hangs in the dining room where guests always ask about it and I have an excuse to tell them about the shared dreams for professional success that this photograph represents.

My experience with these two treasured gifts leads me to observe that a memorable gift should be seen often, reminding the recipient of the giver. In time, such gifts become the icons of friendship.

So, is there a straightforward definition of the perfect present? *The American Heritage Dictionary* defines the words perfect and present (gift) as follows:

Perfect (pur'fikt) adj. 1. Lacking nothing essential to the whole; complete. 2. Without defect; flawless. 3. Excellent and delightful in all respects.

Present (prez'ənt) n. 1. Something that is bestowed voluntarily and without compensation. An offering, token, or remembrance.

Hence, the following extrapolation:

Perfect present (pur'fikt prez'ənt). 1. An excellent and delightful, voluntary, and uncompensated bestowal of a flawless and complete offering, token, or remembrance.

Simple enough? Probably not. One reason it's often difficult to *find* the perfect gift is because it's almost impossible to *define* it. The definition varies with respect to expectations, occasions, needs, interests, and relationships between givers and recipients. The perfect gift for one may produce disastrous

Defining Perfect Presents • Characteristics of the Perfect Gift

or embarrassing results when given to another. The same box of chocolate truffles symbolizing pure indulgence to a self-declared chocoholic may represent an act of sabotage to one resolutely on his or her way to a new waist size.

P*resent Perfect: The Essential Guide to Gift Giving* will assist you in defining pur'fikt prez'ants within a framework of changing circumstances and expectations.

> **Snapshots**
>
> Like a treasured photograph, the perfect gift can say "remember when?"

Characteristics of the Perfect Gift

There is, of course, no single gift that is perfect for everyone, everywhere, for every occasion. If such a gift existed, it wouldn't be long before everyone had more of them than they could possibly want. To illustrate, consider the following shameless example: Although WE think *Present Perfect—The Essential Guide to Gift Giving* is the ideal gift for everyone who gives gifts (which is, in essence, just about every man, woman, and child on the planet), we have to admit that few people will require more than one copy for their personal use. So, once you've given a copy to everyone on your gift list, and they to theirs, and so on down the gift chain, then what? Perhaps the new and expanded edition of *Present Perfect* will be available, in which case you could start the process all over again. (We warned you this would be a shameless example.) If not, you may conclude, as we did long ago, that no gift is perfect for everyone, everywhere, for every occasion. We have observed, however, that the best gifts share seven common characteristics: appropriateness, perceptiveness, selflessness, generosity, indulgence, surprise, and evo-

Characteristics of the Perfect Gift

cation. While volumes could be written about each of these, we have succinctly condensed our observations in the paragraphs below. (You're welcome!)

Appropriateness. The perfect gift is fitting for the occasion *and* the relationship. A sizzling love letter to your spouse for your twentieth anniversary would tell her your romance is still hot! A treadmill to a health and fitness buff for Valentine's Day would let him know your heart is in the right place and that you support his second passion. A hundred dollars to your distant nephew, who you didn't know existed before you received a graduation announcement, would allow him the option of applying your graduation gift to his car loan, college education, or investment portfolio. A tin of homemade Christmas cookies to a coworker would be a thoughtful, innocuous gesture.

Now, just for fun, let's mix things up a little and see what *could* happen. A sizzling love letter to a coworker could cost you your job. A tin of homemade Christmas cookies to a health and fitness buff for Valentine's Day would give him cause to wonder if you knew anything about his health concerns, or what day it was. A hundred dollars to your spouse for your twentieth anniversary might suggest that—after all these years—you still don't know what would please her, don't care what would please her, or won't take the time to find something that would please her. And finally, the graduation of your long-lost nephew probably would not warrant such a significant gift as a treadmill. Furthermore, not knowing of his interests, such a gift could be very insulting. What if he's a confirmed couch potato?

Perceptiveness. Have you ever received a gift that makes you wonder if you are known by the giver? *"Doesn't he know I prefer silver rather than gold jew-*

Power-less

"I learned one thing early in my marriage: Gifts to my wife should not have electrical cords attached to them."

—Michael W.

Characteristics of the Perfect Gift

elry? natural fibers to polyester? wildflowers to roses?" "Isn't it obvious, after all these anniversaries, that the kitchen-gadget-of-the-year is not a fitting present?" The perfect gift reflects the giver's attentiveness to the tastes and preferences of the recipient. In essence, it's a compliment that says, "When I saw this, I couldn't help but think of you!"

Selflessness. Longfellow said, "The greatest grace of a gift, perhaps, is that it anticipates and admits of no return." The perfect gift reveals that the giver's only desire is to please the recipient—expecting nothing in return. This "no-return" policy includes any satisfaction the giver anticipates from the observations of others about the extravagance of the gift *or* the generosity of the giver. For example, if a man gives his wife a stunning piece of jewelry *only* to impress his associates at the upcoming holiday reception, to whom is he really giving the gift?

Generosity. Two young boys went weeks without school lunch to give their mother a strand of pearls. Not old enough to earn a wage, the resourceful boys exercised what appeared to be their only option for obtaining the necessary funds. Their sacrifice and generosity immortalized the gift. Fortunately, in most cases the appropriate degree of generosity can be exercised without squirreling away one's lunch money. Resource-*full* gifts reveal how special the recipient is to the giver. Often, endowments of the giver's time, effort, or creativity are the most generous and memorable characteristics of a gift. Just remember to balance your generosity with the nature of the relationship and the occasion. Too much of a good thing could make the recipient feel obliged, confused, or otherwise uncomfortable.

> **I Get the Message**
>
> A gift serves as a symbol to reinforce the giver's message—"I love you," "Congratulations," "Thank you," "You are special to me," "I'm sorry."

Characteristics of the Perfect Gift

Indulgence. It pampers, it humors, it appeases, it satisfies—the perfect gift says there is something extraordinary about the recipient in the eyes of the giver. After all, doesn't the gift of a lawn mower to Dad send a very different message than the gift of a year's contract for lawn service? The former emphasizes his utility in terms of his labor—and thus his *ordinariness*. The latter shows you value his leisure—and thus his *specialness*. A good question to ask when choosing a gift is, "Will this gift make the recipient feel loved? unique? adored? admired? or just like everybody else?"

Surprise! Do you want to make her eyes widen? make his chin drop? render her speechless? The perfect gift—like the perfect game plan—is a surprise. Careful and discreet planning can catch even the most suspecting recipient off guard or turn an anticipated gift into one that dumfounds. Try these tactics for perfect sneak attacks.

- Give gifts spontaneously. Don't wait for a birthday, anniversary, or other special occasion. Why not give gifts because it's raining, because she just finished reading *War and Peace*, or because his favorite team just won the World Series?

- Give gifts the recipient does not expect. When they must be requested, gifts lose their surprise value. Since the perceptive giver does not need to be told what the recipient wants, the gift chosen is much more likely to be a surprise. From the 15-years-of-kitchen-gadgets husband, a surprise may constitute any gift that is *not* a kitchen gadget.

- Present gifts cleverly. Clever packaging or presentations can heighten suspense and make gift exchanges more memorable. Who could forget the glistening engagement ring wrapped in a bouquet of long-stemmed roses, especially when the

---

Best/Worst

Best: A costume, complete with top hat, cane, and ruffled shirt—because it was a total surprise

Worst: Tasteless adult bric-a-brac—a roll of bathroom tissue with gross messages, trinkets shaped like body parts

—Michael C.

Characteristics of the Perfect Gift • So, Are You a Gifted Giver?

memory is evoked each year with the delivery of a similar bouquet to commemorate the anniversary of the day she said "Yes"? Wouldn't the very scent of roses trigger the memory—for both of you?

Evocation. The moment of truth in any gift exchange comes when the recipient responds to the giver's gesture—the audible gasp, the spontaneous smile, the bittersweet or joyful tears, the loss for words to express the feeling of being completely understood by the giver. The perfect gift moves the recipient. It elicits an emotional response or evokes a sentiment. The enthusiasm—or lack thereof—in the recipient's declaration, "You really shouldn't have!" generally leaves no doubt as to whether the giver has succeeded in finding a perfect gift or whether her efforts could have been better directed.

So, Are You a Gifted Giver?

Some people seem to have an instinct for creatively expressing their feelings through giving. Others find it difficult to convey their sentiments in the form of gifts. A variety of attitudes, practices, and motivations influence gift giving and have direct impact on the messages conveyed through gifts.

Examining your motives and understanding the messages your gifts convey can improve your "giftedness" as a giver. Just for fun, complete the sentences or answer the questions on the next few pages by circling the letter preceding the response that MOST ACCURATELY describes your behavior or feelings. Then, go to page 16 to discover which of four basic profiles best describes you as a giver.

So, Are You a Gifted Giver?

> ### Reasons for Giving
>
> Which of the following reasons most accurately describes why you usually give gifts?
>
> To please the recipient: 47%
>
> Because you like to give gifts: 42%
>
> Because it is expected: 9%
>
> To receive gifts in return: 3%
>
> SOURCE: DISCOVERY RESEARCH GROUP/PRESENT PERFECT SURVEY

1. **The best reason for giving gifts is**
   a. to do the appropriate thing.
   b. to please others.
   c. to make a favorable impression on others.
   d. to receive gifts in return.

2. **When it comes to the cost of a gift,**
   a. money is no object.
   b. I stay within my limits, buying as nice a gift as I can afford.
   c. I spend as little as possible to get something that will do.
   d. I sometimes spend more than I feel comfortable with, often regretting it later.

3. **I usually give gifts that**
   a. will make a good impression.
   b. do not cost much.
   c. are useful and practical.
   d. a person will enjoy but may not buy for himself or herself.

4. **Which of the following factors do you feel has had the most influence on your gift-giving attitudes and habits?**
   a. Family traditions
   b. Peer pressure and the expectations of others
   c. Social customs
   d. Financial constraints

5. **I feel that a gift given by a group of people is**
   a. a good idea because a single item of greater value can be given.
   b. not as personal as an individual gift.
   c. a great way to save money.
   d. not a good way to impress others.

So, Are You a Gifted Giver?

6. When presenting a gift,
   a. I do so with confidence that the recipient will like it because I have good taste.
   b. I suggest it may be returned if it is not satisfactory.
   c. I smile and say, "I hope you like it."
   d. I apologize, saying, "I was going to give something else, but couldn't find it, didn't know what size...."

7. If someone returned a gift I purchased for them,
   a. I would be highly offended, because I have impeccable taste.
   b. I wouldn't care because I don't put much time and thought into gift selections anyway.
   c. I would be hurt because the gift I selected was not satisfactory.
   d. I wouldn't mind because I prefer they have something with which they will be happy.

8. When it comes to giving gifts at the office,
   a. I feel that a collection should be taken to purchase a nice group gift.
   b. I feel it should not be done.
   c. I feel the right gift may be just the thing to insure a promotion, a raise, or cooperation.
   d. I prefer to select my own appropriate gift.

9. When it comes to gift wrapping,
   a. I wrap gifts myself.
   b. I generally have gifts wrapped at the store where they were purchased.
   c. I try to wrap gifts in a box from an expensive department or specialty store other than where they were purchased.
   d. I usually give unwrapped gifts.

Where to Look for Great Gifts

✔ Community bulletin boards

✔ Adult education programs

✔ *The Yellow Pages*

✔ Catalogs

✔ Magazines

✔ Newspaper ads

✔ Weekend classifieds

✔ City magazines

✔ Parks and recreation departments

✔ Country clubs

✔ Commerce department

✔ Public libraries

✔ Museum gift shops and catalogs

So, Are You a Gifted Giver?

> **What's the Occasion?**
>
> At times, the selection of an appropriate gift is simplified or even suggested by an occasion—a housewarming or a themed bridal shower, for example.

10. I prefer to
   a. present gifts at a time I can be alone with the recipient when they open them.
   b. present my gifts in front of a group and have the recipient unwrap them in the presence of others.
   c. make gift-giving presentations as inconspicuous as possible.
   d. present my gifts at an appropriate time and place, allowing the recipient to open them when he or she desires.

11. Do you enjoy receiving gifts?
   a. No, because when someone gives me a gift, I then feel obligated to reciprocate.
   b. Yes, because gifts are a good indication of what others think of me.
   c. No, because receiving gifts makes me uncomfortable and I am not always sure how to respond.
   d. Generally, if they are appropriate for the occasion and the relationship, and the giver is sincere.

12. How do you feel about giving money as a gift?
   a. Giving gifts of money is not a good way to show your creativity and originality.
   b. Giving gifts of money is probably inappropriate, but giving gifts of money eliminates the dilemma of deciding what to give and allows the recipient to purchase what she wants.
   c. Giving gifts of money is generally acceptable if a person has indicated a need or desire for gifts or cash.
   d. Giving gifts of money is okay if you can't think of anything else to give.

So, Are You a Gifted Giver?

13. **How do you feel about handmade gifts?**
    a. Handmade gifts are great if you can't afford to buy something.
    b. Handmade gifts are not appropriate under any circumstances.
    c. Handmade gifts are the best type of gifts because the giver is giving a part of himself or herself.
    d. Handmade gifts are appropriate only for close friends and family members whose tastes you are familiar with.

14. **How much time and thought do you put into selecting a gift?**
    a. I usually get something that the recipient has requested to ensure a positive response.
    b. I spend as little time as possible.
    c. I like to spend a considerable amount of time so I can take into account the likes and interests of others.
    d. I usually put off buying gifts until the last minute and end up purchasing the first thing that will do.

15. **When it comes to holiday gift giving,**
    a. I feel it is an excellent time to enjoy the spirit of giving.
    b. I feel that things are much too commercialized.
    c. I exchange gifts with family members and keep items on hand to give to friends that bring an unexpected gift.
    d. I feel it is a great time to improve relationships by giving carefully calculated gifts.

> **Best/Worst**
>
> Best: Handmade items and gifts of time
>
> Worst: Clothes that don't fit
>
> —HELENA R.

So, Are You a Gifted Giver?

What's Your Motive?

The motivations for giving gifts seem obvious: to give or receive pleasure, and to fulfill or create an obligation. Obviously, this is an oversimplification. A giver's motives are not always clear, nor do they generally fit neatly into a single classification.

16. **What do you consider appropriate thanks for a gift?**
    a. A verbal thank you is enough. Writing notes is a nuisance.
    b. If you really want to impress someone, both verbal and written thanks are necessary.
    c. A preprinted thank-you card with my signature is appropriate.
    d. A handwritten note should be sent as soon as possible after the gift is received.

Quiz Key

On the lines to the right, enter the number of points that corresponds to your response for each question. For example, response "C" to question 1 is worth 4 points. Add the points to arrive at your total score. Then see the profiles on the next two pages.

1	A(2)	B(3)	C(4)	D(1)	_____
2	A(4)	B(3)	C(1)	D(2)	_____
3	A(4)	B(1)	C(2)	D(3)	_____
4	A(3)	B(4)	C(2)	D(1)	_____
5	A(2)	B(3)	C(1)	D(4)	_____
6	A(4)	B(1)	C(3)	D(2)	_____
7	A(4)	B(1)	C(2)	D(3)	_____
8	A(2)	B(1)	C(4)	D(3)	_____
9	A(3)	B(2)	C(4)	D(1)	_____
10	A(2)	B(4)	C(1)	D(3)	_____
11	A(1)	B(4)	C(2)	D(3)	_____
12	A(4)	B(2)	C(3)	D(1)	_____
13	A(1)	B(4)	C(3)	D(2)	_____
14	A(4)	B(1)	C(3)	D(2)	_____
15	A(3)	B(1)	C(2)	D(4)	_____
16	A(1)	B(4)	C(2)	D(3)	_____
				Total	_____

So, Are You a Gifted Giver?

Giver Profiles

- **Profile A (16—27 points).** Avoiding gift-giving occasions whenever possible, you give just enough to get by when the exchange of gifts seems inevitable. Well, take heart. Because presents are never obligatory, you needn't swell with resentment when the next wedding, graduation, or birth announcement arrives. Gift giving will be more enjoyable if you focus on giving spontaneously to those individuals you care most about and for the occasions in which you have a genuine interest.

- **Profile B (28—39 points).** Your heart is in the right place and your gift giving is generally motivated by a desire to do the correct thing (although you are not always sure just what that is). Having become somewhat mechanical in the process of gift giving, your gifts may be predictable and unimaginative. At times, you feel that your gift giving is stifled by financial limitations. Try to be more resourceful and creative and you will be well on your way to becoming a great gift giver.

- **Profile C (40—51 points).** As a gift giver, you are generous within your means and put a lot of time and thought into your gift selections. You feel gift giving is just another way to creatively express your feelings for others. Your gifts are carefully selected and presented at just the right time. They are often accompanied by a personal note. Because your gifts reflect an attentiveness to the needs and desires of others, many consider you to be a perfect gift giver.

- **Profile D (52—64 points).** You may be trying too hard to impress others through giving and often spend more than you can afford, later regretting it. When gifts are given with strings attached, they could be interpreted as manipulative in nature. Because your true feelings are seldom expressed in your gifts, others may not be sure what gifts from

> **Why Give?**
>
> Historically, gifts have been given for a variety of reasons: to appease the gods, to win the favor of fair maidens, to subdue an enemy.

you mean. If you really want to make an impression on others through gift giving, choose presents sincerely and with consideration for the interests of the recipient.

Creating a Personalized Gift Bio

You may think you know someone very well, but when it's time to give him or her a gift, you draw a blank. The solution? Simply create a Personalized Gift Bio for those to whom you give on a regular basis.

The Personalized Gift Bio is designed to inspire a variety of gift ideas based on the recipient's preferences and interests. As you learn of his or her likes, dislikes, pastimes, needs, and wishes, enter the relevant information into the Bio. The next time you need a gift for a friend's birthday or another special occasion, simply refer to his or her Personalized Gift Bio. The more specific the information you fill in, the better your chances of finding a sensational gift.

Personalized Gift Bio forms are shown on the next two pages. Several additional copies are located in the back of the book. These may be duplicated for your personal use.

Points to consider when creating the Personalized Gift Bio can be found throughout the book in sidebars entitled "Consider This."

Creating a Personalized Gift Bio

PERSONALIZED GIFT BIO

Name _____
Birthday _____ Birthstone _____ Flower _____
Other Special Dates _____

FAVORITES

Artists/Composers _____
Books/Authors _____
Celebrities _____
Colors _____
Fabrics _____
Fashion Accessories _____
Flowers/Plants _____
Foods/Drinks _____
Fragrances _____
Games _____
Jewelry _____
Magazines/Newspapers _____
Movies/Stars _____
Music/Performers _____
Pets/Animals _____
Places/Vacations _____
Sports/Teams _____
Other _____

SIZES

Women
 Dress _____
 Blouse _____
 Skirt _____
 Jacket _____
 Lingerie _____

Men
 Suit _____
 Shirt _____
 Pants _____

Accessories
 Shoe/Sock _____
 Sweater _____
 Hat _____
 Ring _____
 Belt _____

AFFILIATIONS

Alma Mater/Other Schools _____
Religious/Cultural/Ethnic _____
Civic/Business/Professional _____
Clubs/Teams _____

Creating a Personalized Gift Bio

Personalized Gift Bio (Continued)

PREFERENCES

Prefers Practical or Extravagant Gifts? _____
Clothing Styles _____
Hobbies or Interests _____
Collections _____
Home Furnishings _____

OTHER CONSIDERATIONS

Wants/Needs _____
Dislikes _____
Transitions _____
Restrictions _____
Major Purchases _____

GIFT IDEAS

_____
_____
_____
_____
_____

RECORD OF GIFTS GIVEN

Date	Occasion	Gift	Comments

Coming Out of the Gift Closet

"Come over to my house," she invited the others, "and within 20 minutes I can select an appropriate present for any of you from my gift closet." That promise was made by a woman who attended one of our gift-giving seminars years ago. Her skill and enthusiasm for gift giving came from years of experience and the development of a system that worked for her. She traveled all over the world with her husband, the former head of a major government agency and then an international business consultant. In her travels, she purchased a variety of gifts that she took home and was later able to match—with great success—to a recipient. Her gift closet—complete with a computerized inventory management system—was like having her own worldwide gift shop. There are numerous variations on the gift-closet theme and you don't have to travel the world to adapt the idea to your own needs. Here are some suggestions.

When you see something you know a certain person on your gift list would like, buy it to give for a future occasion.

Keep a calendar of birthdays, anniversaries, and upcoming weddings, births, graduations, and other events with you at all times so you can gift shop at your convenience.

Keep additional items on hand for last-minute hostess, birthday, and thank-you gifts.

Pre-wrap the gifts in your gift closet. Use coded tags to identify the contents of the wrapped packages. This is especially helpful when your children need a birthday present for a party they failed to mention until the last minute. Furthermore, wrapping

Exercising Options

"My teenaged grandchildren enjoy choosing their own birthday gifts from a selection of unwrapped presents in my gift closet. I enjoy shopping the outlet malls, and when I come across something I know will be a hit, I buy multiples of the same item in a variety of colors or options."

—Reva S.

Coming Out of the Gift Closet

> **Unlock the Closet**
>
> Maintaining a variety of items in the gift closet is key to personalizing gifts to fit individuals.

children's presents ahead of time keeps your own children from seeing—and wanting to play with—the items intended for giving.

A variety of items from elegant to whimsical, in a range of prices, may be included in the gift closet:

- Cedar sachet blocks for drawers and closets, napkin rings, bookends, or small appliances for hostess gifts

- Silver serving pieces, candlesticks, tableware, or luxurious bed, bath, and table linens for wedding gifts

- Waist packs, telescopes, video games, calculators with big keys or in bright colors, an assortment of flashlights, hair accessories, small musical instruments, or percussion instruments for children's birthdays

- Layette or nursery items for baby presents

- Cassette tapes, compact discs, music videos, key chains, locking diaries, canvas tote bags, or beach towels for teens

- Umbrellas, bookends, photo frames, albums, board games, puzzles (the new three-dimensional ones are becoming very popular), ice cream makers, popcorn poppers, desk accessories, automobile accessories, candy dishes, cookie jars, mugs, mini book lights, or department-store gift certificates for general giving

Part Two

Gift suggestions listed alphabetically by holiday, occasion, circumstance, interest group, and gift category

Anniversary Presents

SEE ALSO *Romantic Presents* and relevant interest categories

The best anniversary gifts are the ones that say, "I'd marry you all over again." Early anniversaries—such as the first or the fifth—are sometimes recognized by the couple's parents or very close friends, perhaps those in the wedding party. Special wedding anniversaries—such as the 25th and 50th—are often celebrated with extended family and friends.

For a gift with a sentimental touch, have a bakery recreate a scaled-down version of the couple's wedding cake.

Commission a florist to design a floral arrangement from the same type of flowers used in the bride's bouquet.

Give a certificate from a photographer for a portrait sitting.

Pool your resources with those of other friends and family to give a spectacular gift: a cruise or a second honeymoon vacation; a pair of four-wheelers, snowmobiles, or jet skis; a whirlpool, lap pool, or sauna; a lifetime country club membership; a golf cart; a home gym; or a new deck.

Give a painting, photograph, needlework, or model of something with sentimental value to the couple: their first house, their sailboat, a favored vacation spot, or the place where they met or were married.

Special Presentations

Take her to the place you were married or honeymooned to present her with a special anniversary gift.

Anniversary Presents

> ### Up in Flames
>
> "One of my favorite gifts to give is a cozy fire. I simply tie some firewood, kindling, and newspaper together with a raffia bow and attach a book of matches and a note that reads 'Have a relaxing night by the fire.'"
>
> —Barbara B.

Assemble a memory album of pictures of family, friends, and cherished times spent with the recipients and give it to the couple celebrating their anniversary.

Make—or commission someone to make—a quilt depicting important events in the couple's life together.

Enlarge and frame a photograph of the couple on their wedding day. For the couple married many years, have an old wedding picture restored.

For a fiftieth-plus anniversary greeting from the President of the United States, write to: Greetings Office, The White House, Washington, D.C. 20500. In your request, include the recipients' full names, address, and date of their wedding. Send your request four to six weeks in advance.

Give a matched set of two comfortable chairs, bedside tables, lamps, snack trays, bed trays, bicycles, garden carts, wrist watches, crystal goblets, trees, or shrubs.

Give season tickets for a cultural or sporting series the couple would enjoy attending together.

Many couples give themselves a joint present—a romantic getaway, a television set, a camcorder, a VCR, equipment for a sport they both enjoy, a set of books about a common interest, home furnishings or accessories.

Anniversary Presents

We are often asked about the customary gifts for various wedding anniversaries. Would that we could tell you the following list evolved in some romantic folkloric fashion, but to our knowledge, it was assembled by merchants and others with commercial interests. Nevertheless, here it is if you wish to use it. (Modern gift motifs are indicated in parenthesis.)

First: Paper (clocks)

Second: Cotton, calico, straw (china)

Third: Leather (crystal, glass)

Fourth: Silk, linen, flowers, fruit, books (electrical appliances)

Fifth: Wood (silverware)

Sixth: Sweets, iron (wood)

Seventh: Wool, copper, brass, bronze (desk sets, pen and pencil sets)

Eighth: Bronze, pottery, rubber (linens, laces)

Ninth: Pottery, willow, china, crystal, glass (leather)

Tenth: Aluminum, tin (diamond jewelry)

Eleventh: Steel (fashion jewelry, accessories)

Twelfth: Linen, silk, nylon (pearls, colored gems)

Thirteenth: Lace (textiles, furs)

Fourteenth: Ivory, agate (gold jewelry)

Fifteenth: Crystal, glass (watches)

Sixteenth: (Silver holloware)

Seventeenth: (Furniture)

Eighteenth: (Porcelain)

Nineteenth: (Bronze)

Activity

Go to a mall with your spouse or significant other. Determine a time and spending limit to buy gifts for one another. Meet and exchange your finds in the mall or take them home and wrap them to be opened later. Observe your partner's responses as he or she opens your gifts. This will provide valuable feedback for future gift giving.

Anniversary Presents • Apartment Dwellers

> ### Best/Worst
> Best: My husband
>
> Worst: Incense
>
> —Ardith D.

Twentieth: China (platinum)

Twenty-fifth: Silver (sterling silver)

Thirtieth: Pearl, personal items (diamond)

Thirty-fifth: Coral, jade (jade)

Fortieth: Ruby, garnet (ruby)

Forty-fifth: Sapphire (sapphire)

Fiftieth: Gold (gold)

Fifty-fifth: Emerald, turquoise (emerald)

Sixtieth: Diamond, gold (diamond)

Seventy-fifth: Diamond, gold

Apartment Dwellers

Apartment dwellers put up with a lot—noisy neighbors, cramped quarters, and rogue Chevrolets in their parking spots. Fortunately, there's a lot we can do to make their lives better. Here are a few ideas.

In most apartments, space is at a premium. To save valuable kitchen counter space, give an under-the-cabinet-mounted appliance: a can opener, a coffee maker, a microwave, a toaster, a television, or a radio.

A closet organizing system would enable the apartment dweller to use every square inch of closet space efficiently.

Pay for the services of a professional decorator or space planner to arrange and enhance the quarters of the apartment dweller.

Apartment Dwellers

A breakfast set with a drop-leaf table and two chairs would fit cozily in a small kitchen.

A fresh coat of paint can breathe new life into the dreariest apartment. Give a certificate for the paint and painting supplies (brushes, rollers, drop cloths), and set a date to help paint.

For the young adult setting up housekeeping for the first time, fill a dish drainer or waste basket with such basic housekeeping items as light bulbs, sponges, mops, brooms, household cleaners, paper towels, laundry detergent, and dishwashing liquid.

Give a microwave cart or utility cart for added counter and storage space in the kitchen.

A foldaway ironing board that mounts on a door (or in an attractive cabinet that mounts on the wall) would be both convenient and space efficient.

Floor lamps are compact and can fit in places too tight for a table and lamp.

For those in tight quarters, a change of scenery can do wonders. Give a certificate for a night at a bed-and-breakfast.

To the studio apartment dweller, give a sleep sofa or Murphy bed (a bed that folds into a cabinet that is anchored to a wall).

> **Consider This**
>
> Some people are uncomfortable about receiving extravagant gifts when they are unable to reciprocate with the same generosity.

Arts Lovers

SEE ALSO *Music Lovers*

With paint-by-number simplicity, you can put your signature on a masterpiece for the arts lover. Please tour the exhibit of gift ideas below.

Sponsor her membership in a museum or gallery society. Memberships generally include such privileges as free admission to the museum or gallery, subscriptions to the society's magazines and other publications, and discounts at its shops and through its catalogs.

Give tickets to a symphony, opera, ballet, or gallery opening he would like to attend.

Give books from or about her favorite art galleries or the galleries she dreams of visiting.

Arrange for participation in, or attendance to, an art festival.

Enroll her in a course to study the masters or other artists in whom she has an interest.

For a generous contribution in the name of the arts lover on your gift list, you may be able to arrange for one of the following:

◆ Attendance at a dress rehearsal and a reception with the stars

Best/ Worst

Best: Tickets to an art show in New York City—I live in Virginia

Worst: None

—Jamie F.

Arts Lovers

- Membership in a museum or theater founders' circle
- A theater seat named after him
- An opportunity for her to conduct a symphony
- A private performance or entertainment for a social event

Give him a reproduction of a work of art he favors or a signed, limited-edition lithograph from a favored artist.

With a huge selection of art books, you should be able to find the perfect one for any arts lover on your gift list.

Give a gift subscription to *American Theatre*, a monthly magazine devoted entirely to the theatre. Regular sections include Stages, People, Approaches, In Print, Trends, and Media. Special sections include Season Preview, Theatre Facts, Festival Preview, and published playscripts. Write: *American Theatre*, 355 Lexington Avenue, New York, NY 10017. Phone: 212/697-5230. Fax: 212/983-4847.

Give a classical memory: *Great Arias with Placido Domingo and Friends*, *Brahms Piano Concerto No. 1*, *Kirov Ballet: Classic Ballet Night*, and *Gilbert & Sullivan: Their Greatest Hits* are just a few of the top quality videos available from V.I.E.W. Video. Phone: 800/843-9843. Fax: 212/979-0266.

Shop the Gift Shops

Museum gift shops make easy work of selecting gifts for those interested in the museum's subject. Reproductions of manuscripts, art, and artifacts from the museum's collections can often be found in the museum's gift shop or catalog. Interesting coffee table books, posters, stationery, clothing, and accessory items may also be found.

Arts Lovers • Aviators

> **Celebrate!**
>
> August is American Artists Appreciation Month.

If the arts lover on your gift list is also a dabbler in art, give her a gift certificate and catalog from Cheap Joe's Art Stuff. She will then be able to choose paper, paints, brushes, art books, easels, and other art supplies best suited to her. Phone: 800/227-2788.

Aviators

These folks have their own ideas about off-road vehicles and will go to great heights to view breathtaking landscapes. When it comes to gift possibilities for hedgehopping crop dusters, globe-trotting airline pilots, and other aviators, the sky is the limit. For the Wright kinds of gifts, look (out) below.

Kids from 10 to 99 will enjoy the gift of computer flight-simulator software. For serious simulation, add a yoke and rudder pedals.

Tailwinds is a must-have resource for anyone looking for presents for pilots or others with a passion for flying. Featured items include:

◆ World War II-style leather flight jackets, Air Force flight jackets, and down-filled flight vests

◆ Warm-up suits, sweatshirts, T-shirts, and ties with flight motifs

◆ Whimsical holiday greeting cards and ornaments

◆ Handcrafted model aircraft

◆ Flight videos, posters, puzzles, stamps, jewelry, mailboxes, lamps, clocks, license plate holders, mugs, and more

Phone: 800/992-7737.

Aviators

Gifts of software for the aviator include:

- Logbook programs for tracking and reporting aircraft maintenance, flight cost and classification, tax or reimbursement expenses, flight rule, and instrument currency
- Flight planners for calculating distance, time, ground speed, true course, true heading, magnetic variation, fuel requirements, and best altitude
- Moving flight maps, flying and instrument instruction, business programs, and tax programs

For these programs, check your local flight shops and computer stores, or request a copy of the *Flight Computing Catalog* which is filled with innovative, leading-edge aviation software. Phone: 800/824-5946. Fax: 415/883-7599.

Other gifts for pilots or wannabes include flight computers, gear bags, chart cases, instrument training visors, instructional books, headsets, wind socks, air show seats, in-flight videos, cloud charts, and weather monitors.

Sporty's Pilot Shop features many of the items mentioned in this section as well as an annual Christmas tree ornament and such whimsical items as a stick-on panic button. Call them for information or a catalog. Phone: 800/543-8633.

Give a subscription to *Plane and Pilot* (Phone: 800/283-4330. Fax: 310/826-5008) or *Flying* (Phone: 800/678-0797).

> **Celebrate!**
>
> Surprise your aviator with a gift on the anniversary of Lindbergh's transatlantic flight (May 20-21), or the Wright brothers' first flight (December 17).

Baby Shower Presents

Baby Shower Presents
SEE ALSO *Children—Infants*

Customarily given four to six weeks before or after baby's arrival, showers provide friends and family a chance to deluge the mom-to-be with the tools of her new trade. Lately, it's not uncommon to find men at such gatherings, and showers for expectant couples are becoming more popular. Whatever the setting or the guest list, the purpose remains the same—to shower the expecting with gifts for the expected.

Compile a memory book with pictures of parents, brothers, sisters, and other of the baby's relatives.

Decorate an oval basket with scraps of fabric and lace to resemble a baby bassinet. Fill it with nursery supplies.

Create and frame a family tree or pedigree chart.

Contribute to the purchase of such major baby gear as a crib, bassinet, cradle, high chair, stroller, booster seat, car seat, battery-operated swing, changing table, jogging stroller, portable crib, infant carrier, or portable play yard.

Give nursery equipment or furnishings: an ultrasonic humidifier, an electronic thermometer, a nursery monitor, a mobile, wall hangings, crib bumpers, blankets, quilts, a crib mirror, a nursery clock, or closet organizers.

It's A Wrap!

Wrap a baby gift in a cloth diaper secured with diaper pins. Top it with an assortment of teething rings or rattles.

Baby Shower Presents

Assemble bathtime items in a baby bathtub. Include bath toys, a shampoo hat, a hand-held shower, baby bath soap, shampoo, cotton swabs, towels, and washcloths. Wrap the filled tub with a large sheet of cellophane, tie it with a colorful bow, and top it with an adorable rubber duck.

Equip a diaper bag with gear for outings: a car bottle warmer, a portable changing pad, disposable diapers, baby wipes, baby toys, rattles, and teething rings.

Give a silver rattle, spoon, porringer, mirror, or another keepsake engraved with the baby's initials and the date of her birth, christening, blessing, or other first rite.

Laminate the front page of the newspaper from the day the baby was born.

Make an heirloom-quality quilt, christening dress, or petticoat. Embroider the baby's name and birth date (or christening date) on the item and offer to embroider the same information for each successive recipient. (Granted, you will not likely be around to do this for more than a generation or two, but it's a polite way to suggest that the tradition be initiated and maintained.)

A care package for Mom is a welcome change from the traditional baby shower gifts. Bubble bath, a candy bar, a good book, and a coupon for free babysitting would bring a smile to a tired new mother's face.

> **Best/Worst**
>
> Best: Child care so my husband and I could have a night out
>
> Worst: Silk cocktail napkins
>
> —Katina N.

Backpackers and Hikers

Backpackers and Hikers

Hikers are on top of the world. Literally! And, although not all aspire to ascend Europe's Mount Elbrus, Africa's Kilimanjaro, or South America's Aconcagua, the psychological and physical challenges of hiking propel legions of trekkers over the river and through the woods. Outfitting the hiker should present little challenge for gift givers that do their homework. Does the hiker favor long or short treks? Trail or off-trail hiking? Is the hiking combined with other activities such as camping, skiing, or climbing? Scout out the recipient's preferences, and when it's time to hit the gift-giving trail, consider these possibilities.

Arrange for a hiking adventure. A travel agent can help you plan for trekking the Amazon or climbing the Swiss Alps. Helpful people at a sporting goods store can tell you about hiking in the area.

Give a treadmill, stair climber, cross-country ski machine, or other exercise equipment to keep the trekker in shape between hikes.

Give a first-aid kit to the trailblazer. Even if your hiker is not particularly accident prone, potential perils lie around every corner of the back country. Assemble kit contents from a drugstore, or call one of the numbers below for a complete kit. Be sure to include antiseptics for wound cleansing, an assortment of bandages (adhesive strips, wound closure strips, elastic bandages, triangular bandages), gauze pads and rolls, an irrigation syringe, tape, safety pins, scissors, tweezers, pain killers, and ointments for itching, swelling, and infection. Atwater Carey (800/359-1646) and Adventure Medical Kits (800/324-3517) sell complete outdoor medical kits and components.

What Gives?

Have you ever been party—as giver *or* recipient—to an embarrassing or awkward gift-giving situation? Would you be willing to share your story with us? If we provide you anonymity, would you be willing to share someone else's dilemma? If so, please see page 277.

Backpackers and Hikers

Outfit a backpack with all the necessities for the perfect picnic: dishes, stemware, utensils, a cutting board, a tablecloth, napkins. For a romantic touch, add candle holders, candles, and a book of poetry.

Give gifts of hiking gear and accessories: custom packs, trail maps, binoculars, compasses, hiking boots and insoles, sleeping bags, knives, backpackable lights, portable water filters, bear-resistant food containers, weather monitors, barometers, altimeters, portable radios, trekking poles, protective eye wear, insect repellent, head nets, bug jackets, emergency flares, emergency radio transmitters, or walkie-talkies.

To fuel the hungry hiker, give a cook set and an assortment of trail foods, including energy bars, freeze-dried meals, boil-in-bag foods, beverage powders, and MRE (Meals Ready-to-Eat) entrees and desserts.

Arrange for a gift membership in the National Parks and Conservation Association. Phone: 800/NATPARK.

Make a donation in the recipient's name to the Appalachian Trail Conference, or order a gift from the Trail Store brochure. Write: Appalachian Trail Conference, P.O. Box 807, Harper's Ferry, WV 25425. Phone: 304/535-6331.

A hand-held global positioning system would help the hiker stay on course. If you can't find one at your local sporting goods store, contact Trailhead

> **It's a Wrap!**
>
> Gift bags are great for wrapping odd-shaped or unboxed items in a hurry, and they are available in a wide range of sizes, colors, and patterns.

Backpackers and Hikers • Bar/Bat Mitzvah Presents

Sports (117 North Main Street, Logan, UT 84321, 801/753-1541) or Infocenter, Inc. (800/852-0649).

To keep the hiker astride, give a subscription to *Backpacker*, the magazine of self-propelled wilderness travel. Phone: 800/666-3434.

Bar/Bat Mitzvah Presents
SEE ALSO *Teens*

In the Jewish faith, bar mitzvahs for thirteen-year-old boys and bat mitzvahs for twelve-year-old girls are ceremonies that mark the youth's reaching the age of religious responsibility and maturity. Both are preceded by years of study and preparation. The manner of celebrating a bar or bat mitzvah varies from simple to lavish. Usually it involves lunch or dinner (sometimes both), and often music and dancing are part of the occasion. In spite of the somewhat festive atmosphere, the reason for the celebration is rooted in faith, devotion, and tradition.

Although bar mitzvah and bat mitzvah presents do not necessarily have to be deeply religious, such lasting gifts as jewelry, art, books, poetry, and music by and about Jewish people are especially appropriate for this significant rite of passage.

Arrange for a tree to be planted in Israel (for conservation purposes) in the recipient's name. The recipient will be notified and provided with a certificate. Write to: Jewish National Fund, 114 East 32nd Street, Suite 1501, New York, NY 10016. Phone: 516/561-9100. Fax: 516/678-3204.

Special Delivery

To announce a forthcoming gift, give a miniature toy, ceramic, sculpture, bracelet charm, or trinket relating to the gift.

Bar/Bat Mitzvah Presents • Birders

Sabbath candle holders make nice gifts for a bat mitzvah.

Give a mezuzah—a handwritten scroll traditionally placed in a small container hung on the doorway to a Jewish home.

Monetary gifts—checks, stocks, bonds—are often given.

For a card signed by the President, send a request four to six weeks prior to the bar/bat mitzvah, with the recipient's full name and address, and the date of the event. Mail the request to: Greetings Office, The White House, Washington, DC 20500.

> **Shopping Tip**
>
> Synagogue gift shops and Jewish bookstores are good places to look for bar/bat mitzvah presents. Israel Connection also features Jewish gifts and books. Call: 800/722-5290.

Birders

Olor cygnus, Sitta carolinensis, and Rhynchopsitta pachyrhyncha (a.k.a. whooper swans, white-breasted nuthatches, and thick-billed parrots)...the names roll off the tongue of a birder like the song of a lark. With over 75 million bird watchers in this country alone, that's a lot of singing. The next time you need a gift for a watcher of warmblooded, egg-laying, two-legged, feather-covered vertebrates, consider the following.

Choose a gift from the hundreds of bird books and videos including field guides on birds by region, state, and continent; videos on all types of birds, from songbirds to owls, and hawks to bluebirds; books on constructing bird houses; and even books about the bird watchers themselves.

Present Perfect: The Essential Guide to Gift Giving

Birders

It's a Wrap!

In addition to ribbon in all its varieties (satin, French-wired, acetate moire, lace, Mylar, metallic, cloth, and so forth), many other objects make creative tyings. These include colorful shoelaces, artificial rope pearls, leather strips, vinyl cording, jump rope, strips of netting, paper streamers, paper twist, raffia, hemp rope, twine, and yarn.

To attract birds to the yard of the bird watcher, give a winter roosting box, bird bath, bird house, or bird feeder.

For ornithological excursions, give such equipment as binoculars, field scopes, cameras, tripods, bird callers, and field bags.

The SuperEar Sound Enhancer allows birders to pick up bird calls from 100 yards away, and it attaches to binoculars, pockets, belts, or other gear. From Sonic Technology Products, Inc. Phone: 800/247-5548.

To the bird watcher with a personal computer, give birder computer software for maintaining checklists, notes, records of sightings, and other observations.

CD-ROM programs for computers include such features as field guides to birds, quizzes on bird identification by sight and sound, and action of birds in flight. Call Axia International (800/969-2942) or Thayer Birding Software (800/865-2473).

Arrange a nature tour for the adventurous birder. Many domestic and international tours are offered through bird clubs and travel agencies. Victor Emanuel Nature Tours in Austin, Texas, for example, offers over 100 tours from Antarctica to Zimbabwe. Phone: 800/328-VENT.

Give a subscription to *Bird Watcher's Digest* which features how-to articles on identifying and attracting birds, primers on bird photography, thought-provoking studies, gorgeous photographs, and color illustrations. Phone: 800/879-2473.

Birthday Presents

The charm of a birthday lies in the notion that it's entirely one's own—although the realist would say that it's shared with ten million other people. Use your imagination for fun ways to give a birthday gift as singular as the recipient.

Give as many gifts as the birthday person is old. For example, a dozen roses to a 12-year-old girl from her father would make a young lady feel very special on her twelfth birthday. Other ideas include *16* movie tickets, a three-week (*21*-day) European trip, *30* car wash certificates, *40* pints of Ben & Jerry's ice cream, a strand of *50* pearls, or 5 dozen (*60*) golf balls, fishing lures, or tulip bulbs.

If you are the birthday person's employer, a half or full day off would make a great birthday present.

In a scrapbook or notebook, assemble cards and letters from friends telling about treasured remembrances of the birthday person.

Send a birthday card every day during the month of her birthday, or send as many cards as he is old on his birthday.

Give a video time capsule from the year of his birth. FlikBaks video greeting cards feature news

Hide-and-Seek

"Our family has a tradition of hiding gifts for the birthday person to find."

—Tiffany W.

Birthday Presents

> ### A Bloomin' Birthday
>
> "For my 38th birthday, my friend Barbara "planted" 37 carnations with "Happy" tags in my yard. She later hand-delivered the "Birthday"-tagged 38th flower along with a birthday present."
>
> —Robyn S.

headlines, sports highlights, fashion, and politics from most years of the 1930s, 1940s, 1950s, and 1960s. Phone: 800/541-3533.

For 80-plus birthdays, you can request a card from the President of the United States. Send your request four to six weeks in advance to: Greetings Office, The White House, Washington, D.C. 20500. Include the recipient's full name, address, and date and year of birth.

Take the birthday person to dinner at his favorite restaurant. Arrange for cake to be served, but be sure to mention to the management whether you want the cake to be presented in a discreet or celebratory way. Some people don't like the attention drawn by singing waiters.

For a fun and unique present for children or adults, give a birthday scroll. A birthday scroll from Great Days Publishing is a personalized keepsake filled with news, trends, weather, and other information about the day one was born. Phone: 800/447-7817.

When giving a birthday party, remember that some people don't like surprises or are uncomfortable about having a lot of fuss made about them. For example, it's okay if Sherri gives Larry a surprise party, but he knows better than to give her one!

If asked, a conscientious party host or hostess will offer party guests some direction on gift giving. For example, depending on the type of party, it may be requested that guests bring only inexpensive or humorous gifts. Such suggestions, however, should be

Birthday Presents

conveyed by word-of-mouth rather than printed on invitations. (See *Humorous Gifts* and *Inexpensive Gifts*.)

Birthstones

January: Garnet (generally dark to very dark red)

February: Amethyst (purple or violet)

March: Aquamarine (blue-green) — alternative: bloodstone

April: Diamond (colorless or white)

May: Emerald (strong yellowish green)

June: Pearl (yellowish white) — alternatives: moonstone and alexandrite

July: Ruby (deep red)

August: Peridot (clear green) — alternative: sardonyx

September: Sapphire (blue)

October: Opal (translucent) — alternative: tourmaline

November: Topaz (yellow)

December: Turquoise (light to brilliant bluish green) — alternatives: zircon and lapis

Zodiacal Signs

January 20 to February 18: Aquarius (the Water Bearer)

February 19 to March 20: Pisces (the Fish)

March 21 to April 19: Aries (the Ram)

It's A Wrap!

To create custom birthday wrap, cover the package with plain paper. With colored markers, write the recipient's age in various sizes all over the package.

Special Presentations

Was he born at 2:00 a.m.? Then wake him at 2:00 a.m. with an enthusiastic "Happy birthday!" as he opens his present.

Birthday Presents

Birthday Wishes

According to one survey, parents of 1- to 14-year-olds would urge friends and relatives to buy birthday gifts of the following, by percentage: Books, 33%; Clothes, 26%; Art/Craft Supplies, 13%; Sports Equipment, 11%; Games, 7%; Toys, 6%.

Source: The AFT-Chrysler Report on Kids, Parents, and Reading

April 20 to May 20: Taurus (the Bull)

May 21 to June 20: Gemini (the Twins)

June 21 to July 22: Cancer (the Crab)

July 23 to August 22: Leo (the Lion)

August 23 to September 23: Virgo (the Virgin)

September 24 to October 23: Libra (the Balance)

October 24 to November 21: Scorpios (the Scorpion)

November 22 to December 21: Sagittarius (the Archer)

December 22 to January 19: Capricorn (the Goat)

Birth Month Flowers

January: Snowdrop

February: Primrose

March: Violet

April: Daisy

May: Hawthorn

June: Rose

July: Water Lily

August: Poppy

September: Morning Glory

October: Hops

November: Chrysanthemum

December: Holly

Boaters
SEE ALSO *Water Sports Enthusiasts*

"The happiest two days of a boat owner's life," the old saying goes, "are the days he buys and sells his boat." Nevertheless, for all the days in between, one is captain of his own ship—be it yacht or dinghy, sloop or speedboat. To help keep his screws turning or the wind in his sails, we've charted a bounty of gift possibilities guaranteed not to incite mutiny.

Give a gift certificate for routine maintenance or special detailing of his boat. Or, offer your own services to oil the wood, swab the deck, or polish the trim.

Assemble charts and maps of waterways she wants to navigate. Add chart accessories such as cases, holders, and weights.

Choose a gift from a boatload of boating accessories and equipment: a fishing rod holder, binoculars, navigational equipment, weather gauges, or a weather-channel radio.

Equip the boater's vessel with safety equipment: life vests, a first-aid kit, a fire extinguisher, a smoke alarm, a life boat, floating rescue lights, distress flags, whistles, and flares.

Give tote bags, shirts, scarves, ties, caps, mugs, sunglasses, key rings, and other items with nautical motifs.

Special Delivery

Dress a teddy bear in boating apparel to deliver with a gift certificate to a boater, in workout garb to deliver with a gift of spa membership, in ski clothes to deliver with lift passes, or in a chef's hat and apron to deliver with a gift certificate for dinner at an exclusive restaurant.

Boaters

> **Best/Worst**
>
> Best: 20 pounds of shrimp
>
> Worst: Useless kitchen items
>
> —Eduard M.

Give a framed picture of the boater at the helm of his boat.

Arrange to have a custom boat cover or sail cover made.

Commission an artist to draw or sculpt a replica or paint a picture of her boat.

Give foul weather gear: a poncho, a jacket, a pair of pants, a pair of boots, a hat.

Give a set of signal flags spelling out the recipient's name or the name of her boat.

Assemble an assortment of tools and spare boat parts. In addition, a diving mask, fins, and a snorkel can be invaluable if something below the water line—a propeller, for example—gets fouled.

Make reservations and prepay the slip fee at an exotic port of call.

To the canoeist, kayaker, or other paddle-sport enthusiast on your gift list, give a subscription to *Canoe & Kayak* magazine. Articles and features include adventure paddling destinations, equipment reviews, and various paddling techniques. Phone: 800/678-5432.

Boaters • Bookworms

To the sailor, give a subscription to *Sail,* which features breathtaking color photography, informative articles, and helpful hints to make his sailing adventures more enjoyable. Write: *Sail*, P.O. Box 56396, Boulder, CO 80323-9396.

For more great accessories, toys, clothing, gear, and other gifts for boaters, call for a catalog from E&B Discount Marine. Phone: 800/262-8464.

Bookworms

Nothing brings more joy to a bookworm's heart than curling up in a comfortable spot with a great book. Add a warm fire and bad weather outdoors, and you've created a backdrop for a potentially perfect fantasy! However, every bookworm's fantasy will be different. Use these ideas to start him on his way.

Daedalus Books offers new and remaindered (publishers' overstock) books at a savings of 10% to 90%. Each book offered in the catalog is accompanied by interesting and amusing blurbs written by Daedalus' own reviewers. Phone: 800/395-2665. Fax: 800/866-5578.

Books on tape make great gifts for commuters, runners, and the bedridden. There are many educational and entertaining audio tapes from which to choose. Children enjoy story books that are accompanied by tapes that signal when to turn the pages. Check bookstores for available titles.

Celebrate!

Donate a book to the library in the name of a bookworm friend on the birth anniversary of his or her favorite author.

Bookworms

One for All

A gift to one became a treasure for all. The classic story *Alice in Wonderland* was written by Lewis Carroll as a gift for Alice Liddell, daughter of the dean of Christchurch College.

There are coffee table books that address just about every subject—from fly fishing and film making to folk art and fashion. Give a book about something the recipient is interested in, or introduce her to something new you're sure she'll enjoy.

Many books are now available in braille or large print for people that are visually impaired. Check with your bookstore or librarian.

Survey Scoop! Perhaps not surprisingly, the highest marks for gifts of books come from college graduates. Preference decreases as education and income go down. On average, women rate gifts of books slightly higher than men do.

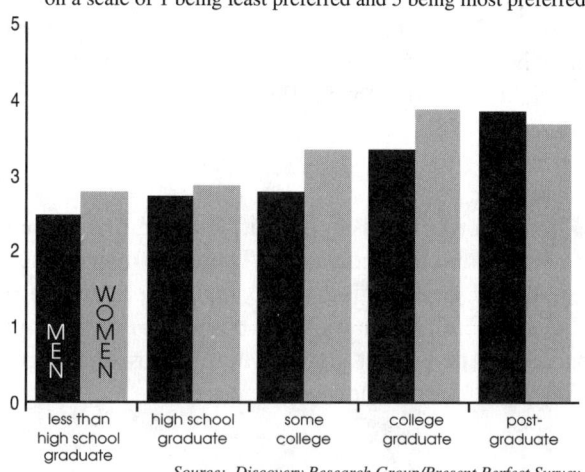

who wants gifts of
BOOKS ?
Preferences for gifts of books, by education, on a scale of 1 being least preferred and 5 being most preferred.

Source: Discovery Research Group/Present Perfect Survey

Bookworms

To the serious book collector, specialist, antiquarian bookseller, or rare book dealer, give a subscription to *AB Bookman's Weekly,* which provides features, news, and other information. Write: *AB Bookman's Weekly*, P.O. Box AB, Clifton, NJ 07015. Phone: 201/772-0020. Fax: 201/772-9281.

A set of encyclopedias or another reference book series would make a great gift for a family with school-aged children.

Give a book in tandem with another gift. For example, give one of the following duos:

◆ A romance novel with an assortment of candles or bath oils

◆ A book on quilting with a quilt rack or set of quilting frames

◆ A book on gardening or flower arranging with an assortment of flower bulbs and seeds

◆ A trail book with a backpack or hiking shoes

◆ A dutch oven cookbook with a set of dutch ovens

◆ A photography book with a camera or camera accessories

◆ A book on the works of great artists and art class tuition

◆ An assortment of novels with a beach umbrella to a friend leaving on vacation

◆ A parenting book and jar of pickles to an expectant mother

◆ A book on bugs and a bug jar to a budding entomologist

> **Once Upon a Time**
>
> The great American tradition of public libraries started in Salisbury, Connecticut in 1803 with a local resident's gift of 150 books. Rural communities throughout the United States have public libraries because of gifts made by the Carnegie Foundation during the 1920s and 1930s.

Bowlers

Bowlers

Whether you're giving to a bowling pro or a beginner, you'll never strike out with these gift ideas for the bowler on your gift list.

Outfit the bowler with a customized bowling ball, bowling shoes, wrist supports, thumb and finger grips, bowling shirts, and bowling towels (to remove lane oils that build up on hands and bowling balls).

Give prepaid lane fees at the bowler's favorite bowling alley.

Bowling's Bookstore boasts the largest selection of books and videos in the bowling world. Book titles include *40 Common Errors in Bowling & How to Correct Them*, *The Complete Guide to Bowling Principles*, and *Bowl Like a Pro*. VHS video titles include *Striking Ladies' Hottest Tips*, *The Perfect 300*, and *Strikes, Spares & Strategies*. Phone: 800/521-BOWL.

Arrange for bowling lessons or a week at a bowling camp such as Dick Ritger's Bowling Camps in New York, Georgia, Virginia, Kentucky, Illinois, Michigan, Minnesota, Missouri, Texas, and Mississippi. Phone: 800/535-0678.

Give a subscription to *Bowling Digest*. *Bowling Digest* features behind-the-scenes information and entertainment for bowlers, including schedules, statistics, and records. It covers men's pro tour, women's pro tour, amateur, junior, senior, and collegiate bowling. Write: *Bowling Digest*, P.O. Box 570, Mt. Morris, IL 61054.

Special Delivery

To add suspense to your gift presentation, buy—or make—a puzzle depicting the gift. The recipient discovers what the gift is by putting together the puzzle.

Business Gifts

SEE ALSO *Employee Gifts* and *Workplace Gift Exchanges*

Choosing an appropriate business gift can be tricky business, indeed. The right gift can give great momentum to a good business relationship. The wrong gift can bring negotiations to a halt. Ideally, the business gifts you choose will reflect your thoughtfulness, creativity, good taste, and attention to detail. Where the gift recipient works, how she gets there, what she does there, how she spends her lunch hour, and her interests outside the office can provide valuable direction for choosing business gifts. Here are just a few ideas:

Contributions to charities important to the recipient are fitting business gifts. Many recipients, as well as givers, find this a satisfying use of gift dollars and a way to avoid the appearance of a conflict of interest or other impropriety. In addition, some charitable organizations send periodic newsletters or magazines to donors. These can serve to remind the recipient of your gift.

Give membership in a professional organization, or a subscription to a journal, magazine, or newsletter relevant to the recipient's job.

Write a letter or memo to her supervisor detailing what a great job the recipient is doing for you or your company.

Does he head for the gym on his lunch hour? A sports cassette tape player (perhaps with your recorded greeting) would make a great gift for the fitness-oriented executive.

> **Celebrate!**
>
> September is Be Kind to Editors and Writers Month. (No, we didn't make this up.)

Business Gifts

It's a Wrap!

A supply of brown packaging paper, packaging tape, markers for addressing packages, and shipping information from the Post Office, UPS, and Federal Express will come in handy when you need to ship packages. For convenience, keep these items with your wrapping supplies.

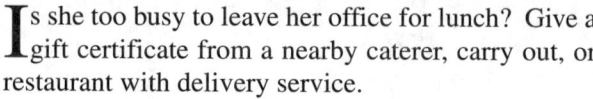

Is she too busy to leave her office for lunch? Give a gift certificate from a nearby caterer, carry out, or restaurant with delivery service.

Is she concerned about the environment? (Who isn't these days?) Environmentally responsible items are popular business gifts. Good choices include reusable canvas shopping bags, flowers and plants, items made from natural materials, contributions to environmental organizations, and trees planted through the National Arbor Day Foundation. Write: National Arbor Day Foundation, 211 North 12th Street, Lincoln, NE 68508. Phone: 402/474-5655.

Are her fingers attached to a computer keyboard or a cellular telephone? Accessories for high-tech equipment are popular gifts for use at home, on the road, or in the office. They are available in a wide range of prices; many cost less than $25. Consider a leather cellular phone case, computer disc storage, a computer game, a graphics package, fun fonts, or a custom mouse pad.

Does he prefer brown bagging to lunching in the company cafeteria? Outfit a basket with table service for one to use at the office. Elegant china, crystal, silverware, and linen can make a tuna-salad sandwich seem like a gourmet treat. If his passion is Chinese carry-out, equip his basket with rice bowls, chopsticks, a teapot, and fortune cookies. Or select a place setting to compliment his office decor. Maybe he's a paper-plate kind of guy. If so, fill his basket with an assortment of recyclable plates, cups, napkins, and flatware.

Business Gifts

In response to the recipient's expressed interest, sign up for the two of you to attend a professional development seminar. The time together can be well spent improving your business relationship. Note: Make certain your presentation reflects your response to the recipient's interest and does not imply a suggestion of improvement.

Make a contribution, in the name of your doctor, to one of the following:

◆ Alzheimer's Association. Phone: 800/272-3900

◆ American Diabetes Association. Phone: 800/401-7590

◆ American Cancer Society. Phone: 800/729-1151

Note to doctors: Make a donation to a charitable or research organization in the names of your colleagues or patients. Send greeting cards, indicating that such a contribution has been made. In addition to accepting donations, many organizations sell greeting cards and other items suitable for gift giving, with profits donated to worthy causes. Call them for a catalog or brochure.

Send a gift that can be shared with her staff. Such gifts include a food basket, a flower bouquet, a catered lunch, an item for the waiting room display case, a potted plant, an art object, or a print that compliments the office decor.

For Counsel boasts the most diverse selection of products for lawyers, including books, bookends, bookcases, jewelry, mugs, posters, T-shirts, ties, and nameplates with legal motifs; prints depicting court room scenes, lawyers, juries, and other legal settings;

Celebrate!

A gift subscription to a general interest magazine such as *People*, *Newsweek, House Beautiful*, or *Women's Day* is sure to be well received at your doctor's office for Doctor's Day (March 30).

Business Gifts

> **Celebrate!**
>
> Celebrate Law Day, May 1, with a gift to your attorney.

and the cuddly, handmade Teddy Barrister with a retainer certificate for your personalization. Our favorite item is a pair of Legal Advice Dice handcrafted from Oregon myrtlewood with laser engraving. To use, just state the issue, then roll the dice—together, or one at a time—to reveal the decision. One says "SUE," "SHOOT," "BEG," "LIE," "SETTLE," and "ASK MOM." The other says "NOW," "LATER," "NEVER," "ASAP," "SOON," and "MAYBE." From the traditional to the irreverent, For Counsel's catalog features hundreds of items that are perfect for giving to your own friendly attorney or your attorney friends. Phone: 800/637-0098. Fax: 503/697-3851.

Getting Down to Business

Appropriateness, timing, and delivery are the keys to successful business gift giving. Consider the following:

♦ *Before* sending a business gift, check with the recipient's company concerning its gift policy. A quick call will help you avoid unnecessary gift gaffes.

♦ Ask yourself three questions when considering gift options: What does the gift reflect about my company and me? Where or how will the gift be displayed or used? Will the gift remind the recipient of my company and me in a positive manner?

♦ Exhibit as much imagination and customization as possible when selecting business gifts. A one-size-fits-all present will not have the same impact as an individualized gift. Do your homework to find out the interests and tastes of the recipient. Create a Personalized Gift Bio for clients, employees, and other business associates to whom you will be giv-

Business Gifts

ing on a regular basis, or for whom gift giving presents a particular challenge. Obtain information about the recipient's preferences from his or her coworkers and known friends or family. (See *Creating a Personalized Gift Bio in Part One*.)

- Choose only quality products and services for business gift giving. First-class products are available in all price ranges.

- Timing is everything, so give gifts when they are pertinent. Give gifts to new clients at the time contracts are signed. Give "thank you" gifts as soon as possible after someone has gone out of his or her way to help you.

- To make your holiday gifts or greetings stand out, send them at Thanksgiving or New Year's instead of Christmas.

- Wrap your gifts with care. Perfect presentations are evidence of your attention to detail. You may want to create a "signature" wrap to reflect a characteristic of the image you wish to convey. Such wraps can be flamboyant, conservative, nostalgic, imaginative, elegant, or meticulous.

- Attach a thoughtful note. The proper enclosure card establishes the relevance of your gift and personalizes the gift to the recipient. For example, attach this note to a "decision-making" dartboard: "Congratulations on your promotion to project manager. Here's something to help you with all the tough decisions you'll now be making."

- Deliver your gift in person, if possible. Your verbal expressions of congratulations, thanks, or encouragement add significant impact to your gift. In addition, presenting your gift in person connects you with the gift in the mind of the recipient.

The Politics of Gift Giving

Whether regulated by federal law or international protocol, gifts play a role in strategic lobbying, contract negotiations, and decision making. Gifts to congressmen and government officials flow into their offices despite federal regulations. The United States Constitution forbids government officials to accept lavish presents from their foreign hosts. The Foreign Corrupt Practices Act disallows congressmen from taking gifts valued at more than $100 from any individual or group with a direct interest in legislation pending before Congress.

Business Gifts

> **Consider This**
>
> Cultural, religious, dietary, space, physical, and other such restrictions should be considered when selecting gifts.

Business Gift Taboos

Common sense dictates that certain business gifts should not be given.

♦ **Do not give gifts that might embarrass or interrupt the work of the recipient or others.** Many people consider strip-o-grams or gifts with sexual overtones to be offensive, not humorous.

♦ **Do not give business gifts to individuals that work for companies with no-gift policies.** At a minimum, such gifts put recipients in the awkward position of returning them or result in breeches of ethics for those that keep them.

♦ **Do not give considerable gifts to those with whom you are in the process of negotiating a business deal.** Such gifts may be interpreted as an attempt at bribery. To ensure their employees are not swayed by front-row tickets to the opera, some companies prohibit employees from accepting any gifts. Others allow employees to receive only gifts of nominal value—say $10 or $20—or gifts the whole office can enjoy such as a food basket or magazine subscription for the staff lounge.

♦ **Do not give logo-bearing gifts for the holidays.** As a general rule, items from your company's product line or bearing your company's name or logo are risky holiday presents. No matter how cleverly you package them, they smack of self-promotion at a time you should be conveying goodwill and appreciation. Reserve product and logo items for more appropriate times such as advertising campaigns. If you feel that your name or logo must appear on the gift to remind the recipient of who gave the gift, place it in the most inconspicuous place possible. However, if you've done your homework, your gift—and you—will long be remembered.

Campers

SEE ALSO *Backpackers and Hikers* and *Fishermen*

The trees, the stars, the mosquitoes, the rain...campers really do sleep better on rocks and roots. And that ruddy, healthy-looking complexion? It's actually the result of using denim for a pillow. The next time you need a gift for the camper on your gift list, try one of these suggestions. In return, you may be invited to share a wilderness adventure over the next three-day weekend!

To keep your camper snug as a bug—or should we say, snug *with* the bugs?—give a sleeping bag, bag liner, sheet, blanket, warmer, foam pad, air mattress (throw in the pump and repair kit), or folding cot.

A hike to the local bookstore would reveal a multitude of books and magazines for campers with a variety of interests. Or, pick up a guide to campgrounds from your travel club to present with your gift to a camper. These guides are free to members and available to nonmembers at a modest price.

Add campsite comfort to the camper's home away from home with a folding chair, stool, lounger, table, hammock, or portable shower.

Equip the chuck wagon with a propane or wood-burning camp stove, reflector oven, butane match, grill and utensils, enamelware camp set, stainless steel cookware, inflatable sink, cooler, bear bag (for suspending food from trees), or bear-resistant food container. An assortment of baking mixes, drink mixes, and freeze-dried meals would also be well received.

Best/Worst

Best: A cabin in the mountains

Worst: Dance lessons shortly after surgery to replace my hip, which was shattered in a car accident

—Richard S.

Campers

Celebrate!

Once a scout, always a scout. Celebrate the anniversary of the founding of the Boy Scouts of America with a gift from *The Official Boy Scout Catalog* which offers hundreds of rough-and-tumble gift ideas. Phone: 800/323-0732.

A ditty bag, duffle bag, stuff sack, backpack, or day pack would help the happy camper haul gear to and from the wild. Compression stuff bags are perfect for reducing such bulky items as sleeping bags.

For roughing it easy, give your camper a new tent. You may find the variety of tents astounding. To mention just a few, there are multi-room cabin tents for family campers, ultralight tents for backpackers, and, for those in a hurry to set up camp, freestanding tents that can be set up in as little as sixty seconds. Lean-tos, cabanas, canopies, and screen houses also provide shelter and privacy. Customized tents are available for use in conjunction with specific vehicles (Plymouth Voyager, Tercel 5-door Wagon, Corolla All-Trac Wagon, Ford Bronco, GMC Jimmy 4x4, Chevy Blazer, Jeep Cherokee, and the list goes on). Camper-top tents convert trucks into complete camping units (available for the Ford Explorer, Mazda Navaho, Chevy S-10 Blazer, GMC S-15 Jimmy, and others).

Still need more ideas? Try one of these: pocket-knife, battery-less razor, reflective emergency blanket, clock-radio-flashlight combination, compass, folding shovel, lantern, axe, binoculars, water filter or purification system, watch (with compass, barometer, or altimeter), first aid or medical supplies, camp clothing, prepaid reservations at a campground or recreational vehicle park, or a gift certificate to rent or purchase camping equipment.

Camping is often combined with other outdoor sports: hunting, fishing, hiking, backpacking, cycling, boating. Each of these activities suggest a multitude of additional gift ideas.

Campers • Car Buffs

The *Campmor* catalog is filled with great gift ideas for campers. Phone: 800/526-4784.

Car Buffs

There is one thing on which car buffs agree: "They just don't build 'em like they used to." With motor oil running through their veins, car enthusiasts rebuild, restore, and replicate their treasured classics. Although you don't need to understand the ins and outs of coachbuilding or engine hibernation to select a winning gift for the car buff, you would do well to note the enthusiast's automotive passions. Here are some cream puff gifts you can give without reinventing the wheel.

Give a limited-edition classic collector's model of his favorite car.

Contract with a builder to construct a garage in which the car buff can protect a vintage beauty.

A customized car cover would make a nice gift for the car fanatic—even if he has a garage in which to store his car.

Arrange for restoration of her classic Mustang (or Thunderbird, or Corvette, or...).

Give a full-color fine art print of a 1950s classic car. Call artist Frank Riley for information and a brochure. Phone: 800/848-9459.

What Gives?

Are there any interest categories or other gift-related topics you would like to see addressed in future editions of *Present Perfect*? Write to us about your ideas. See page 277.

Car Buffs

> **Best/Worst**
>
> Best: A car when I graduated from high school
>
> Worst: A tie
>
> —Brendan O.

Assemble a car cleaning kit. Fill a plastic washing bucket with car-washing mitts, cleaners, sponges, protectorants, auto brushes, camel cloths, wheel brushes, leather treatment, a chamois, and car air freshener.

Give a subscription to *Car Collector & Car Classics* which features antique, classic, special interest, and sports cars, and nostalgic articles relative to car collecting. Phone: 800/877-6119.

Dress up the car buff's car or truck with glueless car tattoos. Designs are printed on clear, removable and reusable film, and are available in a variety of styles at auto-parts stores, through catalogs, and at other retail outlets.

Give a gift certificate to a catalog or store that sells parts to her beloved automobile.

Give car accessories: lamb seat covers, hub caps, steering wheel covers, hood ornaments, or floor mats.

Here's a blast from the past! Big Boy Toys in Springfield, Illinois, offers cruising classics and memorabilia from the 1930s, 1940s, and 1950s. Customized car floor mats, radiator caps, hand-carved rugs, gas pump/ice makers, and dome-top trash cans are just a few of the many items available from Big Boy Toys. Phone: 800/798-2766.

Cats and the People That Love Them

The way to a cat lover's heart is through his cat. So, the next time you're on the prowl for the pur-r-r-fect present, consider one of the following.

Commission a portrait of the recipient's cat—or the recipient and her cat. For best results, find a photographer or painter who specializes in animal portraits.

Give a pet health insurance policy. Check with a veterinarian or pet shop to find out about available policies.

To people that worship their cats and want to read about how to care for them and how to celebrate them, give a subscription to *Cat Fancy*. Phone: 800/365-4421.

Other gifts for cats include heated cat cushions and beds, cat poles, pet doors, litter boxes, scratching pads, automatic cat food and water dispensers, pet sleeping bags, a Protect.A.Pet flashing collar, a pet canteen (for traveling pets), raincoats, sweaters, and caps.

Other gifts for cat lovers include calendars, mugs, T-shirts, and jewelry with cat motifs.

Present Danger!

Animals require a considerable amount of care and expense. To give a pet without consulting a child's parents or being certain of an adult's wishes may be a major imposition on the time and finances of the recipient.

Charitable and Philanthropic Gifts

Charitable and Philanthropic Gifts

Thomas Jefferson said, "I deem it the duty of every man to devote a certain portion of his income for charitable purposes; and that it is his further duty to see that it is so applied as to do the most good of which it is capable." Well, you needn't be a billionaire to be a benefactor. Here are some ideas for making the most of what you have to contribute.

The Council of Better Business Bureaus (CBBB) offers the following tips on charitable giving:

- ◆ Do not give cash; always make contributions by check and make the check out to the charity, not to the individual collecting the donation.

- ◆ Keep records of your donations so you can document your charitable giving at tax time.

- ◆ Don't be fooled by names that look impressive or that closely resemble the name of a well-known organization.

- ◆ Check out the organization with the charity registration office (usually a division of the state attorney general's office) and with the Better Business Bureau.

For more information, and a free copy of "Tips on Charitable Giving," write: Council of Better Business Bureaus, Inc., 4200 Wilson Boulevard, Arlington, VA 22203.

In an effort to help you choose charities that will make the best, most effective use of your contributions, the National Charities Information Bureau (NCIB) publishes periodic reports on national charities. For more information, and a free copy of the *Wise Giving Guide*, write to National Charities Information Bureau,

Park Place

The land we now know as Yosemite National Park was a gift from the state of California to the nation. John D. Rockefeller and other individuals have also given land for the establishment of national parks.

Charitable and Philanthropic Gifts

Inc., 19 Union Square West, 6th Floor, New York, NY 10003-3395.

The Internal Revenue Service has compiled the following lists:

Deductible as Charitable Contributions

◆ Money or property you give to churches, synagogues, temples, mosques, and other religious organizations; federal, state, and local governments, if your contribution is solely for public purposes (for example, a gift to reduce the public debt); nonprofit schools and hospitals; public parks and recreations facilities; Salvation Army, Red Cross, CARE, Goodwill Industries, United Way, Boy Scouts, Girl Scouts, Boys and Girls Clubs of America, etc.; war veterans' groups

◆ Costs you pay for a student living with you, sponsored by a qualified organization

◆ Out-of-pocket expenses when you serve a qualified organization as a volunteer

Not Deductible as Charitable Contributions

◆ Money or property you give to civic leagues, social and sports clubs, labor unions, and chambers of commerce; foreign organizations (except certain Canadian and Mexican charities); groups that are run for personal profit; groups whose purpose is to lobby for law changes; homeowners' associations; individuals; political groups or candidates for public office

◆ Cost of raffle, bingo, or lottery tickets

◆ Dues, fees, or bills paid to country clubs, lodges, fraternal orders, or similar groups

---

Notable Quotables

"Either her judgment or fortune was extraordinary, in the choice of those on whom she bestowed her charity; for it went further in doing good than double the sum from any other hand. And I have heard her say, she always met with gratitude from the poor; which must be owing to her skill in distinguishing proper objects, as well as her gracious manner in relieving them."

—JONATHAN SWIFT
ON THE DEATH OF ESTHER JOHNSON [STELLA]

Charitable and Philanthropic Gifts • Children—Infants

- Tuition
- Value of your time or services
- Value of blood given to a blood bank

Children—Infants
SEE ALSO *Baby Shower Presents*

Infants look, listen, touch, smell, and taste their way through the first year of life as proud parents chart baby's first smiles, rolls, claps, words, and steps. Items designed to stimulate baby's senses and encourage hand-to-eye coordination make great gifts. A few are listed below.

A busy box with fun peekaboo mirrors, dials, spinners, and sliding doors would keep baby occupied for hours. Some are designed for both crib and floor play.

A colorful musical mobile with high-contrast images that face the baby would provide audio and visual stimulation for the very young infant.

Babies love to play peekaboo! Give a framed safety mirror that attaches to the side of the crib.

Pushing and rolling toys, chunky little cars and trucks, and colorful balls are perfect for babies that are starting to get around on their own.

Squeezable, floating tub toys would make bath time fun for little ones.

It's A Wrap!

Top a baby gift with a rattle, a pair of booties, a small stuffed animal, a pacifier, or a teething ring tied to the ribbon or bow.

Children—Infants • Children—Ages One to Two

To lull baby into a gentle sleep, give a tape of lullaby music. Vocal and instrumental versions of the classics as well as new songs are available.

Sturdy cloth and vinyl storybooks with simple images are good choices for the very young. If you choose to give activity books, make sure the detachable pieces are too large to swallow and that such items as buttons and snaps are securely fastened.

If you are artistically inclined, paint a colorful mural on the walls or ceiling of the baby's room.

Interesting wall hangings, pictures, night lights, lamps, switch plate covers, and other nursery accessories also provide visual stimulation.

It's a Wrap!

When presenting several packages to one recipient, form a "tower" by stacking them from largest to smallest and tying them together with a sturdy cord, rope, or ribbon.

Children—Ages One to Two

If it can be pushed, pulled, punched, poked, rolled, doodled on, stacked, turned, cranked, climbed, ridden, or slid down, chances are it would be well received by a busy toddler. Musical instruments and other noisemaking items are also toddler favorites.

Big crayons are just the right size for little scribblers. Give a set with a drawing pad or supply of blank paper.

A sturdy children's tape player is perfect for little music lovers. (As a gift to the toddler's parents, include a generous supply of batteries.)

Children—Ages One to Two • Children—Ages Three to Four

Shopping Tip

Teacher supply stores are an excellent place to find educational presents for preschool and school-aged children.

Toddlers would have "snow" much fun in a sleigh with high sides, a seat belt, and a sturdy tow rope.

Tiny travelers love foot-powered ride-ins. Each year seems to bring new models for touring tots.

For outside fun, give a wading pool, swing, slide, gym set, sand box, toy lawn mower, or play gardening tools.

An indoor gym, slide, or seesaw allows active play on rainy days.

Pop-up toys, puzzles with large pieces and easy-to-grasp knobs, construction blocks, play telephones, or baby dolls and accessories are other great gifts for toddlers.

Children—Ages Three to Four

The pre-schooler's love of pretending is reflected in the stories and television programs she enjoys, the way she plays, the way she dresses, and the art she creates. Give props for playing "all grown up," or gifts that stir the imagination.

Give an assortment of puppets and a puppet stage. With a few yards of fabric and a couple of tension rods, you can construct a doorway stage. Simply drape fabric over the tension rod, or sew parting curtains embellished with decorative trim, cording, or braid. If desired, sew pockets on the curtain backs for storing props and scripts.

Children-Ages Three to Four

A trunk full of dress-up clothes, shoes, gloves, purses, and jewelry inspires hours of "let's pretend." An assortment of hats and other head gear also makes a fun gift. Choose from engineer hats, fire fighter hats, baseball caps, football helmets, straw hats, coonskin caps, yachting caps, sombreros, top hats, cowboy hats, construction hard hats, sailor hats, tennis visors, tiaras, berets, derbies, and crowns to start. ADA Discount Dancewear carries a wide assortment of hats and accessories. Phone: 800/882-9882.

Assemble a collection of project supplies: washable markers, construction paper, crayons, safety scissors, glue, paints, paint brushes, and tape.

Give blocks, blocks, and more blocks: wooden blocks, plastic blocks, giant cardboard blocks, magnetic blocks. To accessorize the block structures for creative play, include small animals (farm, zoo, and wild), cars, trucks, dinosaurs, and people.

For hours of hands-on fun and creativity, give Play-Doh or homemade dough with a rolling pin and an assortment of big cookie cutters.

Remember the Slinky, the Etch-A-Sketch, and Tinkertoys? These classic toys, along with other favorites from yesteryear, can still be found at toy and department stores.

A rhythm band set, a chalkboard, a tricycle, a dollhouse, a painting easel, a nonelectric train set, and storybook tapes are also great gifts for three- and four-year-olds.

Classic Wheels

"One of the few possessions I remember from my childhood is a little red wagon. This classic toy was the perfect gift for our daughter Lauren's third birthday. I'm sure she and her brothers will always remember the hours they spent together pulling and pushing her up and down the hills of our neighborhood in her Radio Flyer."

—SHERRI

Children—Ages Five to Eight

Children—Ages Five to Eight

Children's play and interests become more sophisticated during the early school years as social skills, motor dexterity, and formal instruction increase. They still like to play make-believe, but require more realistic props. Many participate in organized sports. Most want the latest trends in playthings. And they have an insatiable need to know how things work. With these things in mind, it shouldn't be hard to find a gift to delight a five- to eight-year-old.

The Way Things Work, by David Macaulay (Houghton Mifflin Company), explains the mechanics of such concepts as leverage, engines, lasers, stereo, and more, in terms a child can understand.

Pleasant Co.'s "American Girl" collection features dolls with a history. Each doll is dressed in period clothing. Storybooks, furniture, accessories, craft kits, clothing, and matching girl-sized outfits are available separately. Phone: 800/845-0005.

Arrange for dance, swim, karate, gymnastic, or music lessons.

An electronic keyboard is a fun way to introduce a young person to playing the piano. Kids like the percussion features and various instrumental sound options. Parents like the peace and quiet made possible through plug-in headphones. Rechargeable batteries make the keyboard portable.

To a young nature lover, give a birdhouse, a bird feeder, or a bug-collecting bottle and book.

Best/Worst

Best childhood gift: A Daisy BB-gun

Worst childhood gift: Porcelain soldiers I wasn't allowed to play with—I wanted plastic Army men

—Mike B.

Children—Ages Five to Eight • Children—Ages Nine to Twelve

Parents and grandparents would enjoy selecting gifts of toys, games, and activities from the HearthSong catalog. Choose from modeling beeswax, roller beetles, Halfpenny doll and storybook sets, Topsy Turvy Trolls, and more. Phone: 800/325-2502.

To kids that like to scope things out, give a periscope, microscope, geoscope, or kaleidoscope.

An assortment of colored chalk and a chalkboard (or a sidewalk) would bring out the artist in just about any child.

Hire a clown, magician, or face painter for the child's birthday party or another activity.

> **Celebrate!**
>
> On the first truly warm day of the year, one Pacific Northwest mom greets her children coming home from school with treasure maps. After a joyful, noisy twenty minutes, each is clutching her treasure—a plastic pail and shovel—and they are off to the beach to celebrate the coming of summer.

Children—Ages Nine to Twelve

Motorized, computerized, electronic, and remote-controlled are the hallmarks of gifts to please the nine- to twelve-year-old. Kiddie versions of grown-up toys will just not do. Older children demand the real thing in sports gear, musical instruments, audio/video equipment, fashion accessories, and tools for their chosen hobbies.

Replace children's sports equipment with the genuine articles. Give regulation gear: basketballs and backboards, footballs, baseballs and bats, soccer balls and nets, tennis racquets and balls, volleyballs and nets.

Give craft kits that challenge older children's creative skills. A pottery wheel, papermaking kit,

Children—Ages Nine to Twelve

Blockbusters

"The only playthings our children have consistently requested since they were five years old are Legos, Legos, Legos, and Legos. Countless action figures have gone the way of the dinosaur, but their interest in Legos has never waned."

—Lee W.

weaving loom, rock-polishing kit, or jewelry-making kit are good choices.

Give educational posters or maps to hang on bedroom walls. Framed posters or maps are especially fun.

Walkie-talkies are a great way for kids to communicate while playing spy games or hide-n-seek. For just a few dollars more than the toy walkie-talkies, you can get a simple version of the real thing from Radio Shack.

Air hockey and table-tennis tables are popular among nine- to twelve-year-olds.

Arrange for a child to attend a summer camp related to her interest—music, sports, writing, or space exploration, to name a few.

Give a book or magazine subscription related to a hobby or interest. (Refer to the relevant interest categories for ideas.)

Give admission (for two or more) to play miniature golf, play pinball, swim, or drive go-carts at a local sports park.

Computer programs and games are available for a wide range of interests. The encyclopedias and atlases on CD-ROM are so much fun, kids don't even care that they are actually learning something in the

Children–Ages Nine to Twelve • Children's Magazines, Gifts of

meantime. For advice on educational software, consult the child's teacher.

Give an electric train, racing set, or anything with a remote control.

Give a junior membership in the National Geographic Society. Membership includes a subscription to *World* magazine, a membership card, an official certificate, and an iron-on insignia. Phone: 800/638-4077.

The *Exploratorium to Go!* catalog features gifts and learning tools from the Exploratorium in San Francisco. Choose from sound kits, hands-on science kits, nature calendars, note cards, videos, cookbooks, and more. Phone: 800/359-9899.

> **Try This!**
>
> Children love the gift of your time. Fill a container with strips of paper on which you've written fun activities or outings. On a regular basis—weekly, monthly—set aside a time to participate in an activity the child selects from the container.

Children's Magazines, Gifts of

Magazines make wonderful gifts for children and provide a monthly reminder of your thoughtfulness. Preview magazines at a bookstore or library and then check with the child's parents to avoid duplication. Send the child a wrapped issue of the magazine—not just a gift subscription announcement—so he can have something to open and see. Here are just a few of the many publications of interest to children.

Highlights helps children ages 2 to 12 sharpen their observation skills, develop their ability to make decisions, increase their attention span, and improve their language skills through stories, games, puzzles,

Children's Magazines, Gifts of

riddles, jokes, experiments, exercises, and craft projects. Phone: 800/255-9517.

Cricket is for young people (ages 9 and up) that are curious about their world, love to read, and have adventurous minds and imaginations. Stunning illustrations complement superb text and original covers to make each issue a treasure. Also of interest are *Cricket's* own special cartoon characters, word and number games, hands-on projects, and monthly art and writing contests. Phone: 800/827-0227.

Stone Soup features stories, poems, book reviews, and art by children from all over the world. Budding writers and artists (through age 13) are encouraged to submit their work. *Stone Soup* is a very high-quality publication. Phone: 800/447-4569.

Boys' Life is a general service magazine for boys. Contents deal with scouting adventures and skills, sports, amusements, hobbies, science, careers, bicycling, fishing, collecting, magic, books, ecology, movies, and other topics of interest to boys. Write: *Boys' Life*, P.O. Box 152079, Irving, TX 75015-2079. Phone: 214/580-2088.

Ranger Rick is a nature magazine for kids ages 6 to 12, published by the National Wildlife Federation. Through the highest quality photographs, art, and text, the magazine aims to inspire a greater understanding and appreciation of the natural world and our place in it. Phone: 800/432-6564.

Best/Worst

Best: A subscription to *Mad* magazine when I was 11 years old

Worst: A cheap, tasteless, synthetic tie

—Dan J.

Children's Magazines, Gifts of

Barbie, *The Magazine for Girls*, is all about being a girl who's into crafts, sports, celebrities, best friends, cooking, *and* Barbie. Write: *Barbie, The Magazine for Girls*, Welsh Publishing Group, 300 Madison Avenue, New York, NY 10017. Phone: 515/243-4543.

The following are available from Cobblestone Publishing. Call for more information or to place an order. Phone: 800/821-0115.

- *Faces* is a magazine about world cultures for the 9- to 14-year-old. It aims at instilling an interest in and respect for different people, their customs, art, food, and so on.

- *Cobblestone* brings to life past events and people in American history. Aimed at 8- to 14-year-olds, each thematic issue includes historical and nostalgic articles, interviews, photos, illustrations, recipes, and activities that offer a multifaceted look at the subjects.

- *Calliope*, a world history magazine for 8- to 14-year-olds, invests history with reality through articles, stories, activities, and regular departments devoted to word origins, archaeology, maps, and time lines. The magazine covers world history through 1800 A.D.

- Featuring astronomy and space exploration, *Odyssey* gets its 8- to 14-year-old readers to take their imaginations and understanding where they have never gone before. Each issue includes articles, stories, photography, and activities centered around a specific issue or topic.

It's a Wrap!

✔ What little boy wouldn't love a package with a generous assortment of colorful rubber bands stretched around the box? (Don't be offended if—at least initially—he finds the rubber bands more amusing than what's inside the package.)

✔ Top a little girl's present with an assortment of colorful shoelaces, hair ribbons, barrettes, or bows.

✔ Place small balloons, balloon-twist animals, a box of crayons, or an assortment of crazy straws on top of a child's wrapped gift.

Chocoholics

Chocoholics consider chocolate the foundation that supports the entire food pyramid. Furthermore, chocolate—in all its varieties—enhances foods from each of the basic groups. Here are some fun ways to give a gift of chocolate to those for whom there seems to be no maximum daily requirement.

If the chocolate lover on your list craves Reese's Pieces, Mr. Goodbar, Hershey's Kisses, Krackel, Almond Joy, or other Hershey's candies, call for a catalog from Hershey's. Each one is filled with fun gift possibilities. Phone: 800/454-7737.

Give a chocolate gift reflecting the profession or an interest of the recipient. Molded chocolate replicas are made in all shapes and sizes:

- Telephones, typewriters, computers, and compact disks, for desk dwellers (Cummings Studio Chocolates, 800/537-3957)
- Porsches, Ferraris, Corvettes, and Mercedes for car enthusiasts (Chocolate Catalog, 800/325-8881)
- Footballs, baseballs and mitts, basketballs, golf clubs, golf balls, skis, and ski boots for sports enthusiasts (Cummings Studio Chocolates, above)
- Birth announcements and chocolate cigars with chocolate matches (for giving by or to proud new parents) can be found in many in hospital gift shops

Other chocolate gifts include fresh chocolate-dipped fruit (or fresh fruit and a jar of dipping chocolate), chocolate cheesecake, chocolate truffles in all their glorious varieties, chocolate pancake and

---

Indispensable

"Our children thought they found the perfect gift for Sherri when they gave her an M&Ms candy dispenser. They love replenishing it, too!"

—LARRY

Chocoholics

waffle mix, chocolates wrapped in love notes, and chocolate-covered nuts.

To toast a very special occasion, give a wine bottle made entirely from Swiss chocolate and filled with chocolate-covered toasted almonds. This and other fabulous chocolate gifts are available from Essentially Chocolate. Phone: 800/243-7466.

If the chocoholic on your gift list also likes to cook, give a chocolate cookbook and the ingredients for a specific recipe from the book.

If brownies are his passion, choose from white chocolate brownies with white chocolate chips, peanut butter brownies with milk chocolate chips, double chocolate brownies with dark chocolate chips, butterscotch brownies with white chocolate chips...or choose them all!

Leave a trail of chocolate kisses that leads to a basket filled with gourmet chocolate treats.

Give a certificate to a store or catalog that sells fine chocolates.

Give tickets to a chocolate festival. Many are charity fund-raisers ranging from one-day affairs to week-long extravaganzas. Activities include tastings, demonstrations, bake-offs, raffles, and auctions. For a list of chocolate festivals, events, and celebrations across the country, or for information on organizing a festival in your own community, write to American

High See's

"For as long as I can remember, See's Candies were the only chocolates given by my father to his business associates and good friends. A box of See's was his way of saying, 'Thanks,' or 'You're special.'"

—SHERRI

For mail order information, call See's Candies. Phone: 800/347-7337.

Chocoholics • Christmas Presents

Chocolate Week Events, 708 Third Avenue, Suite 1100, New York, NY 10017.

Christmas Presents

Does your next year's Christmas shopping start at this year's day-after-Christmas sales, or does the annual sight of tinsel and tree trimmings mingled with Halloween decorations at the mall make you want to shout "Bah humbug!"? Either way, we hope you'll find some holiday cheer in the following pages.

Give tickets to *A Christmas Carol*, *The Nutcracker*, *The Messiah*, or other Christmas entertainment.

Fill a decorated basket with twelve wrapped packages. Put one item in the first package and label it "On the first day of Christmas...." Put two items in the second package and label it "On the second day of Christmas...," and so forth. The presents can be as simple or elaborate as you wish. Each day the anticipation mounts. This is an especially fun gift for someone who lives alone or is away from family for Christmas. It is also fun to do anonymously.

For another twist on the above idea, give an advent basket with 25 individually-wrapped packages. One item per package will do. Children love this idea and it gives them something to look forward to each day leading up to Christmas.

Offer to wrap and store a friend's Christmas packages.

Best/Worst

Best: A needlepoint nativity scene

Worst: A face-cream warmer

—Carmen E.

Christmas Presents

Decorate a storage box with holiday wrap and fill it with Christmas lights, ornaments, candles, wrapping paper, ribbon, greeting cards, and traditional holiday recipes for a couple's first Christmas.

Give a Christmas-morning breakfast basket to your holiday host or hostess. Fill with pancake or muffin mix, flavorful syrups and jellies, gourmet cocoa mixes, fresh fruits, and napkins with holiday motifs.

For friends that stop by during the holidays, fill a basket with Christmas crackers (exploding cylinders filled with small favors), ornaments, or small wrapped gifts. Choose generic gifts—candy, puzzles, mugs, notepads, picture frames—or wrap gifts in different papers to indicate which ones are for women (scarves, compacts, potpourri sachets), men (holiday tie tacks, sports magazines, car fresheners), or children (marbles, Silly Putty, washable markers). Let each guest choose a present as he or she leaves.

A present for the family pet would endear you all the more to the recipients. Fill a Christmas stocking with treats and toys for Phelix or Phideaux. (See *Dogs and the People That Love Them* and *Cats and the People That Love Them*.)

Assemble a holiday activity box to occupy children while parents prepare for holiday parties, shop, or wrap presents. Be sure the activities are age-appropriate and can be completed without supervision. Here are a few ideas to get you started: Christmas coloring books and crayons, sticker books, stencils, ornament kits, safety scissors, construction paper, glue sticks, glitter, buttons, string, beads, and tape.

> ### Holiday Treasures
>
> "Nearly every year our friend Susan and her children make Christmas crafts of one sort or another to give to friends and relatives. The angel they made for the top of our tree and the nativity set they created for us are among our most treasured holiday decorations."
>
> —SHERRI & LARRY

Christmas Presents

Mail Call

Mail packages early to reduce costly overseas rates and to ensure delivery before Christmas. The Post Office suggests a deadline of October 1 for surface mail to Africa, the Middle East, and South and Central America, and November 1 for surface mail to Australia, the Caribbean, Europe, the Far East, and Southeast Asia. Check with the Post Office for other suggested mailing dates.

Give a Rubbermaid Wrap'n Craft box or another suitable container filled with rolls of gift wrap, ribbons, bows, scissors, tape, gift cards, markers, and other wrapping supplies.

Stocking stuffer ideas for kids of all ages include trading cards, stickers, gloves or mittens, personalized pencils, jewelry, magazines, small books, flashlights, flower bulbs or seed packets, boxed fruit juices, small wallets or change purses filled with cash (bills or coins), cosmetics, brushes, hair accessories, dried fruits, nuts, small puzzles, magic tricks, fragrant drawer sachets, cedar blocks, film, gourmet treats, movie passes, markers, chalk, colored pencils, coloring books, refrigerator magnets, soap, lotion, powder in a favorite fragrance, fishing lures, golf tees, tennis balls, or small items related to the recipient's favorite sport or hobby.

Christmas-theme gifts are great for giving to hostesses of pre-holiday parties or others with whom you exchange gifts before Christmas. Here are just a few suggestions:

◆ Christmas table linens—cloths, runners, placemats, napkins

◆ A welcome mat with a holiday greeting

◆ Tableware—plates, glasses, serving pieces, centerpieces

◆ Holiday decorations—tree ornaments, crèches, stocking holders, wreaths, bells, yule logs, candles, tree skirts, tree angels, imported wood carousels, snow globes, or music boxes

◆ An assortment of mugs with wassail spices and cinnamon sticks

Christmas Presents

- Audio tapes or compact discs of Christmas music
- A book or collection of treasured Christmas stories
- A ceramic cookie platter or jar filled with holiday cookies
- Fashion accessories with a holiday motif—earrings, ties and tacks, socks, scarves, hats, mittens
- Flowers and greens—poinsettia, Christmas cactus, mistletoe, pine boughs, garland
- A lap quilt, sweater, or painted sweatshirt of your own design
- An advent calendar
- A basket of peppermint candy
- Videos—*It's a Wonderful Life*, *Miracle on 34th Street*, *White Christmas*, *A Christmas Story*, *The Santa Clause*

R.E.D.U.C.E. Your Holiday Gift List

- **R—Record** the names of people to whom you feel you want or need to give holiday gifts, and how much you plan to spend on each gift. When making the list, consider your parents, siblings, grandparents, spouse, children, grandchildren, aunts, uncles, nieces, nephews, neighbors, friends, church associates, paper boy, mail carrier, housekeeper, secretary, and coworkers, and your children's teachers, activity leaders, and coaches.

- **E—Examine** your gift-giving priorities. Decide what is really important to you as far as gift giving goes. Remember that your priorities will change from year to year depending on your outlook, family situation, time, energy, and finances. Here are

---

Surprise, S-u-r-prise!

"When I was a child, we were always given one present to open on Christmas Eve. The gift was always the same—new pajamas. I later learned that the reasoning behind this annual gift was to look our best for pictures on Christmas morning. From speaking with others, I've learned this is a fairly common practice."

—MICHAEL W.

Christmas Presents

All the Trimmings

"For our first Christmas after we were married, some friends gave us a boxed set of 24 Christmas tree ornaments. They were simple, painted wooden figurines, nothing extravagant, but it was the perfect gift for us as newlyweds, since we didn't have anything with which to decorate our tree. We have since added lots of ornaments to our collection, but each year as we trim the tree, we think of our friends and our first Christmas together."

—Kristen B.

a few gift-related holiday priorities: hand make all gifts, complete gift shopping by November 15th, include family members in the selection and giving of gifts, give time and means to a worthy charity, cut back on overall gift expenses, reduce or eliminate the commercialism of the holidays, center holiday gifts and activities around a person or family with special needs, or beautifully wrap and creatively present gifts.

◆ **D—Delete** from your gift list all those with whom gift exchanges have become meaningless, those whom you haven't seen or heard from for years, those from whom you never receive notes of thanks for gifts given, and those that do not fit your gift-giving priorities.

◆ **U—Unload** yourself of some of the gift-giving responsibilities. Recruit your husband and children to help with gift giving. Decide, as a family or couple, who will select, shop for, order, wrap, and deliver each gift. Take advantage of such resources as mailing or shipping, in-store gift wrapping, personal shopping services, and UPS pick up.

◆ **C—Combine** recipients and resources. Pool your resources with those of your siblings to give your parents something you cannot afford to give by yourself. Or, instead of giving individual gifts to your aunt, uncle, and each of their six children, give a single gift the whole family can enjoy. Give a joint gift to the office instead of a separate gift to each staff member.

◆ **E—Evaluate.** Keep a list of gifts you gave to and received from others. Record responses made by the recipients about the gifts as well as your own impressions as to how they felt. List the budget busters, the time busters, the sanity busters, and the successes.

Christmas Presents

Special Delivery

Few occasions or events allow the bearer of gifts as many options for creative presentation as do the Yuletide holidays. Create wonder, excitement, anticipation, surprise, or adventure with your special deliveries.

◆ Don a Santa suit before you deliver your gifts to neighborhood children, your young nieces and nephews, or children in the hospital.

◆ Bundle up for family carolling and gift delivering.

◆ Are you the fun-loving or old-fashioned type? Hire a horse-drawn sleigh with driver to convey you and your packages to your delivery destination(s).

◆ Whet dinner guests' appetites with gifts wrapped to coordinate with your centerpiece. Put a gift at each place setting, with the gift tags doubling as place cards.

◆ Imagine the grandchildren's anticipation as Grandpa pulls one gift after another, after another, from a large Santa sack.

◆ For a touch of mystery, discreetly leave your gift under the recipient's tree, but with no giver's name on the card. Enclose your greeting inside—to be discovered only after the package is opened.

◆ Hang a variety of ornaments from a small tree near the front door and allow holiday guests to choose one for a gift as they leave.

◆ Wrap a gift and label it with the recipient's name. Place the wrapped gift in a box. Wrap and label it with the name of another person who will be present when the gift is to be opened. Repeat the process, changing the name on the label each time you wrap another box. When it's time to open gifts, the pack-

---

Special Request

"For Christmas I would like peace on earth, unless you're really giving out holiday gifts, then I could use a new waffle iron."

—Jack Lemmon

Christmas Presents

> ### Time for a Change
>
> **"**My friends and I have reached a point in our lives where if we want something, we can go get it. It's time to exchange cards.**"**
>
> —Barbara B.

age will be passed from one person to another until the true recipient opens the box containing the gift.

◆ And finally, who can resist the romance of exchanging gifts with that special someone in front of a cozy fire?

Scrooges Unite

According to founder and Executive Director Chuck Langham, the Society to Curtail Ridiculous, Outrageous, and Ostentatious Gift Exchanges (SCROOGE) was founded in 1979 to provide good-natured moral support for those that want to change their holiday gift-giving practices—to stop wasting large sums of money on gifts that don't seem to make anybody all that much happier. With thousands of members worldwide, SCROOGE's principles are:

◆ Try to avoid giving and receiving extremely expensive gifts (particularly the heavily advertised fad/status symbol items that so often are not very useful or practical).

◆ Make every effort to use cash—not credit cards—to pay for the gifts you do give.

◆ Emphasize gifts that involve thought and originality—handcrafted items you can make yourself, for example.

◆ Celebrate and enjoy the holidays, but remember that a Merry Christmas is not for sale in any store for any amount of money.

Lifetime SCROOGE memberships are available for $2.00 to cover the cost of preparing and mailing the annual newsletter. For more information, write to SCROOGE International Headquarters, 1447 Westwood Road, Charlottesville, VA 22903.

Clergymen

"The most acceptable service of God is doing good to man," said Benjamin Franklin. Those that devote their time and energies to our spiritual well-being are worthy of our utmost attention. We hope you'll find some inspiration in the following ideas.

Offer to visit ill or hospitalized members of his congregation or to take meals to shut-ins.

Provide, or arrange for, regular gardening, lawn, or housekeeping services for the house of worship or the clergyman's residence.

Arrange an evening out for the clergyman and his wife and baby-sitting services for their children.

Give a book, magazine subscription, or other gift relating to her interests outside of her ecclesiastical duties. (See relevant interest categories.)

Volunteer your services to help with answering telephones, typing, word processing, or other clerical duties.

Host a reception in her honor.

Contribute your time to a fund-raising activity or charitable event.

What Gives?

If you have any great gift ideas for clergy men and women, we would love to hear from you. See page 277.

Collectors

Collectors

My friend Catherine's penchant for collecting almost makes finding a gift for her too easy. Pewter picture frames grace the top of her antique baby grand piano. Clever groupings of rustic old farm tools adorn the walls of her living room. Handmade wooden ornaments bedeck the 12-foot noble fir that is the centerpiece of her annual holiday party. Many of her collectibles are gifts from observant friends. Adding to—or starting—a collection for someone who has or wants a collection could simplify gift giving for years to come. As a collection grows, give shadow boxes, curio cabinets, shelves, and cases for displaying the items.

There are thousands of possibilities for collectibles. Here are just a few:

- Antiques (dishes, linens, tools, toys, bird cages)
- Sports cards (baseball, football, basketball)
- Records, comic books, music posters
- Memorabilia from an era (Elvis Presley, Coca Cola, the 1950s)
- The works of a favored artist, composer, writer, or performer
- Models (trains, airplanes, automobiles)
- Candlesticks (crystal, brass, silver, ceramic)
- Picture frames (pewter, wood, silver)
- China service or silverware (keep lists from friends' wedding registries)
- Household items (clocks, teapots, cookie tins, cookie cutters)
- Stamps or coins (from a particular time or country)

Consider This

The expert collector may have very specific wants. If you are sure about her wants, add to her collection. Or, if you know the person would enjoy it, start a new collection to which you may add objects on later occasions. Gifts relating to a theme or given in sequence can also be fun.

Collectors

- Books (cookbooks, rare books, first editions, collections by a specific writer, or a collection on a specific topic)
- Charms for a bracelet, pearls or stones for an add-a-bead necklace
- Dolls, dollhouses, and furnishings
- Quilts
- Music boxes

Children also love to collect things. Try adding to or starting a collection of rocks, insects, sea shells, autographs, buttons, baseball caps, mugs, action figures, or paraphernalia related to their favorite television program or movie.

Arrange for attendance to a collector's fair, convention, workshop, lecture, or museum.

Arrange and prepare for an appraisal of the recipient's collection.

Give a "treasure map" showing areas in which to find collectibles of interest. Have "X" mark the spot where the collector will find a treasure—a collectible you have purchased for her.

Make the effort to track down and purchase a rare or hard-to-find item the collector is interested in adding to his collection.

Give a book or pricing guide about the type of item the recipient collects. History books for the

> **Present Danger!**
>
> Do not give gifts beneath the recipient's standards. For example, just because you can't tell the difference between the kind of pottery she favors and factory imitations does not mean the shoddy imposter will find a place in her collection. Choose something else.

Collectors • Computer Buffs

> ### Best/ Worst
>
> Best: Glass bells—I collect them
>
> Worst: Candy dishes we received for our wedding
>
> —Monique D.

period in which the collector is interested also make great gifts.

Arrange for a stay in New York City, London, Glasgow, or another city, and pay for seats at an antiques auction.

Computer Buffs

Computerese may not be as romantic as French, but it's the language of love to the computer buff. And, once this affair has begun, there is no end to the list of enticing gift possibilities.

For the neophyte, a class in basic skills would ease the transition into the world of computers. Arrange for instruction through a computer store, community education program, or private instructor. Tutoring software is available for those that prefer to be taught by the computer itself.

Gift choices of hardware and peripherals include fax modems, mouses (but not mice!), joysticks, scanners, digitizers, printer stands, surge protectors, virtual reality accessories, and antiglare screens.

> ### It's A Wrap!
>
> Wrap presents to the computer buff in computer paper or pages from a computer magazine.

Most computer buffs have mile-long lists of software wishes—and it's no wonder, with all the options for database management, financial analysis, desktop publishing, word processing, computer-aided design, art, music, education, games, entertainment, graphics, fonts, utilities, and other software. The *800 SOFTWARE Catalog* is filled with descriptions and comparison charts for software, hardware, and network products, making it a valuable resource to you in choos-

Computer Buffs

ing and giving gifts to the serious computer buff. Phone: 800/SOFTWARE.

Give ergonomic helps for those that spend lots of time at the computer: touch pads, wrist rests, ergonomically-correct keyboards, and keyboard trays.

If there is one thing computer users just can't have too much of, it's diskettes for backing up files, and storage for those diskettes. Before you shop, find out the size and brand of diskettes your recipient uses.

Give a subscription to one of the many computing magazines. Pick one up from the newsstand or bookstore and mail in the subscription card, or call the following magazines:

- *Computer Gaming World* is a computer magazine for serious computer game players. Phone: 800/827-4450.

- *Window Sources* is a magazine for Windows experts. Phone: 800/365-3414.

- *PC Magazine* is an independent guide to personal computing. Phone: 800/289-0429.

- *PC/Computing* is a magazine for business computing experts. Phone: 800/365-2770.

- *MacUser* is a Macintosh resource. Phone: 800/627-2247.

- *Computer Shopper* is a computer magazine for direct buyers. Phone: 800/274-6384.

- *Family PC* is devoted to software for families, especially kids' software. Phone: 800/413-9749.

> **It's a Wrap!**
>
> For padding fragile objects, use paper streamers, Easter grass, shredded paper, popcorn, or unshelled peanuts.

Consumable Gifts

Consumable Gifts

Sherri celebrated her 38th birthday within days of hauling our family's earthly possessions across the country in a moving van. After weeks of sorting, discarding, donating, and packing more than five tons of tables, chairs, books, clothing, pots, dishes, toys, computers, filing cabinets, bicycles, stuff, stuff, and stuff, the last thing we needed was more stuff. She thought the message, "I want nothing for my birthday," was loud and clear. But when the inevitable day rolled around, friends and family gathered with gifts to bestow. As Sherri began to unwrap each of the gifts, she soon realized they all had one thing in common—they were consumable. Among the gifts she found a box of fine chocolates, a dozen red roses, and a gift certificate to her favorite restaurant. Within two weeks, the only thing left was memories. There was nothing to store, clean, or maintain. She will never forget the cleverness of those givers that added to her joy without adding to her stuff.

Ideas for gifts that leave only memories include:

- Tickets to a cultural or sporting event
- A party
- Lift passes for the skier, green fees for the golfer, prepaid court time for the racquetball player
- The services of a personal trainer or tutor
- Art, music, flying, race car driving, scuba diving, or other lessons
- Tuition or fees for a class or seminar of interest to the recipient
- Dessert-of-the-month club enrollment
- Long distance debit cards—perhaps with a note about how much you'd like to hear from him

Consider This

Consumable gifts are great for those that have everything as well as for those that have limited space.

Consumable Gifts • Cooks

- Certificates for spending time together
- Lawn or housekeeping services
- Car washing and detailing
- Gift certificates for a manicure, pedicure, hairstyling, or facial
- Movie passes and concessions
- Travel
- Admission to an amusement park, zoo, or other such attraction
- A carriage ride, a sleigh ride, or limousine service
- A hot-air balloon, parasailing, or scuba diving adventure

> ### Let's Be Practical
>
> "How about giving gifts people can really use—a box of laundry detergent, a bottle of dishwashing liquid, or a pack of light bulbs, for example."
>
> —Barbara B.

Cooks

SEE ALSO *Hosts and Hostesses* and *Outdoor Cooks*

For some, cooking is a pastime. For others, it's a passion or profession. On any level, masters of the culinary arts can really dish it out. For kudos from the cooks on your gift list, try one of the following recipes. You could have them eating out of your hand for a change.

Not every course should be served on an ordinary dinner plate or in an all-purpose bowl. No, no, no! When giving to cooks that like to entertain, your choices are many: pasta bowls, chili bowls, popcorn bowls (they filter out the unwanted unpopped kernels), corn-on-the-cob dishes, onion soup bowls, ramekins (for puddings, mousses, soufflés, and crème brûlée), cheese plates, and espresso cups to name a few. Or, choose a gift from the wide range of serving platters, trays, tureens, and bowls.

Cooks

It's a Wrap!

Wrap a kitchen gift in a pretty dishtowel. Tie it with a colorful bow and attach a wooden spoon or wire whisk.

Most gourmet cooks have specific preferences about pots and pans and a good supply of basic cookware. Specialty items in the recipient's preferred line of cookware would be sure gift winners. In addition to the essential sauce pans and stock pots, you can choose from a variety of omelet pans, stir fry pans, sauté pans, roasting pans and racks, fondue pots, quiche and au gratin dishes, lasagna pans, pasta inserts, fish and vegetable steamers, bread pans, crepe pans, deep fryers, double-boilers, griddles, skillets, and other such items.

Today's kitchen appliances can make just about any cook look like a pro. In addition to making quick work of KP, these items are also fun to give: pasta machines, bread makers, Belgian waffle irons, rotisserie grills, food processors, yogurt makers, food dehydrators, frozen dessert makers, and malt mixers.

If there is a garlic lover on your gift list, you're in luck! There are enough garlic gizmos to make garlic lovers everywhere rejoice. These include garlic braids, garlic roasters, garlic presses, garlic peelers, garlic slicers, garlic bakers, and garlic keepers—all in a variety of styles and sizes. (Did you know there are specially engineered garlic storage pots that provide precisely the correct amount of ventilation to keep garlic from sprouting or growing fungus?)

Most of the items on the cook's kitchen wish list can be found in two excellent cooking catalogs: *Chef's Catalog: Professional Restaurant Equipment for the Home Chef* (800/338-3232) and *Williams-Sonoma: A Catalog for Cooks* (800/541-2233).

Cooks

For added workspace in the kitchen, give a kitchen island cart, baker's rack, or folding table. If you're married to the cooped-up cook, you may even consider giving him a kitchen makeover. (Caution: Due to the potential strain on a relationship brought on by a major renovation, the giving of this gift is better left to those who will have to endure the disruption.)

Give a gadget with the food on which it will be used: a zester with a basket of lemons or oranges, or a melon baller with an assortment of melons, a cheese knife with a wedge of cheese.

Many cooks would love a few culinary tips from the pros. If a trip to a French cooking school is not in the gift budget, give him a video cooking series featuring a chef he admires or a cooking technique he would like to learn.

Great cooks are always looking for savory ways to please the palate. Flavored vinegars and oils, exotic spices, extracts such as vanilla and almond, gourmet cheeses, and fresh herbs make welcome gifts.

A recipe for an exotic dish and the special ingredients and cookware with which to prepare it would make a nice gift.

Local or specialized cookbooks are great gifts for cooks. Many of Sherri's favorite recipes for entertaining can be found in the Junior League cookbooks she's been given by friends from all over the country.

It's in the Mail

✔ Mail jams and jellies in plastic containers with tight-fitting, twist-on lids.

✔ Pack baked goodies in popped corn, puffed cereal, or peanuts (either the unshelled or the polystyrene foam variety).

✔ Ship uncut cookie bars in the pan in which they were baked to keep them moist and crumble free.

✔ Bake fruit and nut breads in metal food cans. Remove them from the cans to cool. Wrap the breads in plastic wrap and put them back into cleaned cans for wrapping and shipping.

Couch Potatoes

After years of sitting and snacking, there's nearly as much starch in a couch potato as in his or her vegetable counterpart. Although you may be tempted by good intentions to give the couch potato an exercise bike to ride while viewing ball games, soap operas, or videos, one of the following may be more well received.

Fill a large bowl with assorted snacks and drinks. Throw in a game schedule or television guide and a coupon for uninterrupted viewing of an upcoming sports event, movie, or special television program.

Make your sweet potato comfortable with a fluffy pillow, cozy afghan, sturdy footstool, recliner, snack trays, or TV trays.

One television set is not enough for the TV addict. Give a portable, wrist, mounted-under-the-cabinet, or big-screen television.

Give cable service or a satellite dish to the couch potato who desires more channel choices.

To the channel surfer, give a remote control, video headset, split-screen television for viewing two programs at once, or a VCR on which to record one program while watching another.

Give clothing, home furnishings, and accessories like those seen on the set of her favorite television series.

Celebrate!

February is National Snack Food Month. This lends itself to gift baskets galore! Tell someone you love them with a Twinkie.

Couch Potatoes • Country Western Fans

Movie posters (originals and reproductions), pressbooks, stills, and lobby cards for movies made since 1945 are available from Movie Poster Warehouse. Write: Movie Poster Warehouse, 335 Lesmill Road, Don Mills, Ontario, Canada, M3B2V1. Phone: 416/391-0133.

Signals: A Catalog for Fans and Friends of Public Television is filled with quality gifts that inform, enlighten, and entertain. Videos of award-winning public television programs, shirts with witty sayings, glorious music, beautiful art posters, jewelry, books, and more are available from *Signals*. Phone: 800/669-9696.

The people at A Million and One World-Wide Videos are video detectives. They buy, sell, trade, rent, broker, and auction every video in the world. Contact them if you need help finding inactive, out-of-print, sold-out titles, or active new releases. Phone: 800/849-7309. Fax: 800/849-0873.

> **Present Danger!**
>
> Do not give gifts that hint of self improvement or change on the recipient's part. The treadmill to the couch potato, the gourmet cookbook to the casserole cook, or time management classes to the unorganized would not evoke gushing thanks, even if such items are—in the giver's estimation—exactly what the recipient needs.

Country Western Fans

Country western tunes are hymns from America's heartland. Blending rock and bluegrass with the wail of steel guitars, modern artists celebrate love and life, and lament cheatin' hearts and other done-gone-wrongs. If your gift list includes a country western fan, fiddle around with these heel-stompin', toe tappin', gift possibilities.

Give a biography, signed photograph, poster, or calendar of the country fan's favorite star.

Country Western Fans

> **Special Presentations**
>
> To build suspense, leave hints about a forthcoming gift for the recipient to find during the days or weeks preceding the giving of the gift.

Give western apparel—a shirt, a vest, a pair of jeans, a duster—or western accessories—a belt buckle, a hat, a pair of boots, a bandana, or a piece of jewelry.

Assemble a collection of cowboy songs, stories, or poetry. Our neighbor once gave us a book of cowboy poetry written by his father. It's not something we would ever have thought to buy for ourselves, but we have enjoyed it immensely. Through the poems, we've seen an insider's view of a very interesting lifestyle and profession.

Arrange a trip to Branson, Missouri, or Nashville, Tennessee.

When in San Antonio, we attended a party at which line dancing was taught. It was really fun! It's also great exercise. Many instructional videos are available that would make great gifts for the country western fan, as well as others on your gift list. (See B&S Video under *Dancers*.)

Give a country cookbook filled with recipes for down-home cookin'.

Give a set of the Academy of Country Music collector's cards. The cards feature information about country music superstars Hank Williams Jr., Minnie Pearl, Clint Black, Sawyer Brown, Roy Clark, Patti Page, and others. The cards are available at baseball card and hobby shops and through Music City News. Write: 50 Music Square W., Suite 601, Nashville, TN 37203. Phone: 615/329-2200.

Cyclists

There are almost as many reasons for cycling as there are cyclists. And whatever the reasons—fitness, fun, or frugality, competition, convenience, or commuting—cyclists are really going places. Here are some gift ideas to help get them there.

A bike trailer, cart, or child carrier is a great gift for the cyclist who wants to take the kids along.

A bicycle storage rack is an ideal gift for the college student living in a dorm, apartment, or condo.

Bike bags, baskets, and panniers (designed to fit on handlebars, frames, seats, and racks) are great gifts for those that use their bikes to commute or trek.

For the adventurous cyclist, arrange through a cycling club or travel agency for a bike tour.

Tire pumps, work stands, tool kits, or bicycle maintenance and repair books are great gifts for the avid cyclist.

Safety lights, reflectors, horns, mirrors, and reflective biking vests would help protect the cyclist on your gift list. A bike security system or lock would help protect her bike.

Handlebar wrap is a fun gift and is available in many colors and patterns.

Celebrate!

May is American Bike Month. Give a catalog and gift certificate from Bike Nashbar, 800/627-4227, or Performance Bicycle, 800/727-2453. Call now for a catalog! Both have 24-hour-a-day service.

Cyclists • Dancers

Today's cyclists are making fashion statements as well as fitness statements. Wearable gift possibilities include jerseys, skin suits, tights, and shorts in high-tech fabrics, and lightweight, wind resistant, and waterproof jackets and parkas. And don't forget the head-to-toe accessories: helmets, sunglasses, fanny packs, bike gloves, cycling shoes, and socks.

Give a subscription to *Bicycling Magazine*, the world's #1 road and mountain bike magazine. It covers all aspects of the sport, including fitness, training, and equipment. Phone: 800/666-2806.

A subscription to *Bike Magazine* would give the cyclist a fresh new look at the sport of mountain biking. It features travel articles, adventure stories, and behind-the-scenes interviews with the pros. Phone: 800/765-5501.

Dancers

They clog and jig, hip-hop and tap, leap, twirl, sashay, and hoof it— in lines and in squares, alone and in pairs. When it's time to give to the dancer, the following suggestions may help you keep in step.

To a dancer, what could be more fun than dancing the night away? Find out what type of dancing he enjoys or where his favorite dance spot is, and make reservations to dance 'til dawn.

Give clothing, shoes, jewelry, accessories, posters, or music relevant to the recipient's specific dance interests.

Dancers

Give tickets to a dance performance, competition, or exhibition in which she has expressed an interest in attending or participating.

Arrange and pay for dance lessons.

The *ADA Discount Danceware Catalog* is filled with gift possibilities for dancers. Choose from shoes (ballet, pointe, jazz, tap, character, and lyrical), danceware for men, women, and children (leotards, skirts, dresses, and unitards), wigs, hats, accessories, and makeup. Phone: 800/882-9882.

Do you know someone who is hankerin' to learn the Cowboy Cha-cha, the Hawaiian Hustle, or the Boot Scootin' Boogie? Instructional video tapes on these and other country, line, and novelty partner dances are available from video and chain stores, and via mail order. For a small, refundable fee, B&S Video will send a "Video Sampler/Catalogue Tape" for your review. Phone: 800/858-5518.

Give a subscription to *Dance Magazine*, a monthly look at today's exciting world of dance. *Dance Magazine* features picture stories of the latest performances, interviews with leading personalities, profiles of outstanding dance companies, behind-the-scenes commentary, dance news from around the world, a calendar of upcoming events, and reviews of dance books, television, and film productions. *Dance Magazine* also offers a quarterly publication for young audiences. It's called *Young Dancer Supplement*. Call them for more information. Phone: 800/331-1750.

It's a Wrap!

For added interest, embellish your presents with baubles, fresh or dried flowers, ornaments, trinkets, potpourri sachets, balloons, small toys, or knickknacks.

Desk Dwellers

Desk Dwellers
SEE ALSO *Home Office Dwellers*

Desks. They can be found in dorm rooms, offices, and nooks and crannies of homes around the country. And behind each desk, you'll find a desk dweller assuming the role of student, executive, telecommuter, or home-based entrepreneur. Whether bound by the grade, the paycheck, or sheer determination, your desk dweller may enjoy the following gifts.

Give a book or article on power napping along with a comfy pillow and audio tapes of relaxing music or white noise.

Arrange to have lunch or dinner delivered when he can't get away from the office.

Fill a whimsical or elegant candy dish with a supply of favorite confections to give to the desk dweller with a sweet tooth.

A picture of you, framed for desktop display, may remind your significant other that she has a life away from her desk.

Assemble a contingency kit containing just-in-case items such as socks/stockings, cologne/perfume, tie/scarf, tie tack/earrings, comb/brush, sewing kit (buttons, thread, and scissors), and antistatic spray.

Interject a few minutes of fun in the workday routine or provide amusement during boring phone calls by giving such gifts as executive games, over-the-door

Best/Worst

Best: Books and computer programs

Worst: Cheap tools—I have about 400 Phillip's screwdrivers

—Bob F.

Desk Dwellers • Dogs and the People That Love Them

basketball hoops, decision-making dartboards, puzzles, and kaleidoscopes.

Give a desk accessory: bookends, paperweights, nameplate, business card holder, desk clock, desktop globe, letter opener, writing instruments, reference book, stapler, tape dispenser, stationary box, desk lamp, stamp box, pencil cup, leather clipboard, or notepad.

Order a custom-made, ergonomically-correct chair for a gift she'll thank you for again and again.

> **It's a Wrap!**
>
> Keep a pair of scissors, a stapler, and a pen with your wrapping supplies and guard them jealously—unless you don't mind searching for them when needed.

Dogs and the People That Love Them

"Like me, like my dog." That's what our friend Sarah said of man's best friend (or in this case, woman's best friend). In any case, most people appreciate gifts for their beloved pets. Here are some dog-gone great gift ideas.

Give a book on canine history, health care, breeding, showing, or training. T.F.H. Publications, the world's largest publisher of dog books, has over 400 titles on these and other dog-related topics. Order through your local pet shop and save 10%, or contact T.F.H Publications. Write: P.O. Box 27, Neptune, NJ 07753. Phone: 908/988-8400.

For dogs on the go, give a collapsible dog crate, portable exercise pen, or a pet barrier for the back of the car. Check your local pet supply shop, or call Kennel-Aire, Inc. Phone: 800/346-0134.

Dogs and the People That Love Them

Dog owners might enjoy a subscription to *Dog Fancy*. The magazine offers articles on dog care, health, training, behavior, grooming, and various breeds of dogs. Phone: 800/365-4421.

To breeders, exhibitors, hobbyists, and professionals in kennel operations, veterinary medicine, and pet supplies, give a subscription to *Dog World*, the world's largest all-breed dog magazine. Contents include dog health care, veterinary medicine, grooming, legislation, training, and breed articles. Phone: 800/361-8056.

Other gifts for Rover include grooming products, grooming tables and dryers, whelping boxes, heated pet cushions or beds, automatic timers and feeders, raised dog bowls, cordless pet grooming vacuums, retractable leashes, dog doors, pet washers, pet taxis, dog pillows, rawhide bones, rubber toys, boarding or grooming services, and pet life preservers.

The pros insist "Old dogs *can* be taught new tricks." A video featuring training techniques, or tuition for his dog to attend obedience school might be a gift much appreciated by an exasperated owner.

Still stumped over what to give or where to find it? The people at J-B Wholesale Pet Supplies are self-proclaimed knowledgeable and friendly "dog people." With a complete selection of professional dog products and equipment, they will help you pinpoint the perfect canine gift. Phone: 800/526-0388.

Bow, Wow!

"A young man I dated made a great impression on my dad when he brought treats for the family dog."

—ALYSE R.

Easter Presents

The word "Easter" finds its roots in the Anglo-Saxon goddess of Spring, Eostre. Traditionally, a day was set aside to worship her and celebrate the Earth's awakening with the changing of seasons. Such symbols as the egg and the hare first appeared in this setting. Easter has taken on even greater significance in the Christian world. For Christians, Easter commemorates the resurrection of Jesus Christ after three days in the tomb. Many consider it a most sacred Christian holiday and find life, hope, and a new beginning in Easter. Here are some ways to renew their spirits.

Give a religious book, bookmark, hymnal, inspirational recording, or subscription to a religious magazine or publication.

A framed Easter poem or scriptural verse might be appropriate.

Make a contribution to a church, shelter, or other charitable organization in the recipient's name.

A personal journal may be a nice present to a friend making a new start.

Flowers are a traditional gift at Easter time. Easter lilies, potted plants, colorful bouquets, and corsages are popular choices. Floral door wreaths and table centerpieces also make nice presents, as do outdoor plants and trees.

What Gives?

What is the most sentimental, most thoughtful, most generous, most delightful, most romantic, or most sincere gift you have ever received? See page 277.

Easter Presents • Employee Gifts

> **It's a Wrap!**
>
> It is said that good things come in small packages. Put a ring or other small piece of jewelry in a plastic egg, then place the egg in a basket with other eggs filled with the usual Easter treats.

Easter eggs are fun to create and exchange at Easter time. Many women's and children's magazines feature instructions for creating beautifully decorated eggs. Other eggs-cellent gift ideas include egg cookbooks, egg timers, egg poachers, egg-shaped gelatin molds, deviled egg plates, wire egg baskets, egg beaters, quiche pans, and omelet pans.

Bakeries and candy stores are filled with egg-, chick-, and bunny-shaped cakes, cookies, and confections for Easter giving. Homemade versions of the same are also welcome gifts.

Fill an Easter basket with goodies to delight a friend or neighbor of any age.

Costume jewelry, accessories, and clothing with bunny, egg, or chick motifs might be appropriate for some recipients.

Employee Gifts
SEE ALSO *Business Gifts* and *Workplace Gift Exchanges*

Beyond cake breaks for birthdays and gold watches for retirement, employee gifts can increase morale and reinforce the notion that employees are valued assets. To get the best return on your organization's human capital, invest in the following portfolio of gift ideas.

As with other gifts, the positive impact of gifts to employees is magnified by attention to detail and personalization of the gift to the recipient. Although the sheer volume of employees in some organizations inhibits ultimate customization, some gifts lend them-

Employee Gifts

selves to at least some degree of personalization. For example, instead of ordering the same general gift basket for all employees, divide the order among broad interest categories—sports, gardening, barbecuing. It doesn't require much effort to tally preferences for each option. Gifts of tickets to the recipient's choice of a sporting or cultural event can be similarly tallied and administered.

A Denver-based computer firm hired an office parent to pamper its employees. In addition to stocking a plentiful supply of company-paid-for snacks and making sure the coffee machine doesn't run dry (and that there is always real cream to go with it), she keeps track of anniversaries, sends flowers to parents of new babies, and throws a monthly birthday bash at the office. The company president says she is paid to spoil them because it just makes a nicer place to work.

An office manager we know said his company always celebrates employee birthdays with a surprise cake. When asked how it could be a surprise when everyone knew of the custom, he explained that the cakes are decorated to depict an interest of the recipient, and that it's always fun to see what interests coworkers pick up on. Try this clever solution to a common dilemma!

Give a day of leisure for which the employee will not be held accountable.

Our friend David, an attorney in Washington, D.C., has a brilliant knack for choosing meaningful client gifts. The genuine interest David takes in his clients' hobbies, professional concerns, and family status is reflected in the gifts he gives. Does this make

Consider This

Although dislikes are not always expressed, close observation may reveal a recipient's indifference to certain styles, colors, food, music, or literature.

Employee Gifts

a memorable impression? You bet it does. By chance, Sherri recently met the wife of one of David's clients over 2,500 miles from Washington, D.C. When they discovered they had a mutual acquaintance, she told Sherri about a gift David had given her husband over ten years ago!

Most employees prefer—and many have come to expect—holiday gifts of cash. Amounts vary from company to company and are often based on the employee's tenure and position, and the company's profits over the past year. If gifts of cash are the custom, employees will anticipate each year to receive an amount equal to or greater than the previous year's gift. We suggest that you, as an employer, notify employees well in advance of a change in policy or profitability. (Note: A bonus as provided for in an employment agreement isn't a gift, it's compensation.)

In addition to year-end gifts, cash is often given for employee birthdays or as an award for safety, service, productivity, sales, or attendance. There are many clever ways to present gifts of cash. Here are a few:

- A dozen rosebuds made from $10, $20, $50, or $100 dollar bills

- Sheets of uncut bills

- Cash sealed in a metal can (perhaps one emblazoned with the company's logo)

- A stack of bills glued on one end to resemble a notepad (yes, they can be torn off and spent!)

Establish a company tradition for holiday gifts to employees:

Special Presentations

Take time to think of clever and memorable ways to present gifts of money.

Employee Gifts

- Commission an artist to create limited edition holiday ornaments.
- Start a collection of quality picture frames, music boxes, stemware, or Christmas plates.
- Give an annual gift of holiday greens for decorating the house, or a beautiful centerpiece of greens, pine cones, and candles.

Be unconventional! Imagine the excitement that will build as the holidays approach and your employees are wondering what outrageous or fun gifts you will come up with next:

- Foot-long fortune cookies with your holiday greeting and gift certificate inside
- Party favors and confetti for a festive New Year's celebration
- Tickets for hot-air balloon rides

Where's The Turkey?

Unfortunately for management, one year's "gift" to its employees can turn into next year's "entitlement" in the eyes of employees. This concept is perfectly illustrated by the following story, told to Sherri by a human resource manager. A few years ago, the company for which he worked gave its employees 12-pound turkeys to commemorate a year of brisk business. The next year, speculation commenced among the employees about when they would receive their turkeys. However, due to sluggish sales, the company had not planned to "gift" its workers as in the previous year. As time passed, highly-pressured management was forced to call the poulterer to repeat the previous year's order. Getting 300 turkeys on short

Poultry Geist

We have been trying for some time to determine the origin of the turkeys-to-employees-at-Christmas-time tradition. To date, we've traced the practice to 1843, when Ebenezer Scrooge gave such a gift to the Cratchits. However, you will note that this turkey was not any ordinary turkey, but the big, prized turkey—twice the size of Tiny Tim. It was given anonymously, with delight, and—as you may recall—was not Scrooge's only gift to the Cratchits. Bob Cratchit received a raise and a pledge from his employer to assist his struggling family.

Employee Gifts • Environmentalists

> **What Gives?**
>
> How does your company handle holiday, birthday, wedding, new baby, get-well, incentive, and other gifts to employees? Please share your ideas with us. See page 277.

notice was going to present only one hitch: the birds were not all going to be the same size. This, however, seemed a small plight. Management was relieved to have dodged the bullet of insurrection, and they distributed the awaited turkeys to pacified employees. Nevertheless, conjecture arose in the parking lot when workers began to compare their "gifts" and speculate why one received a 10-pound turkey, another a 12-pounder, and another a 14-pounder.

Southwest Airlines maintains an inventory of gifts for the following:

◆ "Reward the troops" gifts (jackets, caps, and T-shirts) to boost morale among its more than 16,000 employees

◆ Goodies for frontline employees that receive no complaints for six months

◆ "We're sorry" gifts for inconvenienced passengers

In addition, the company sends all of its employees cards on their birthdays and on the anniversary of their employment with the company.

Environmentalists

When it comes to the Earth, many feel that Mother's Day should be a daily celebration. Their cries to "think globally while acting locally" can be heard from the tropical rain forests to the inner-city green spaces. The following ideas should help you clean up your act as a gift giver without requiring a superfund to implement them.

Give note paper and other paper products produced from recycled paper.

108 • Present Perfect: The Essential Guide to Gift Giving

Environmentalists

Lease a sugar maple tree, a lobster trap, or an acre of Minnesota red wheat; hire a honey hive; or rent a sheep, pecan tree, or Mineola angelo tree. A company called Rent Mother Nature contracts with growers that share their concern for the environment to bring you wholesome, distinctive, natural, and memorable gifts. Call for a catalog. Phone: 800/232-4048.

Give videos from PBS's acclaimed series *Conserving America*, which profiles people across the United States dedicated to preserving endangered animals, landscapes, and natural resources. The *Conserving America* series includes four video cassettes: *Champions of Wildlife*, *The Rivers*, *The Challenge on the Coast*, and *The Wetlands*. For more information on these and other environmental videos, contact V.I.E.W. Video. Phone: 800/843-9843. Fax: 212/979-0266.

Make a contribution to—or give a gift from—the National Wildlife Federation. Choose from books, T-shirts, toys, holiday ornaments, cards, and more. Profits fund the federation's programs. Call for information or a catalog of environmentally friendly gift ideas. Phone: 800/432-6564.

Give a reusable shopping bag.

Give a stuffed animal, a toy, a piece of jewelry, or a knickknack depicting an endangered species. These and other interesting items are available from the World Wildlife Fund. Profits support the fund's programs to protect endangered species and their habitats. Phone: 800/833-1600.

> ### It's a Wrap!
> Make reusable gift bags from silk, taffeta, burlap, chintz, or another fabric, or from dishtowels, doilies, or pillow cases. These are great for odd-shaped and oversized presents and are easily customized to any dimensions. Embellish the bags with applique, embroidery, lace, trim, or buttons and tie them closed with ribbon, yarn, cord, or raffia.

Environmentalists • Expectant Parents

Give a set of recycling receptacles, and, where available, arrange for regular curbside pick up of recyclable items.

Arrange for a landscaper or nursery to deliver and plant a tree of the recipient's choice.

Make a contribution to The National Arbor Day Foundation. A letter will be sent to inform recipients of gifts made in their honor. Choose from several gift options including the Gallatin National Forest reforestation project, the Rain Forest Rescue program, or construction of a conference center at Arbor Day Farm in Nebraska City, Nebraska. Write: The National Arbor Day Foundation, 211 North 12th Street, Lincoln, NE 68508. Phone: 402/474-5655.

> **Celebrate!**
>
> Give an environmentally friendly gift to the conservationist on your gift list in honor of Earth Day, April 22.

Expectant Parents

The nine months before Junior arrives can seem to last nine years for excited, expectant parents. A thoughtful gift would let them know you share their excitement. The following ideas were conceived to help you fill the expectations of parents-to-be.

Give a hospital bag filled with items to celebrate the new baby's arrival. Include a supply of writing paper and stamps, a pen, addresses and telephone numbers of those to be notified, a long-distance calling card, and nonalcoholic champagne.

Present a photography studio gift certificate in a baby picture frame or photo album.

Expectant Parents

Pickles 'n' ice cream, or any other unusual food combinations that appeal to the mother-to-be, make fun gifts.

Books on parenting and child development are pertinent gifts for expectant moms and dads.

Arrange a getaway for the expectant couple. Note: This gift would also be much appreciated after the baby's birth, but should then include an offer to babysit.

Contract with a cleaning service to help ready the house or apartment for Baby's arrival.

Every new mom—and dad—needs a comfortable rocking chair.

Pay for tuition to a birthing class or a refresher course.

Give a subscription to *Parents Magazine,* which is filled with articles about child development and behavior, marriage and family relationships, and health and education research. Write: 685 Third Ave., New York, NY 10017. Fax: 212/867-4583.

Give a subscription to *Working Mother Magazine.* The magazine features helpful articles about trends, child development, and issues pertinent to working mothers. Phone: 800/627-0690.

Great Expectations

"My best friend had just moved out of the state when I found out I was expecting our first child. I called to tell her the news, and shortly thereafter, we received our first baby gift—a tiny pair of newborn socks and a congratulatory card. I often held the incredibly tiny socks and dreamed about the baby who would fill them. It was my friend's thoughtfulness that meant the most to me—it showed that my news meant a lot to her, too."

—Paige V.

Families

Tommy wants some in-line skates, Stacy wants a Barbie, Kelly wants a gory book...the list goes on and on. So how do you choose a single gift the whole family will enjoy? When choosing gifts for the entire family, base them on a theme: an activity the family enjoys together—camping, hiking, photography, or the arts; a family project—remodeling the house or landscaping the yard; or a family concern—the environment or education.

To celebrate the purchase of a new house, give home and patio furnishings or accessories the entire family can enjoy.

To thank a family in whose home you've been a guest, give a food basket, board game, or accessory for the family's home entertainment equipment.

For family presents exchanged between grown siblings with children, give handmade crafts, holiday ornaments, family albums, or video greetings.

If the family enjoys being outdoors, give a gas grill; a colorful wind sock; a patio lantern; wind chimes; a hammock with a pillow and canopy; a porch swing; lawn and patio furniture; a bird feeder, bath, or house; a sundial; or outdoor planters.

For a bit of friendly outdoor competition, give lawn games: croquet, badminton, tetherball, lawn billiards, horseshoes, or volleyball. A swing set or sand box would make a fun gift for a family with young children.

It's a Wrap!

Wrap oversized gifts in pillowcases, paper table cloths, butcher paper, or lawn and leaf bags. Tie with rope or wide ribbon and attach an extra-large gift tag. (To find oversized boxes, check with furniture and appliance stores.)

Families

For indoor family fun, give a mini table tennis or billiards table, electronic dart game, or game table and chairs.

Give tickets to a sporting event, concert, or movie of interest to all family members.

Give an ice cream maker with all of the ingredients for homemade ice cream, or a popcorn popper and a gourmet popcorn recipe book.

Outfit a picnic basket with dishes and flatware for the entire family.

Engage the services of a genealogist or historian to research the family's genealogy or write the family's history.

Commission an audiovisual production service (listed in *The Yellow Pages*) to produce a video of a family reunion, wedding, or other special event. The specialist can incorporate sound effects, computer graphics, and multi-image effects into the video. Order copies for everyone involved.

Pay for family membership at a recreation center or swimming pool.

Give something special for the family pet. (See *Cats and the People That Love Them*, *Dogs and the People That Love Them*, and *Horses and the People That Love Them*.)

Tag Along

"The first year my husband and I were married, I thought my mother-in-law kept forgetting to remove price tags from clothing items given as gifts. However, it didn't take long to figure out that she enjoyed shopping and tried to please us, but knew that while living on a meager income, many times we would exchange an expensive item for two or three generic-type articles. Now the price tags left on gifts of clothing are a joy to see and remind me of what a wonderful, practical woman she is."

—Julie W.

Families

Consider This

If your gift-recipient-to-be has recently made a major purchase of a VCR, computer, microwave, recreational vehicle, or the like, finding a gift should be simple. Accessories for all of the above are available in a wide range of prices and are perfect for giving as gifts.

Give audio/video equipment the whole family can enjoy: a split-screen television, a video recorder, pre-programmed audio/video remote controls, wireless videophones for the television or VCR, a remote control rack, a stereo system, a compact-disc changer.

Have color slides, home movies, or family photographs transferred to video cassettes.

Give a speaker phone so family members can all join in on conversations to loved ones.

Collect as many favorite family recipes as possible. Format, copy, bind, and give family cookbooks as gifts to all those that contributed. (Sherri wishes someone in her family had done this. There are still favorites the grandchildren try to duplicate, but, without the original recipes, they have not had much luck.)

Give a supply of the family's favorite snack foods or soft drinks—ours are Pringles, Snickers, and 7-Up.

Fill a basket with movies and blank video cassettes. Add popcorn, candy, a gift certificate for movie rentals, and a catalog of video reviews.

As a sequel to the gift above, purchase a video storage cabinet or large video storage case and fill it with the items above. Add cordless headphones, remote controls, and so on as your budget will allow.

Farewell Presents

It's always hard to say farewell to dear friends. Moving to a new house or transferring to a new job are bittersweet occasions filled with apprehension and anticipation. To relieve a bit of the separation anxiety, bid adieu with one of the following.

Give a memento of the area from which the recipients are leaving. When we moved from northern Virginia, we were given a flag that had flown over the United States Capitol. It brings back a flood of memories about the time we spent working and playing in the nation's capital.

Give a framed photo, watercolor, or sketch of the house they are leaving.

Arrange for a newspaper subscription from their old area to be delivered to their new house.

Host a farewell party in their honor.

Give an address book, stationary, stamps, and a nice pen. Let friends handwrite their own addresses in the book.

Arrange for the delivery of a tree or plant to their new house. Or, send bulbs or clippings from your yard with them.

> ### Movin' Right Along
>
> "We treasure a scrapbook of pictures and good wishes of those that attended a farewell party in our honor. It's just like having a snapshot of a certain place and time in our lives."
>
> —SHERRI & LARRY

Father's Day Presents

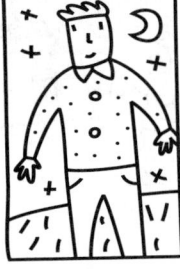

Patriarch, father, dad, the one with the remote control. What politician holds a more influential office? What doctor works longer hours? In spite of how deserved they are, Father's Day presents are notoriously outlandish, obnoxious, and even (gasp!) tacky. Here, then, are a few ideas guaranteed to be as popular with fathers as Dad's Day itself.

Mothball the lawn mower and give Dad a contract for lawn service.

How about season tickets to a sporting event for which he has a passion?

Help Dad with a project around the house—repaper or paint a room, plant a garden, mend a gate.

Pamper him with a bounty of shower accessories: a massaging shower head, shower clock-radio, non-fogging mirror, back brush, Turkish towel, and bathrobe.

Give Dad a handsomely framed picture of you and your siblings to put on his desk or bedside table.

Give Dad a subscription to the hometown newspaper from where he was born, grew up, or lived for a long time—this is a great way for him to keep up with what's happening with old friends.

Take Note

Whatever investigative method you use to identify gift possibilities, be sure to keep notes about what works and what doesn't.

Father's Day Presents

Take him back in time with a collection of trading cards from his youth, a recording of songs from the "good ol' days" (many are now available on compact discs), or a video of a favorite old movie.

Surprise him with a vacation to a place he has always wanted to visit.

Install a garage door opener, security system, or motion-sensor lights to make his life more safe and convenient.

Arrange for a reunion with a former teammate, coach, college roommate, business associate, or friend. Or, make a "This Is Your Life" audio or video tape of friends and acquaintances from days gone by.

A few years ago, Sherri helped our three children write notes to attach to the following items. The items were placed in a basket and presented to Larry for Father's Day. The idea is easily adaptable to your own situation:

- On a candle: "No other dad can hold a candle to you."

- On a can of shaving cream: "You're the crème de la crème."

- On a light bulb: "We appreciate your bright ideas."

- On a package of chewing gum: "We chews you as the best dad in the world."

- On a can of Pringles potato chips: "We are chips off the old block."

Present Danger!

Do not disguise an item intended for family or group use as a gift to an individual. "Hey Dad...here's the boat you've always wanted...I dibs it for Memorial Day, Independence Day, and Labor Day...John has planned an outing with friends near the end of July...and Uncle Bob has asked to use it for the family reunion the third week in August."

Father's Day Presents

> **It's a Wrap!**
>
> To mislead shakers and squeezers, add marbles, bells, weights, or padding to your package before wrapping it.

- On a Matchbox sports car: "You're a dad in the fast lane."
- On a Sugar Daddy: "You're so sweet, Daddy."
- On a coupon attached to a bottle of car cleaner: "Good for one free car wash."
- On a Mounds candy bar: "You're mounds of fun."
- Wrapped around a pencil: "You're so sharp, you always get the point."
- On a box of tissues: "Our love for you is nothing to sneeze about."
- On a measuring tape: "You always measure up to our expectations."
- On a flashlight: "Your love for us shines through."
- On a pen: "You are write on."
- On a note pad: "For a noteworthy dad."
- On a map: "You're really going places."
- On a can of soda: "You're the best, Pop."

Survey Scoop! Ratings for gifts of tools rise with household income in the $20,000 to $75,000 brackets. Scores rise sharply in favor of gifts of tools as men leave their fathers' homes (and tools) to set up their own domiciles. According to Brookstone's Vice President of Marketing, Donald O'Brien, Brookstone's catalog customers are more mature and affluent men that have been in their homes longer. A high percentage have home workshops with a good supply of basic tools and are looking for specialty tools. "What they seem to like—and what we try to provide—are things that are a little bit out of the mainstream," says O'Brien. "They are probably not going to buy a hammer, but

Father's Day Presents

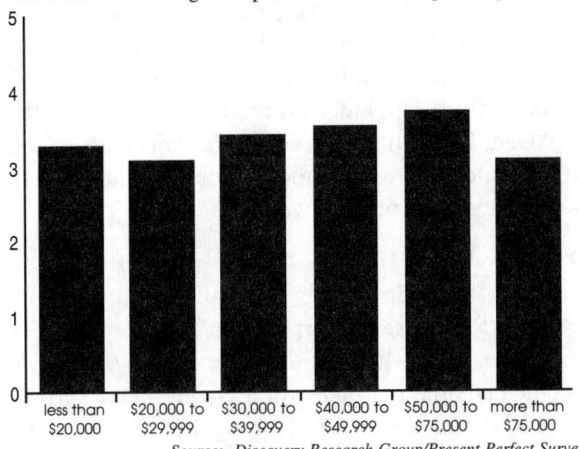

who wants gifts of TOOLS?

Men's preferences for gifts of tools, by income, on a scale of 1 being least preferred and 5 being most preferred.

Source: Discovery Research Group/Present Perfect Survey

Best/Worst

Best: A 35-mm camera

Worst: Socks and ties

—CARL C.

they may buy an all-purpose tool that includes a hammer and 18 other functions."

Father's Daze

According to dads across the country, memorable Father's Day gifts are often handmade, humorous, and heartfelt.

◆ **The Camera Never Lies.** Robert Wood, Dean of the Center for Naval Warfare Studies at the Naval War College in Newport, Rhode Island, was amused one Father's Day when his four 16- to 30-year-old daughters presented him with a video tape in which they took turns imitating his characteristics (in a loving and sensitive way, of course). He was sur-

Father's Day Presents

> **Super Sleuth**
>
> When brainstorming for gift ideas, list everything that pops into your mind, whether it's within your budget or not. You may find related items in your price range that would make great gifts. Here are a few ways to uncover gift possibilities:
>
> ✔ Observe interests and needs through the way he lives, works, and plays.
>
> ✔ Look through catalogs and magazines pertaining to his interests and affiliations.
>
> ✔ Go window shopping with him.
>
> ✔ Ask his friend or relative what he might like.
>
> ✔ Exchange wish lists or "carelessly" leave them where they may be found.
>
> ✔ Listen for hints.
>
> ✔ Use your intuition.

prised by how accurately they captured the essence of his particular mannerisms.

◆ **Taking Dad to the Cleaners.** In McLean, Virginia, the five Colton children (ages 15-25) have maintained a long-standing Father's Day tradition of breakfast in bed for dad, Kent Colton, CEO of the National Association of Homebuilders. In addition, Colton recalls a card once given to him by one of his daughters. It read something like this: "Dear Dad, I love you so much. This Father's Day I would like to do some chores for you. I'll start by cleaning out your wallet."

◆ **Away From Home—Alone.** Bruce Bennett, father of 3 children (ages 5-12) and Deputy Program Director for Rand Corporation in Moorpark, California, says when his daughter was $2^1/_2$ years-old she declared her plans for a Father's Day surprise. She announced that beginning the third Sunday in June, she would go to the church nursery by herself. Nobody could have been happier about her "gift" than Bruce, since he had been the one to accompany her there each week for the previous year.

◆ **A Snowball's Chance.** Although he was secretly hoping for a fly rod, Steve Thacker, City Administrator in Cañon City, Colorado, appreciated the book of coupons he received from his children one year. The certificates were redeemable for a variety of indulgences (breakfast in bed), chores (weeding the garden), and activities (a snowball fight). It's just as well, though. With six children between 4 and 16 years old and a busy job, Steve had as good a chance for finding time to use a fly rod as he did for a snowball fight in June.

◆ **Just Her Size.** Andy Wahlquist, International Trade/Government Relations Consultant in Washington, D.C., remembers a Father's Day gift from one of his two twenty-something daughters. "She gave me an oversized tennis shirt. It was big and baggy—just the size she likes to wear." Somehow, he has managed to retain custody of the shirt. He was wearing it at the time Sherri spoke with him about the gift.

> **Best/Worst**
>
> Best: My child
>
> Worst: Clothes
>
> —Dan M.

- **All-Star Hugs.** Dave Westergard, general counsel for Micron in Boise, Idaho, remembers the love that went into making the three gifts his daughters (then ages 3-9) gave him a few years ago. From one, he received an envelope filled with colorful stars—each redeemable for a hug. From another, he received a shoe box diorama of the family's house. And from his preschool daughter, he received a footprint with a precious verse.

- **Morning Glory.** Breakfast in bed definitely appeals to the sybarite in Greg Krogel, Exxon's country manager in Guam. A few years ago, his 7-year-old son and 10-year-old daughter prepared their own version of scrambled eggs and orange juice and served it in style for a memorable Father's Day gift.

Fishermen

There are almost as many ways to fish as there are fishermen (and women)—bowfishing, float fishing, bottom fishing, deep-sea fishing, clamming, crabbing, and fly-fishing, to name a few. Many of the gifts you choose for the fisherman will depend on the type of fishing he does. Bait him with one of the following piscatory gifts and you may catch his attention—hook, line, and sinker.

Make arrangements through a travel agent or tackle shop for a fishing expedition or lessons from a pro fisherman.

Fishermen

Taking the Bait

"My husband was born to fish. He catches anything and everything, and consequently, he seems to have everything he needs. One Christmas, I wanted to buy him some new lures, but didn't have any idea what kind he needed—or wanted. To me, they all looked the same. So I cut large fish out of construction paper, stapled a dollar bill to each of their mouths, and wrapped them in a box with a note that said he could take the money to buy the lures he really

(Continued on next page.)

Give a cellular phone so the fisherman can call with the latest fish story.

Fill a new creel with the recipient's favorite fish condiments and side-dish ingredients.

To a good-natured fisherman, give a gift certificate from the local fish market.

Arrange to have her largest catch of the season stuffed and mounted.

Give her a waterproof, floating camera to catch the big one on film.

Give a cast iron skillet for frying fresh fish lakeside, riverside, or oceanside.

Enroll the fisherman in a fly-tying course.

To the fly-fisherman, give a subscription to *Fly Fisherman*, a magazine featuring detailed expert advice on the latest fly fishing techniques, tackle, and fly patterns. The magazine highlights the best destinations for trout, salmon, steelhead, bass, and saltwater species around the world. Phone: 800/435-9610.

Give fishing apparel and accessory items: caps, boots, vests, hats, hip waders, sunglasses.

Fishermen • Fitness Buffs

Other gift ideas for the fisherman include a belly boat, a rod holder, a fly-tying kit, a tackle box, a thermos, an ice chest, a boat seat cushion, a folding fishing chair, lures, and other tackle.

Give a sterling silver or hand-carved wood and bronze trout sculpture or trout jewelry from Gill's. Write: 1586 Tomahawk Drive, Salt Lake City, UT 84105. Phone: 801/322-1683.

> (Continued from previous page.)
>
> wanted. I solved the problem of which lures to get, and my husband got just what he wanted!"
>
> —Julie R.

Fitness Buffs
SEE ALSO *Runners and Walkers*

A fitness buff has muscle tone where some of us don't even have muscles. For some, fitness is an obsession. For others, it's a chore. For most, it's a way to maintain psychological and physical well being. Whatever the motivation, the following gifts would help your fitness buff stay in shape.

Contract for the services of a personal trainer to coach the fitness buff.

Give a sports watch with a built-in lap counter, stop watch, and other nifty features.

Arrange and pay for membership at a spa, gym, fitness club, or pool.

Fitness buffs enjoy monitoring their progress. Give a stopwatch, lap counter, caliper, professional scale, pulse monitor, or blood pressure monitor.

Celebrate!

May is National Physical Fitness and Sports Month.

Fitness Buffs

Better with Age?

Many sports scientists now believe that certain aspects of athletic performance can be maintained or even improved in one's late 30's, 40's, and beyond. Optimal training and nutrition are key elements. Your gift to the fitness buff can show your support for his or her efforts.

Give a cargo bag, weekender bag, fanny pack, gym bag, sports attaché, portable locker, or rucksack according to the enthusiast's sports interests and needs.

Choose from a wide array of home gym and exercise equipment: floor mats, chin-up bars, rebounders, step exercisers, slant boards, hand grip exercisers, jump ropes, weights (ankle, wrist, waist, hand), rowing machines, cross-country ski machines, stationery bicycles, treadmills.

Give a book or video on aerobics, weight training, cycling, health and nutrition, or other fitness interest of the recipient.

Plan a weekend around the recipient's favorite fitness activity: biking, swimming, running, or a week at a health spa. A travel agent can help you with the details.

Give a shower massager, vibrating heat massager, or pressure point massager to relieve tired muscles. Or, give yourself a video to teach you how to give him a relaxing massage.

A Skimmer ultralight rowing craft is the ultimate gift for the fitness buff who has everything. Less cumbersome and more stable than a traditional rowing shell, the Skimmer is suitable for almost any condition from choppy seas to glassy lakes. This would be a gift to last—and perhaps extend—a lifetime. Prices start around $5,000. Phone: 800/233-2060.

Flowers and Plants, Gifts of

According to Emerson, "Flowers...are always fit presents...because they are a proud assertion that a ray of beauty out values all the utilities of the world." Here are a few tips for picking the right flowers.

Flowers make appropriate gifts for just about any occasion. However, there are a few considerations to keep in mind when giving gifts of flowers:

◆ Flowers should be chosen with care to keep from appearing to be a last-minute gesture (as it often is).

◆ While some people prefer arrangements of rare, exotic, or short-lived blooms, others prefer long-lasting potted flowers and plants. As always, choose according to the recipient's preference. (We know a woman who prefers wildflowers but whose husband—conditioned by the media, we suppose—gives her roses instead.)

◆ When giving fewer than a dozen flowers, an uneven number of blooms is generally more aesthetically pleasing than an even number.

◆ To those for whom the scent of fresh flowers is all too fleeting, give baskets, bowls, or other containers filled with fragrant potpourri.

◆ When taking flowers to a host or hostess, present them in a bowl or vase. Unarranged, cut flowers require the host or hostess to search for an appropriate container while guests and other duties go unattended.

Survey Scoop! Ninety-five percent of American men and women agree that flowers continue to be

Around the World

The Japanese cherry trees surrounding the tidal basin in Washington, D.C. were a gift of gratitude for the United States' mediations of the 1904-1905 Russo-Japanese War.

Flowers and Plants, Gifts of

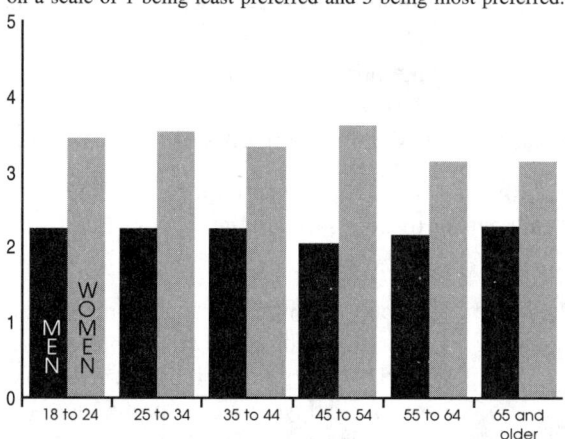

who wants gifts of
FLOWERS?
Preferences for gifts of flowers and plants, by age, on a scale of 1 being least preferred and 5 being most preferred.

Source: Discovery Research Group/Present Perfect Survey

a universal sign of romance, according to a survey for the American Floral Marketing Council. Flowers are rated the best "I Love You" gift by 54% of men and 42% of women according to the same survey. However, when it comes to receiving flowers and plants, our survey notes a definite gender gap. (To successfully bridge the gap, see our suggestions for giving flowers to men in the section on gifts to *Men*.)

To the romantic, flowers are so eloquent. Their meaning may be translated into friendship, infatuation, adoration, devotion, love, or passion. A spirited liaison may be carried on by sending flowers according to their meanings. The language and sentiment of flowers may be outdated according to some, but it will never go out of style among romantics. Here are a few select interpretations of this florigraphical language from the Society of American Florists:

Best/Worst

Best: My whole house filled with flowers from my husband

Worst: A sterling silver spaghetti server

—Michelle T.

Flowers and Plants, Gifts of

Bleeding Heart: Wounded affections

Camellia, pink: "Longing for you"

Camellia, white: "You're adorable."

Camellia, red: "You're a flame in my heart."

Carnation, yellow: "You have disappointed me." Rejection

Carnation, pink: "I'll never forget you."

Carnation, red: "My heart aches for you." Admiration

Carnation, white: Sweet and lovely, innocence

Carnation, striped: "Sorry I can't be with you." Refusal, no

Daffodil: "You're the only one."

Daisies: "I'll never tell." Innocence, loyal love

Gardenia: "You're lovely." Secret love

Lilac, purple: First emotions of love

Lilac, white: Youthful innocence

Lily of the Valley: "You've made my life complete."

Orchid: Beautiful lady

Pansies: "I'm thinking of you."

Primrose: "I can't live without you."

Spider Flower: "Elope with me."

Sweet Peas: "Goodbye." "Thank you for a lovely time." Departure

Violets, white: "Let's take a chance on happiness."

Violets, blue: "I'll be true—always."

Notable Quotables

"What am I to whom these sweet hints are addressed?"

—Ralph Waldo Emerson

Flowers and Plants, Gifts of

> ### Celebrate!
>
> Groundhog Day is February 2. If Punxsutawney Phil sees his shadow, there will be six more weeks of winter. Cheer someone up with fresh flowers. Better still, how about some flower bulbs or seeds to be planted later?

According to the Rose Information Bureau, each rose color has a special meaning, as do certain combinations of rose colors and arrangements of roses in various stages of bloom. To help you compose just the right sentiments in your rose designs, the Rose Information Bureau and Roses, Inc. (the national association of rose growers) put together the following list of the most widely accepted meanings for different rose colors, blooms, and arrangements:

- Red roses say "I love you" and also stand for respect and courage.

- White roses have several meanings: "You're heavenly," reverence and humility, innocence and purity, and secrecy and silence.

- Pink roses symbolize grace and gentility.

- Yellow roses usually stand for joy, gladness, and freedom.

- Coral and orange roses denote enthusiasm and desire.

- Together, red and yellow roses stand for jovial and happy feelings.

- Pale-colored roses convey sociability and friendship.

- Rosebuds symbolize beauty and youth.

- A single rose stands for simplicity.

- Hybrid tea roses mean "I'll remember you always."

- Two roses wired to form a single stem signal a forthcoming marriage.

- A rose in full bloom placed over two buds signifies secrecy.

- A crown made of roses signifies reward of virtue.

Food or Candy, Gifts of
SEE ALSO Chocoholics

Gifts of food are easily customized because everyone has a passion for an epicurean delight of one sort or another. Giving a gift of food can be as simple as raiding the refrigerator section of the local grocery store, dropping by the corner deli, or opening a gourmet catalog and picking up the telephone.

Some of our best-loved food gifts are regional specialties sent from friends and family around the country. Larry's mother sends dried cranberries and maple syrup from New England. A friend in New Mexico sends southwest seasonings. Whether it's pastries or pasta, sauces or sausages, a basket filled with regional favorites would be a wonderful gift for a friend who has moved from one part of the country to another.

We've never met a cookie we didn't like. Come to think of it, we've never met a person who didn't like cookies. (That's not to say everyone does!) Fresh-baked cookies usually make a welcome gift. Present them arranged in a reusable basket or decorative tin. For an elegant presentation, deliver them on a beautiful silver or porcelain platter.

A loaf of bread right from the oven is a warm way to welcome a new neighbor or delight an old friend. Place the bread on a cutting board, cover with a pretty towel, and tie with a cheerful bow. Perfect!

Give a spring-form pan with a cheesecake recipe and the necessary ingredients.

Celebrate!

✔ June is National Fresh Fruit and Vegetable Month.

✔ July is National Hot Dog Month.

✔ July is National Ice Cream Month.

✔ October is National Dessert Month.

✔ October is Vegetarian Awareness Month.

Food or Candy, Gifts of

Give a fondue pot with recipes and ingredients for cheese or chocolate fondue.

To give a fresh-baked, custom-decorated cake for any occasion to anyone in the United States, call Cakes Across America. A yummy cake will be created and delivered by a baker in the recipient's home town. Phone: 800/422-5387.

Choose from a club plan to have flowers, fruits, cookies, or other goodies delivered each month of the year.

Give a cheeseboard and knives with assorted cheeses and crackers.

Flavored homemade vinegars make wonderful hostess gifts for those that like to cook. They are so easy to make and can be presented in decorative glass bottles. A set of six such bottles is available from Williams-Sonoma. Phone: 800/541-2233.

Give a basket of low-fat or low-sodium goodies to a friend on a restricted diet.

Give a gift certificate to a favorite restaurant or arrange to have lunch or dinner delivered to the recipient's house or office.

Find out what her favorite childhood food was and learn to prepare it the way her mom did.

It's A Wrap!

As a thoughtful touch when giving gifts of food, include cooking, reheating, or storage instructions.

Food or Candy, Gifts of • Friendship Gifts

If you receive rave reviews for your desserts, exclusive membership in your personal dessert-of-the-month club would make an excellent gift to a friend with a passion for sweets.

Give an ice cream freezer with ice cream recipes and ingredients.

Assemble the ingredients, recipe, and any unique utensils required to make a dish, and give them to a friend who has requested the recipe.

> **Around the World**
>
> To complement the culinary tastes of the French, gifts of food should be of the highest quality. Very fine chocolates and pastries—not bread—are generally good gifts.

Friendship Gifts

We don't know what else to call them—those little gifts and thoughtful gestures that acknowledge our connection with friends, colleagues, and neighbors. They're tokens that say, "I'm glad we're friends," "Thanks for your help with the project," or "Sorry to hear the bad news—I'm here for you."

Deliver a batch of fresh-from-the-oven sweet rolls on a busy school morning, hot homemade soup or chowder on a cloudy day, or a pot of hot chocolate or wassail on a bitter winter afternoon.

Offer your fruit tree's overabundant crop and your help making jam or preserves.

Deliver lunch on moving day or dinner to a new mom when she comes home from the hospital with her baby.

Friendship Gifts

Circle of Friends

"Our friends Bill and Gerri called late one Friday night to tell us to look on our front doorstep before breakfast on Saturday morning. There we found a box of fresh Krispy Kreme doughnuts that we enjoyed with warm fuzzy thoughts of the givers."

—Sherri & Larry

Prepare a batch of cookie dough or homemade bread. Deliver it—with baking instructions—to a friend or neighbor and let him enjoy the aroma while the goodies bake.

Kidnap a friend for lunch or an afternoon of uninterrupted shopping. Arrange for a baby sitter, if needed (this would be a nice gift in itself!).

Tuck a cheerful note into a bouquet of fresh flowers from your garden and give it to a friend who's feeling down.

Give a jug of fresh-pressed cider, spices and directions for making hot cider, and a set of mugs to celebrate Fall.

Fill a wok with fortune cookies into which you have inserted your own "fortunes."

Assemble an assortment of birthday, anniversary, wedding, new baby, and other greeting cards and give them to a busy friend. Present them with a supply of postage stamps, a small calendar, and an address book.

Make holiday cookies for the neighborhood children. Decorate cloverleaves for St. Patrick's day, hearts for Valentine's day, pumpkins for Halloween, or stars for the Fourth of July.

Gardeners

"A garden is like those pernicious machineries which catch a man's coat-skirt or his hand, and draw in his arm, his leg and his whole body to irresistible destruction." So says Emerson. The gardener responds, "What a way to go!" Once gardening gets into the man, it's hard to get the man out of the garden. Gifts for his garden would at least ensure a place in his thoughts and heart for you. Here is a bouquet of gift ideas for the gardener on your gift list.

A variety of structures lend themselves to the beauty and function of a garden. Arrange for the construction of a gazebo, fountain, pond (complete with fish, frogs, lily pads, and bridge), pergola, trellis, or shed in the gardener's garden.

A cordless telephone is a useful gift for the gardener whose phone rings every time she's halfway to the garden shed.

Give a gift of membership in The American Horticultural Society. Membership includes 12 issues of *American Horticulturist* (featuring information on travel tours, books, and special events), numerous fact sheets and garden guidelines, and other member services. Call The American Horticultural Society for details. Phone: 800/777-7931 or 703/768-5700.

Garden accessories that serve as focal points are fun gifts for gardeners. Give a birdbath, birdhouse, sundial, or garden bench.

What Gives?

How would you define the perfect gift? See page 277.

Gardeners

> **Celebrate!**
>
> Nurture the seeds of friendship with a gift to the gardener for National Garden Month (April).

Fill a planter box full of blossoming blooms to give to the flower gardener.

Enroll the flower gardener in a community course on flower arranging.

Give a cookbook featuring recipes, or canning, freezing, or drying instructions for the vegetable gardener's produce. Your help in canning, freezing, or drying would also be a valued gift.

Gifts of tools for the gardener include irrigation kits, hose reels, lawn claws, garden markers, watering cans, garden trikes, scuffle hoes, spading forks, shovels, trowels, hand pruners, knee-saver mats, water timers, adjustable rakes, and garden scissors.

To present a gift of gardening tools, "wrap" them in a shiny galvanized garbage can or wheelbarrow and tie a big bow through the handles.

Other gifts for the gardener include a personal stereo or compact-disc player with a headset, seeds, a gardening apron, a hat, garden stakes (markers), and hose guards.

Give a composting unit, chipper, or shredder.

Gardener's Supply Co. has a wide selection of gifts for the gardener. Call them for a catalog. Phone: 800/955-3370.

Gardeners • Genealogists

Smith & Hawken has a marvelous array of lawn and garden furnishings and accessories as well as gardening tools and clothing. Phone: 800/776-3336.

Give a gift subscription to *Fine Gardening*, which offers how-to information and inspiration about ornamental gardening for the gardening enthusiast. Phone: 800/926-8776.

> **Best/Worst**
>
> Best: Flowers to plant in my garden
>
> Worst: A potato chip slicer/cooker
>
> —Tia B.

Genealogists

So, he's your mother's cousin's sister's nephew. How are you related? A genealogist can tell you. Who else can look at a census and write your grandfather's life story? If you know a genealogist, here is a list of great gifts for him or her. If you don't know a genealogist, then introduce yourself to one—soon. You might uncover your roots.

If the genealogist is a member of your own family, pass on the old family bible. Many old bibles contain records of births, marriages, and deaths.

With billions of genealogical records now on CD-ROM, many genealogists that would otherwise have no use for computers are introduced to the world of computers through their research. Enrollment in a beginning computer course or genealogy course using computers could add a whole new dimension to your genealogist's interest. To the computer user who has not yet obtained genealogy software, give the program of his choice.

Arrange a genealogical excursion to the country from which her ancestors migrated.

Genealogists • Gift Baskets

> **Celebrate!**
>
> Heighten the family historian's awareness of Family History Awareness Month (October) with a gift of genealogical supplies.

Have old family photographs restored and copies made.

Give genealogical books, forms, binders, and charts. Everton Publishers has a huge selection of these and other supplies. Write: 3223 South Main, Nibley, UT 84321. Phone: 801/752-6022.

Gift Baskets

Do you want to give a gift that is fashionable, flexible, and fun? Gift baskets—and other self-contained gifts—are the answer. Pick one up from the grocery store, the department store, a specialty shop, or a mail-order service, or assemble your own. We've harvested a cornucopia of ideas to help you.

Basket Case

Gift baskets and other self-contained gifts are easily customized for specific recipients or for specific occasions. Use your imagination and before long you will be creating delightful, customized gift baskets. Just follow these simple steps:

◆ Assemble related items and a basket or other container (tote bag, leather carryall, garbage can, children's lunch box, backpack, wheelbarrow, canister, ceramic pitcher, cookie jar, or pinata).

◆ Line the basket or container with cloth napkins, popcorn, shredded paper, streamers, paper Easter grass, confetti, dishtowels, hand towels, fabric, peanuts in shells, straw, fabric doilies, leaves, small wrapped candies, or tissue paper. Arrange the items in the container.

Gift Baskets

- Wrap the filled container in clear or colored cellophane or a large plastic bag.

- Adorn the container with a festive bow and accessorize with ribbon, flowers (fresh, dried, or silk), baby's breath, small toys, knickknacks, pine cones, greens, or holiday ornaments.

To prepare gift baskets and other self-contained gifts on a last-minute basis, simply buy related items in a single location: grocery stores, drug stores, and bookstores, for example. (See *Last-minute Gifts*.)

To delight a homebound child, fill a basket with cookie cutters, a loaf of sliced bread, a jar of peanut butter, assorted preserves, a box of raisins, and a jar of sesame seeds for making fun-shaped open-face sandwiches. Or, how about a homemade cookie kit with cookie cutters, sugar cookie dough and ready-made icing?

Cheer a discouraged friend with a ginger jar filled with fortune cookies into which you have inserted your own timely "fortunes."

Fill a watering can with bulbs or seeds, gardening gloves, and small gardening hand tools.

Pamper someone special with a European spa basket filled with loofah sponges and mitts; body, nail, and complexion brushes; fragrant bath oils, gels, and lotions; and a luxurious terry robe.

When More Is Better

It's always fun to get a lot of a little something you like. Turn the ordinary into the extraordinary by giving in excess. Fill a decorative jar, basket, tin, box, or another container with one of the following: golf balls or tees, fishing lures, napkin rings, candles, rolls of film, dollar bills or coins, movie tickets, romance novels, garden seeds, gourmet pasta, scented bath soaps, favorite candy, embroidery floss, or nail polish. For children, try one of these: personalized pencils, hair ribbons, miniature toy cars, balloons, marbles, trading cards, fun straws, wacky shoe laces, or markers.

Gift Baskets

It's a Wrap!

Wrapping tissue is now available in many patterns and colors. Some are designed to coordinate with outer wraps, but it's fun to use your own creative flair to mix and match patterns.

Fill a wire or wicker napkin basket with colorful cloth napkins and whimsical napkin rings.

For a delicious twist on the typical fruit basket of bananas, apples, oranges, and pears, fill a generous-sized basket with fresh pineapple, kiwi, strawberries, blueberries, raspberries, and mangos. Or, assemble a basket full of farm-fresh vegetables or salad fixin's.

Stuff a gym bag with the recipient's favorite sports balls: tennis, golf, softball, baseball, squash, racquetball, or table tennis.

Fill small crocks with fragrant herb butters (mix one to two teaspoons of basil, thyme, dill weed, or tarragon per stick of butter) and garnish with a fresh herb sprig. Present the butters in a bread basket with a fresh-baked loaf of bread.

Fill a dish drainer with dishtowels, dishcloths, dishwashing liquid, scouring pads, and bottle brushes, and give it to someone setting up housekeeping.

Load a sturdy outdoor trash container with lawn and leaf bags, garden hoses, rakes, brooms, and other yard tools and give it to a new homeowner.

Fill a basket with low-sodium, low-fat, or low-sugar goodies for someone on a restricted diet.

Stock a reusable canvas shopping bag with a supply of kitchen spices, flavorings, and staple foods

Gift Baskets • Gift Certificates

and give it to the cook leaving mom's kitchen to go solo.

Stuff cushioned socks, a stop watch, and a pedometer into a pair of running shoes and give them to a serious runner.

Gift Certificates

Some certified gift givers maintain that giving gift certificates ensures the recipient will get exactly what he wants. Some gift recipients maintain that giving gift certificates is an easy way out on the part of the giver. Like everything else, giving gift certificates seems to depend on the circumstances.

Most businesses and services offer gift certificates. Treat someone to his favorite dining, recreational, shopping, or educational experience, or introduce him to a new restaurant, store, or amusement. Gift certificates are available for the following:

- A pair of tickets to a sporting event, a concert, or the theater
- An all-expenses-paid weekend getaway, vacation, or honeymoon
- A tuition-paid adult education class
- A tree or shrub from a nursery or garden center
- Membership at a pool, spa, gym, or country club
- Dinner at her favorite restaurant
- A hair styling, manicure, pedicure, or facial at a salon
- A color consultation or wardrobe analysis

Best/Worst

Best: A bookstore gift certificate

Worst: A toilet seat without a lid—it was a white elephant gift

—LAYNE B.

Gift Certificates • Golfers

Keynote

"I gave Sherri a gift certificate for piano lessons by contracting with a friend who could teach her. The friend was also artistically inclined and she created an elegant gift certificate.**"**

—LARRY

- Art, music, dance, or voice lessons
- Tennis, karate, or swim lessons
- Long-distance phone calls
- Movie tickets and concessions

Purchasing holiday gift certificates from the recipient's favorite department store, specialty shop, or mail-order catalog allows him to take advantage of after-holiday sales.

Books of discount coupons, such as those sold for school fund-raisers, are fun gifts for people that like to shop, travel, or dine out.

Make your own gift certificates for food treats or services such as car maintenance, lawn care, or baby/child/pet sitting. (See *Self, Gifts of*.)

Golfers

You don't have to be a pro to choose pertinent gifts for golfers. Their basic needs are simple: a place to play, balls to hit, clubs with which to hit them, something in which to haul the lot, comfortable apparel, and ongoing instruction for shaving strokes off their games. These needs suggest a profusion of gifts. Here are just a few.

Golfers are very opinionated about the tools of golf. If you decide to give golf clubs as a gift, let the recipient do the choosing. Present your gift by giving a gift certificate along with an accessory item.

Golfers

Give tickets to a professional golf tournament (in Hawaii, perhaps?)

Slider shorts, pants, slacks, knickers, golf shirts, ties with golf motifs, cushioned socks, hats, and golf gloves are gifts that would keep your golfer stylish on and off the course.

Give lessons from the pros. Arrange for golf instruction at a country club. Or, give the latest instructional video, available from the golf course pro shop, the video store, or through a golf catalog.

Country club memberships or greens fees make great gifts! Just ask any golfer.

If you will be giving golf gifts on a regular basis, call for a copy of *Austad's Golf Catalog*. Phone: 800/759-4653.

Give a gift membership in the United States Golf Association. Membership benefits include a year's subscription to the USGA's *Golf Journal*, the *Rules of Golf*, and a personalized USGA bag tag and ID card. Phone: 800/223-0041.

Other great gifts for the golfer include headcovers, golf bags, golf carts, golf balls in her brand of choice, practice nets, golf umbrellas, score card holders, electric putting cups, golfer's record books and diaries, travel putter sets with cases, and golf totes.

Present Danger!

Do not give gifts you hope to "inherit" from the recipient. These gifts speak loudly and clearly. They say such things as, "When you are no longer interested in golf, you can pass these great clubs on to me," or "Oh, silly me, I forgot you look dreadful in this color. I'll just have to keep it for myself."

Graduation Presents

SEE ALSO *Students*

After years of studying, a graduate must find something else to do. Most graduates are delighted to be in this predicament, and are usually inclined to celebrate. After the confetti is swept clean and the mortarboards are packed away, graduates leave behind good friends, a comfortable niche in school, and the carefree security of youth. Mortgages pick up where tuition bills leave off, and finding employment for a college grad these days is challenging at best. A graduation gift shares in the joy of a job well done and prepares for the start of a hopeful, yet demanding, new life. Whether it's on to college or on to a career, a thoughtful graduation present will always be looked upon with a special kind of fondness. Life goals—higher education, employment, marriage, and family—often suggest possible gifts for graduates.

For the graduate moving to her first apartment, gift possibilities are endless. Outfit the kitchen with plates and mugs, a mini microwave, a popcorn popper, or other small appliances. Help furnish the living areas with rugs, tables, lamps, or wall hangings. Supply the bed and bath with colorful linens or accents. A folding table and chair set could used in a variety of areas.

For many graduates, a job may be a most appreciated and practical gift. Offer your assistance as a reference or make appropriate introductions to prospective employers. Or, arrange and pay for professional résumé or job-hunting services.

Give a reference book in the graduate's field of interest.

Wheels of Fortune

"In 1969, my neighbor received—as a high school graduation gift from his father—a $1,000 dollar bill rolled up and tucked inside a Match Box convertible car."

—ROBERT A.

142 • Present Perfect: The Essential Guide to Gift Giving

Graduation Presents

An image or wardrobe consultation would give the graduate starting a new job a professional look as well as a boost of confidence.

For the college-bound dorm dweller, a closet organizing system, bookcase, small refrigerator, or other such convenience would make a great gift.

A laptop or personal computer with software and peripherals would make a most welcome gift to a high-school graduate on her way to college.

Electronic spellers, dictionaries, thesauruses, organizers, portable drafting systems, compact-disc players, boom boxes, stereos, calculators, luggage, backpacks, and book bag are also useful gifts for college-bound graduates.

Gifts of enduring or increasing value, such as jewelry, silver, stocks, bonds, or other investments, serve as lasting reminders of the giver and the occasion.

For the graduate staying at home after high school graduation or moving back home after college graduation, a room renovation with a sophisticated look would make your graduate feel welcome. If a complete makeover is not in the budget, add a few accessories or conveniences such as a new desk or work area or a private telephone line with a phone and answering machine.

> **Consider This**
>
> Current and forthcoming transitions often suggest changes in physical or emotional needs. Is the recipient preparing for parenthood, an empty-nest, or retirement? Is she starting a new job, leaving home to attend school, or embarking on a military career?

Grandparents

Grandparents

Ask the right questions, and you'll likely find these folks to be the easiest people to engage in conversation—complete with anecdotes and pictures. Many will tell you it's truly the grandest way to be a parent. Here are some gift ideas for telling your grandparents how grand you think they are.

Create a scrapbook of grandchildren's art work, pictures, progress reports, and programs from school plays, concerts, or sports events.

Give long-distance calling certificates or a telephone credit card for keeping in touch with far-away grandchildren. Or, have an 800 line installed on which they can call their grandchildren.

Give a mail box with the promise of weekly or monthly letters from the grandchildren.

Present a grandchild's best art matted and framed or reproduced on a plate or mug.

Commission a genealogist to prepare a family tree, genealogy, or history of the recipient's ancestors and descendants.

Produce a day-in-the-life-of-the-grandchildren photo album. Specify a day on which you and your siblings will photograph and chronicle the activities of your children. Assemble the photos and narratives in an album and present it to your parents.

It's a Wrap!

Wrap presents to grandparents in their grandchildren's artwork.

Grandparents

Make an audio cassette of their grandchildren singing, playing musical instruments, reading, or talking. Or, make a video cassette of their grandchildren playing on a Little League team, performing in the school concert or play, building a tree house, learning to ride a bike, or taking their very first steps.

Organize a trip for her to her birthplace. If possible, arrange for her to see the house in which she was born or raised, or to meet with friends from long ago.

How about a nice visit with grandma and grandpa or a family outing to a place they choose?

Make a tablecloth decorated with the handprints of the grandchildren.

Grandparents' Day

In 1978, Congress proclaimed the first Sunday after Labor Day as National Grandparents' Day. Through the efforts of Marian McQuade and others interested in preserving their family heritage, Grandparents' Day was instituted to honor grandparents, to give grandparents an opportunity to show love for their children's children, and to help children become aware of the strength, information, and guidance older people can offer.

Mrs. McQuade's suggestions for observing Grandparents' Day are in themselves gifts to and from grandparents. They include:

◆ Passing on such talents as cooking, sculpting, or quilting to those that display an interest

> **Present Danger!**
>
> Do not give gifts that require maintenance, assembly, or installation the recipient is not able or willing to perform—unless, of course, you are willing to do it yourself. You wouldn't think of giving a child an unassembled bicycle, so why leave Grandma's bookshelf in the box marked "assembly required"?

Grandparents • Hanukkah Presents

- Sharing old family music, songs, and dances—along with meanings and origins—to maintain a strong sense of family background

- Keeping a family history

- Preserving particular ethnic or religious beliefs by recording ideas, recipes, and family traditions

- Updating family albums with names, dates, and other information while those that remember such information are still around to share it

Hanukkah Presents

Hanukkah, or the Feast of Dedication, is one of the great festivals of the Jewish faith. The tradition began in 165 A.D. when a Hebrew army under Judas Maccabeus defeated the Syrians and recaptured the Temple of Jerusalem. The temple was cleansed and rededicated in a joyous, eight-day ceremony, the triumphant worshippers feasting and lighting numerous candles and lamps to celebrate their victory. Today, Hanukkah is celebrated by many Jewish families in a festive way with a nightly lighting of the menorah, followed by food, games, and gift giving. Although gift-giving practices vary with each family, presents are typically given to the children each night. Often, the grandest gift is reserved for the last night of Hanukkah. Gift exchanges are generally made between, but not necessarily limited to, immediate and extended family.

Because Hanukkah is typically viewed as a festival rather than an observance of a rite, gifts generally don't have religious significance. Base your gifts on the interests of the recipient and the nature and strength of your relationship.

Present Danger!

Do not give gifts prohibited by the recipient's ethnic, moral, religious, or political beliefs. Such gifts as liquor to a teetotaler, fur to the animal activist, or a Hanukkah present wrapped in Christmas paper are in poor taste. Such gifts indicate a lack of knowledge about and sensitivity toward the recipient.

Hanukkah Presents • Have Everything, Those That

When selecting and presenting Hanukkah gifts or cards, avoid any connection to the symbols of Christmas such as Santa, reindeer, nativity scenes, stars, or Christmas trees.

Make a donation to the recipient's favorite charity. Many people of the Jewish faith include charitable giving as an integral part of Hanukkah celebrations.

Have Everything, Those That

"You can't have everything," a wise man once said. "Where would you put it?" Well, some people seem to have found their way around this little obstacle and own at least one of everything. This makes gift giving tricky, but by no means impossible. Let the following ideas inspire you in your search for gifts to those that—seem to—have everything.

Give gifts high in sentiment:

◆ A framed picture of the two of you on vacation together

◆ A needlework portrait of her beloved horse

◆ A gift shop souvenir or gift certificate from the resort where he skis every winter

◆ Something from her alma mater

◆ A watercolor of her first sailboat, a sculpture of his beloved childhood pet, a sketch or charcoal drawing of her lakeside cabin

---

Best/Worst

Best: Albums filled with pictures of my children

Worst: Skimpy lingerie

—Marta S.

Have Everything, Those That

Make a contribution to an interest of the recipient:

- Donate in her name to a charitable organization
- Contribute to his alma mater or another university of importance to him
- Sponsor a Little League team or another youth sports team in her name
- Make a donation to a community recreation center, art project, or library

---

Take your cues from existing collections and accumulations. (See *Collectors*.)

- Does he surround himself with impressionist art? Give a biography about one or more of the impressionists.
- Has her collection of rare books overflowed the existing bookshelves? Give her an antique bookcase.
- Is his childhood baseball card collection still housed in old shoeboxes? Organize it in notebooks and have it appraised. Or, give the latest edition of a baseball card pricing guide.

Order a custom jigsaw puzzle from Bits & Pieces. Phone: 800/544-7297.

For an experience he or she will never forget, give a week on a Montana cattle drive. Laredo Enterprises provides the opportunity to ride the range with genuine cowboys and cowgirls, work cattle, and sleep

---

You Shouldn't Have!

How do you graciously receive a present you don't care for?

✔ "Simply say, 'Thank you for thinking of me and remembering the occasion with a present.'"

✔ "You should, at a minimum, be able to force a polite 'thank you'—if not for the present, for the giver's thoughtfulness.'"

✔ "Be sensitive to the time, money, and emotion that went into giving the present."

✔ "Receive it with graciousness—gifts are discretional, not obligatory."

✔ "Graciously accept it and keep it as you may appreciate it more later on." (Now that's vision!)

—Source: Present Perfect Survey

Have Everything, Those That

under the stars in the Big Sky Country. Phone: 800/535-3802.

Chances are she doesn't have one of these:

- A newspaper from the day she was born (available through Historic Newspaper Archives). Phone: 800/221-3221.
- A teddy bear that plays a message in your own voice, available through Great Days Publishing. Phone: 800/447-7817.
- A star named after her. Call the Ministry of Federal Star Registration (800/528-7827) or the International Star Registry (800/282-3333) for more information.

For the intrepid explorer, arrange for an African safari, an Amazon cruise, or Alaskan adventure. Contact a travel agency for details.

The Brookstone store and catalog are filled with unique items that make great gifts for those that have everything. Phone: 800/926-7000.

Still stumped? Let the folks at Neiman Marcus show you an extraordinary collection of exceptional gift ideas in their annual *Christmas Book*. Each year, Neiman Marcus buyers search the world for unique services and items of unsurpassed quality. Phone: 800/825-8000.

> **Shopping Tip**
>
> Shopping by mail is a great way to find unique gift items and to save time. Most mail order businesses have toll-free 24-hour phone service and offer such timesaving services as gift wrapping, express shipping, and gift certificates.

Heirloom Gifts

Heirloom Gifts

Passing on a family treasure can create a special bond between giver and recipient. A personal note describing the history of the heirloom would help the recipient understand its particular significance. If such a treasure is passed on to you by a dear relative, find out all you can about the object's history so that you can record the information for the future when you pass it on to your own son, daughter, niece, or another relative. For gifts that will nourish the roots of the family tree, consider the following.

Give a hand-sewn christening dress or another baby outfit previously worn by a family member.

Pass on Grandma and Grandpa's love letters or other special letters from family members

---

Give a needlepoint pillow, crocheted dresser scarf, cross-stitched sampler, hardanger table cloth, knitted afghan, or handmade quilt.

Make copies of family photographs and give them with as much detail as possible about the people in the photos and the circumstances under which they were taken.

Hand down a family history, photo album, or journal.

Pass on a treasured locket, brooch, ring, pocketwatch or another piece of jewelry.

> ### Best/Worst
>
> Best: A necklace of my grandmother's, given to me—by her—just before she died
>
> Worst: A box of chocolates—I'm allergic to chocolate
>
> —Heather T.

Heirloom Gifts • Home Office Dwellers

Share a wedding dress and veil that have been in the family for generations.

Pass on sports medals, armed service awards, diplomas, certificates, or a family bible.

Hand down treasured dishes, serving pieces, centerpieces, and silverware.

> **Best/Worst**
>
> Best: A chess set my father gave me 20 years ago
>
> Worst: I can't think of any—I'm pretty easy to please
>
> —Claus V.

Home Office Dwellers
SEE ALSO *Desk Dwellers*

Millions of people are taking their work home with them, for good. Telecommuters, entrepreneurs, and cottage industrialists are beating rush hour traffic by just staying home. The list of gift possibilities is almost as long as the morning commute they are avoiding.

Give such office equipment and furnishings as a copy machine, fax machine, paper shredder, telephone answering machine, caller ID equipment, cellular telephone, beeper, electronic organizer, bookshelves, desk chair, sturdy lock box, or fireproof safe for private documents and important certificates.

Fill a portable file box or small filing cabinet with file folders, envelopes, stationary, stapler, scissors, tape dispenser, and labels, and give it to a friend or relative starting a home-based business.

To help manage the inevitable flow of incoming and outgoing correspondence, give business forms and stationery, a copy center or courier service account,

Home Office Dwellers • Homeowners

> ### Top Brass
>
> "My friend Julie gave me a brass plate with my name and a title engraved on it to put on my office door at home."
>
> —SHERRI

a monogrammed or engraved letter opener, a business card indexer, an address file or electronic directory, or a bulk mail permit.

Arrange for membership in a business, trade, or service organization, or give a subscription to a trade journal, magazine, newsletter, or business or government directory related to the recipient's business or professional interests.

Give a subscription to *Home Office Computing*, a magazine filled with advice on using technology to get the most out of a home-based business. Phone: 800/288-7812.

A gift certificate to an office supply store would allow the home office dweller to choose the supplies he needs to stock a home office. Office Max sells office supplies, computers and software, business electronics, and office furniture at discounted prices in stores across the country and through its catalog. (Gift certificates are not available through the catalog.) Phone: 800/788-8080.

Homeowners

SEE ALSO *Housewarming Presents*

Homeowners need to mind their manors! This being the case, we've constructed the following list of home improvements.

To the recipient who has moved to a new community, you may wish to give a family membership to a private club or public pool; enrollment in a children's museum program; a subscription to the lo-

Homeowners

cal paper; season tickets to a local concert series, sports event, or community theater; change of address announcements; stationery with new address; passes to a nearby amusement park; or a gift certificate from one of the area restaurants or stores. (Less expensive gifts include single-event tickets to the above.)

Give tickets to a decorator's show house or tour of homes.

A security system or burglar alarm may be appropriate.

Frame an enlarged photograph of the recipient's house or commission an artist to paint a house portrait.

Home furnishings and accessories make great gifts for homeowners. Occasional tables, lamps, rugs, bar stools, planters, clocks, mirrors, and art objects are possibilities.

The purchase of a new house opens up many gift possibilities. With savings accounts drained from down payments and closing costs, an appropriate gift might include the services of a professional landscaper to design a special family space outdoors. (Depending on your price range, this could be scaled down to a consultation or limited space.) Or, how about hiring a decorator for a few hours to help arrange furniture (existing or new) and accessories in the new house? When we recently moved to a new house, we could have used the services of a handyman to hang blinds and curtains, or to install extra shelves in the closets.

Consider This

When selecting gifts of furniture or home accessories, note the recipient's style preferences—contemporary, traditional, art deco, country, eclectic—as well as the scale and color scheme of his or her furnishings.

Horses and the People That Love Them

Although the automobile has long since replaced the horse as basic transportation, there remains a certain romance between rider and steed. Glamorized in history and media by the likes of Robert E. Lee and Traveller, Roy Rogers and Trigger, and the Lone Ranger and Silver, this relationship endures. The following resources and catalogs will provide a multitude of gift possibilities for the equestrian on your gift list.

To the clotheshorse, give riding apparel, riding rain gear, horse-motif sweaters, chaps, a felt hat with a hat case, hand-tooled boots, a leather jacket, and silver accessories (belt buckles, earrings, button covers, key chains, or bolo tie).

From artists' renderings on T-shirts to games, books, and all-natural horse care products, Back in the Saddle claims to have something for every horse lover. A few of our favorites include a sturdy canvas and suede grooming bag, Dark Horse chocolates, jumping horse ornaments, and handcrafted sterling silver jewelry—a three horses pin, a horse cuff bracelet, and running horse earrings. Phone: 800/435-3633.

Back in the Saddle also features a wonderful assortment of gifts for children, including adorable galloping pull toys; miniature stables, lofts, stalls, tack room, trucks and trailers, horses, saddles, blankets, and other horse and stall accessories; games; stamp sets; and horse lollipops. Phone: 800/435-3633.

> **What Gives?**
>
> What is the most outrageous, most absurd, most inappropriate, most insensitive, most manipulative, or most shallow gift you have ever received? See page 277.

Horses and the People That Love Them

Forus Enterprises' Horsetrak software would help the horse lover on your gift list with all the paperwork of horse management—vaccination and worming schedules, feed management, a personal journal, farrier services, genealogy charts. For those that make a business of horse management, give Horsetrak Business, which includes all of the above plus bookkeeping, billing, and calendering. Phone: 800/798-4422.

Everything your riding enthusiast could want is available at discount prices through State Line Tack's *Huntseat* catalog featuring brand name, first quality tack, apparel, medicines, stable supplies, reference materials, and more. Phone: 800/228-9208.

Order a sweat shirt, mug, book, or art work from the American Horse Protection Association, Inc. Write: 1000 29th Street, NW, Suite T-100, Washington, D.C. 20007. Phone: 202/965-0500.

The Meadow Tree Catalog offers hundreds of equestrian books and videos on training your horse, English and Western eventing, health care, grooming, conditioning, foal care, showing, and more. Write: The Meadow Tree, 3716 Effingham Place, Los Angeles, CA 90027-1428. Phone: 213/660-3949.

To a backyard horse owner and rider, give a subscription to *Horse and Horseman*. Each issue has training, veterinary, money-saving feature, and articles about celebrity horse owners. Write: *Horse and Horseman*, 34249 Camino Capistrano, Box 2429, Capistrano Beach, CA 92624. Fax: 714/240-8680.

The Horse's Mouth

The immortal caution to recipients against excess scrutiny of a gift is given by Hudibras, a 17th-century fictional character created by English writer Samuel Butler. In a lengthy satire of Puritan hypocrisy and bigotry, Butler coined the phrase "looking a gift horse in the mouth."

Hospitalized or Ill Persons

It's a form of hospitality no one wants any part of, but it's inevitable that at some time or another, most will be duly accommodated. Just about everyone will spend at least some time in a hospital or sick in bed at home. To make the bedridden comfortable, alleviate boredom, or nurse her back to health, add the following personal touches to intensive care.

Give the recuperating person something to look forward to, such as a pair of tickets to a cultural or sporting event scheduled after his expected recovery.

A stylish new bed jacket or robe is a perfect gift for patients that feel well enough to receive visitors.

With the doctor's approval, arrange a visit from a magician or clown to a hospitalized child.

After checking dietary restrictions with the doctor or nurse, fill a colorful lunch box with snacks and goodies to take to a child in the hospital. For grown-ups, use a small cooler or picnic basket to "smuggle" in the goodies.

An assortment of letters, cards, and pictures of family and friends is a gift the patient would look through again and again. Your offer to read the cards and letters (sometimes again and again) would also be a welcome gift.

It's a Wrap!

Wrap a get-well gift in Ace bandages. Make a bow from strips of gauze and top with a bottle of aspirin or a thermometer.

Hospitalized or Ill Persons

If the patient has a healthy appetite (and, again, with doctor's approval), arrange for a meal to be delivered from his favorite restaurant.

Arrange for services such as hair styling, a manicure, a massage, or a facial for the hospital patient or homebound convalescent.

A portable compact-disc player or personal stereo with headset—along with compact discs or cassette tapes—may help fill the hours. Cassette choices include music, books on tape, foreign language lessons, motivational speeches, comedy routines, and movie sound tracks. Note: Since hospitals disavow responsibility for a patient's personal belongings, be sure there is a place to store equipment out of sight while the patient sleeps or is away from the room.

Hand-held video games for kids of all ages are great gifts for the bed-bound (just don't expect kids—of any age—to put them down after recovery!)

For those that enjoy them, a collection of crossword puzzles, math problems, or brain teasers can be a fun gift for the bedridden. A deck of playing cards and instructions for solitaire games might also be appreciated.

A wicker bed tray—its side pockets filled with hair and grooming supplies—makes a nice gift to a bed-resting friend or neighbor.

Bedside Matter

To a family member or friend who spends hours in the hospital waiting room or near the ill person's bedside, give a tote bag filled with such items as a writing tablet, note cards with envelopes, a pen, address book, stamps, a long-distance calling card and telephone numbers (for keeping others updated on the ill person's condition), books, magazines, word puzzles for passing the long hours, snacks, drinks, gum, a hair brush or comb, and a toothbrush and toothpaste.

Hospitalized or Ill Persons • Hosts and Hostesses

To Your Health

"When we were ill with strep throat, our neighbor Julie delivered dinner in a bag on which she had written 'Happy dinner to those that have been strepped of their health.'"

—SHERRI & LARRY

Provide or arrange for care of an ill friend's pet, garden, or lawn.

To a child confined to bed, give a Magna Doodle, Etch-a-Sketch, Lights Alive, kaleidoscope kit, or other creative activity.

Give a project box filled with paper, scissors, markers, glue, tape, stickers, and buttons to occupy a hospitalized or bed-resting child.

A book about origami and a generous supply of paper would please an older child.

Hosts and Hostesses
SEE ALSO *Cooks* and *Outdoor Cooks*

Hospitality, it has been said, is the art of making your visitors feel at home, even when that's where you wish they really were. Whether you're invited for dinner or the whole month of July, it's nice to show your appreciation to the host and hostess with the most and mostess.

If your host or hostess entertains on a regular basis, a guest book would make a nice gift.

To adorn the table of the hostess on your gift list, give a dessert plate stand, centerpiece, table linens (cloth, placemats, runners, and napkins), place card holders, trivets, candlestick holders, chafing dish, serving trays, or napkin rings.

Hosts and Hostesses

Flowers are a nice dinner hostess gift. Send them the day of the dinner party or the day after with a personal note. As a courtesy, do not take cut flowers to a dinner with you. It puts the hostess in the awkward position of leaving her guests to search for a suitable container.

Hors d'oeuvre knives and forks, condiment servers, cheese boards, punch bowls, dessert plates and bowls, cruets, serving utensils, salad bowls, trifle bowls, soup tureens, and bread baskets are other hostess gift possibilities.

Unless you know your host or hostess enjoys alcoholic beverages, it's better to avoid giving gifts of liquor. If you do bring wine, do not expect the host to serve it with dinner as he will most likely have planned the drinks around his menu.

Food items such as homemade jams, chutneys, or pickles from your pantry, flavored vinegars, chocolates, or other food indulgences your hostess can enjoy *after the party* make wonderful hostess gifts. Desserts and food items the hostess might feel obliged to serve at the party should not be given.

If you are an overnight guest and an early riser, slip out in the morning to get fresh bagels, croissants, or muffins from the bakery. Add an assortment of flavored butters, jams, jellies, and fresh fruit.

When you are a houseguest, offer to babysit your host's children while he takes a break. Or, take

> **Noteworthy**
>
> "Some of our most treasured hostess gifts are thoughtful notes of genuine thanks from dinner and house guests."
>
> —SHERRI & LARRY

Hosts and Hostesses • Housewarming Presents

A Welcome Break

Take your hosts to dinner periodically during an extended stay. Pick up the tab for your lunches when shopping or sightseeing. Bring home a bag of groceries every now and then. Order a pizza or another carry-out meal. These are gifts your hosts will remember when issuing next year's invitations.

the children to the movies, the park, the miniature golf course, or the zoo—your treat.

As a house guest, you can't help but observe your hosts' taste in food, home decor, literature, and music. Use these clues for selecting appropriate gifts.

A gift for the hosts' children or household pet would also be well received. (See *Children*, *Dogs and the People That Love Them*, and *Cats and the People That Love Them*.)

The *Crate & Barrel* catalog is filled with items perfect for the hostess, many of them exclusively designed for Crate & Barrel. Choose from interesting vases, wreaths, pitchers, centerpieces, and serving pieces. Phone: 800/323-5461.

Housewarming Presents
SEE ALSO *Homeowners*

Be it castle or condo, purchasing and moving into a new abode is cause for celebration. Often, the celebration takes the form of a housewarming—an open-house hosted by the new homeowners and attended by families bearing gifts for the new house. One may also wish to take a gift to a shower or party given by friends and relatives for the new homeowners, or when visiting a friend's new apartment or house for the first time. Such gifts need not be costly or extravagant. Consider the following hearth-warming ideas.

Outfit a small tool box (a combination tool box/step stool would be fabulous) with picture and mirror hangers, hollow door and wall anchors, nails,

Housewarming Presents

screws, hooks, a flashlight, light bulbs, and small hand tools such as hammers, screwdrivers, and wrenches.

Choose a gift for the fireplace. Ideas include fireplace gloves, a cast iron fire starter, a log cart, a fireplace screen, a hearth mat, long matches, or a popcorn popper designed for use in a fireplace.

Home furnishings and accessories make nice housewarming gifts if you are familiar with the recipient's tastes. Gift choices include dried flower arrangements, bar stools, coat racks, umbrella stands, bookends, kitchen/bed/bath linens, nesting tables, canister sets, spice racks, and area rugs.

To adorn the house's exterior, give a weather vane, new house numbers, a brass door knocker or kickplate, a doormat, decorative door knobs or handles, a custom mailbox, solar night lights, or the services of a landscaper.

Other gift ideas for new homeowners include a folding stepladder, state-of-the art kitchen appliances, coffee table books, a guest book, an indoor/outdoor digital thermometer, closet and drawer organizers, or a subscription to the local newspaper.

Give a customized map of the community. Highlight doctor's offices, schools, shopping centers, playgrounds, parks, libraries, and the Department of Motor Vehicles and add helpful information such as library hours and telephone numbers for trash collection, newspaper delivery, licensing bureaus (car, business, pets), and utilities.

> **Best/Worst**
>
> Best: Thoughtful around-the-house gifts
>
> Worst: An appliance I already had
>
> —Victoria W.

Housewarming Presents • Humorous and Whimsical Gifts

To a do-it-yourselfer, give a book on home repairs or do-it-yourself projects and a gift certificate to the local hardware store or home improvement center.

Many more unique, high-quality gift ideas for new homeowners can be found in the *Preferred Living* catalog from Sporty's. Phone: 800/543-8633.

Humorous and Whimsical Gifts

"People need to know that laughter is a great way to cope. It's cheaper than vodka and Valium, and restores the body's chemical balance, oxygenates the blood, stimulates circulation, and aids digestion," says humorist Larry Wilde. He adds that Norman Cousins cites laughter as an effective tool for promoting the healing process. In Cousins' words, "Laughter is internal jogging." Hence, a humorous gift may be just what the doctor ordered.

Give a collection of jokes or humorous anecdotes, or an anthology of columns by a favorite humorist —Dave Barry, Andy Rooney, Erma Bombeck.

Remember the equation: disaster + time = humor. Give a home video of a funny or disastrous event—after sufficient time has passed, of course.

Find (or have made) a witty bumper sticker, button, badge, or poster expressing the recipient's views or personality, such as "Who cares who's on board?" or "My wife says if I go fishing one more time, she'll leave me. Gosh, I'm going to miss her."

Celebrate!

Look for fun gifts to commemorate National Humor Month (April). But, be careful! Humorist Larry Wilde cautions, "Humor is very personal. What you think is funny, someone else may not."

Humorous and Whimsical Gifts • Inexpensive Gifts

Give a video tape or compact-disc recording of the recipient's favorite comedian—Jay Leno, Paula Poundstone, Jerry Seinfeld, Jeff Foxworthy.

To the kid in him, give a kite, a water gun, a giant bubble blower, a hula hoop, a pogo stick, rollerskates, or a skate board. Find more ideas in the *Toys to Grow On* catalog. Phone: 800/421-5354.

Give a book of comic strips—The Far Side, Calvin and Hobbes, Garfield.

Give a token representing a funny moment shared with the recipient.

Inexpensive Gifts
SEE ALSO *Self, Gifts of*

More unsuitable gifts are given through lack of forethought rather than lack of funds. The following are high-impact, low-cost gifts for just about everyone on your gift list. With a little creativity and time you can come up with more ideas to stretch your gift dollars.

For a bit of nostalgia, order a cassette or compact disc of her favorite vintage radio show. Adventures in Cassettes has a huge selection of comedy, mystery, detective, western, science fiction, drama, and other great old-time radio programs, many for well under $10. Choose from *Lum & Abner*, *The Fred Allen Show*, *I Love a Mystery*, *The Green Hornet*, *Great Lone Ranger*, and many more. Phone: 800/328-0108.

Nothing Ventured, Nothing Gained

"Whenever I ask my friend Robyn what she wants for her birthday, Christmas, or other occasion, her reply is always the same, 'Nothing.' So I once gift wrapped a package with nothing in it. Now, whenever she tells me she wants 'nothing,' I simply ask how big of a box she would like it in."

—BARBARA B.

Inexpensive Gifts

Play It Again

"I've found one of the most fun ways of making To and From tags is to recycle. I save Christmas and birthday cards, and shower and party invitations. I cut out smaller designs and pictures from the cards, and write my messages on the backs. To hang a tag from ribbon, I cut the design a little bigger on one side, use a hole punch to make the hole, then thread the ribbon through."

—Kristen B.

For your little slugger (of any age), Official Major League Baseballs, Automatic Curve Balls, and Pitch Like A Pro balls are available from the Baseball Hall of Fame. Other gifts under $10 include team mugs, the Baseball Legends Card Game, and Abbott & Costello's "Who's On First" audio cassette. Write: P.O. Box 590A, Cooperstown, NY 13326. Phone: 607/547-2445.

If she lives at her desk, your gift of a unique or clever paper weight, letter opener, door or desk nameplate, stamp box, pencil cup, or business card holder would keep you on her mind. A snack pack consisting of canned juices, crackers, and cheese would also be well received.

A gift for man's best friend is sure to endear the giver to the recipient. After all, it has been said, "Like me, like my dog." Give Rover a raised dog bowl, leash, dog pillow, rawhide bone, or rubber toy, or give a book on training or grooming to his owner.

Do you know someone who enjoys being pampered? In some parts of the country, you can find manicurists that will do a manicure for under $10. One office manager we know gave such a gift to all the secretaries in the office. The recipients gave the idea a beautiful thumbs-up!

Gifts from your kitchen are a delightful way to thank a host or hostess. Choose from flavored vinegars or butters, sugared pecans, caramel popcorn, fresh herbs from your window garden, or the fruit preserves or hot salsa you bottled last summer.

Inexpensive Gifts

To the oh-so-dear-but-not-so-near, give prepaid long-distance calling certificates from one of the long distance carriers. These can be purchased from convenience and grocery stores for as little as $5.

A couple of movie tickets to the matinée or discount theater should leave enough change from a 10-spot to throw in a few concessions for a reel treat.

Give a puzzle the family can put together together. It's a fun way to spend quality time together. You may wish to include a jar of puzzle paste to preserve the picture.

A variety of clocks and watches can be found for less than $10. Give a whimsical windup alarm clock to the early-rising college student or a cartoon character watch to the grade schooler.

Many grandparents wish they could see their grandchildren more often. The gift of a framed photo of their precious ones is sure to find a prominent place on a kitchen shelf or bedside table. If one picture just won't do, fill an inexpensive photo album or Grandma's brag book with several pictures and add to the collection throughout the year.

Are you a cook who receives constant requests for your recipes? If you don't mind sharing them, compile your most-requested recipes and organize them in a cookbook format. Include notes about old family recipes and other interesting tidbits about the origin of favorite dishes. For just a few dollars each,

Alma Mat(t)ers

"You owe me," said Bridger when presenting his sister, Paige, with a set of University of Wyoming cups. Paige wanted the huge cups from her alma mater for ice cream shakes, and Bridger had drawn her name for the family gift exchange. What Paige didn't realize at the time was that Bridger, a struggling college student, gathered the eight cups under the bleachers after a ball game and then took them home to sterilize them with bleach. (The idea came from Bridger's resourceful wife.) Years later, Paige and her husband still treasure the cups that have little monetary but great sentimental value.

Inexpensive Gifts

> ### Shopping Tip
>
> Tag sales, flea markets, rummage sales and garage sales are great places to find unique and inexpensive items for gift giving. When giving secondhand gifts, attach a thoughtful note, such as "You came to mind when I found this cobalt vase at a neighbor's garage sale. I hope it's perfect for your collection."

you can have the books printed and bound for giving to family and friends.

Are you a poet still looking for an enlightened publisher who will print your life's work? Self-publish a selection of your writings to share with friends and family that have enjoyed, inspired, or encouraged your efforts.

Garden markers, gloves, knee-saver mats, or gardening hand tools are all inexpensive gifts for the gardener. During the winter, bring the outdoors inside with the gift of a small potted plant (a flowering plant might be especially nice).

Calculators make great gifts for moms that hate to balance the checkbook, dads that like to comparison shop, and kids seeking a shortcut to long division. Many can be found for under $10, and who couldn't use an extra calculator to keep in the car, stick in a purse or backpack, or stash in the desk drawer for incalculable predicaments?

Question: What does an armchair athlete hate more than commercials that interrupt televised games? Answer: Getting up from the easy chair to go to the refrigerator. So, why not give the couch potato a cooler in which to place an afternoon's worth of game-time drinks, sandwiches, and snacks?

Bestow the book lover with book ends, bookplates, clip-on reading lights, bookmarks, or remaindered (publishers' overstocked) books.

Inexpensive Gifts

Indulge the chocoholic with a generous supply of a favorite candy bar, fudge sauce, or a mug and an assortment of gourmet hot chocolate mixes.

Mousepads are now available in hundreds of motifs for computer buffs everywhere.

Garlic bakers, beaded pie-weight chains, stainless-steel wire whisks, rolling mincers, and professional cooking utensils are all available for under $10 from Chef's Catalog. Phone: 800/338-3232.

A backpacker's folding grid, hot dog fork, camp stove, waterproof matchbox, utility stuff sack, stainless steel knife/fork/spoon kit, trailblazer compass, and scout trail light are just a few of the many wonderful gift ideas from the *Official Catalog of the Boy Scouts of America*. Phone: 800/323-0732.

Children can amuse themselves for hours with a variety of cookie cutters and Play-Doh or homemade salt dough. Pizza wheels and spatulas also come in handy while creating with dough.

Give a plastic piggy bank with several rolls of pennies. (Caution: Do not give this gift to children that are in the put-everything-in-mouth stage).

A disposable camera would make a great gift for a child. The pictures he takes of the family vacation, championship Little League game, or class field trip will be a long-lasting reminder of your gift.

It's a Wrap!

To measure the amount of wrapping paper you will need to cut from a roll, wrap a piece of string or yarn around the package and cut it to length. Then, use that to measure the paper.

International Giving

International Giving

An understanding of gift customs and traditions will allow you to give appropriate gifts in any situation—whether you are a businessman or woman, a tourist, an exchange student, or a guest hosted by a friend from another country. To show you really are from the same planet, consult the GGPS (Global Gift Positioning System) below.

A book from the current best-seller list would make a great gift for foreign friends and business associates fluent in English. Coffee table books with pictures of American sports, history, scenery, and culture are also popular.

Gifts of paintings, sculpture, ceramics, and other artwork by American artists are especially appreciated.

Many people enjoy receiving gifts that are not readily available in their country. Such gifts include state-of-the-art electronic gadgets and the latest electrical appliances. (Include a voltage converter, if necessary.)

Trendy blue jeans, athletic shoes, T-shirts, and sweatshirts with sports team logos or clever sayings make fun clothing gifts.

Accessories, desk sets, luggage, scarves, ties, handbags, and costume jewelry by top designers or from distinctive stores are well received.

Foreign Affairs

"There are indeed cultural differences that are easily overlooked or ignored, thus turning a well-meant token of affection into a Pandora's box!"

—REGULA PICKEL,
SWISS NATIONAL
TOURIST OFFICE

International Giving

Give food items from your region of the country—peanuts from Georgia, maple syrup from Vermont, cheese from Wisconsin. Where applicable, gifts of food should be in accordance with Kosher or other religious food laws.

Musical recordings—classical, jazz, country, folk, rock—make interesting intercultural gifts.

Posters of pop artists, sports heroes, and television and movie stars are hits with teenagers from other countries.

Children enjoy American toys and sports equipment—Frisbees, in-line skates, baseballs and bats, footballs, and basketballs. Be sure to show the youngsters how to use the items.

Paying import taxes on gifts you bring into a foreign country is a thoughtful and appreciated gesture.

As a general rule, give only gifts of high quality that will serve as lasting reminders of your visit.

Be careful not to give gifts that conflict with cultural or religious values. For example, alcohol of any kind, books or magazines containing photographs of immodestly dressed persons, and sculptures depicting human or animal forms conflict with the practical aspects of Islam.

> **Worth Waiting For**
>
> The Statue of Liberty—icon of liberty and beacon of hope—was given by the people of France to the people of the United States in celebration of the 1876 centennial. Completed in Paris in 1884 and unveiled two years later in New York harbor, the statue was definitely a gift worth waiting for.

Last-minute Gifts

Last-minute Gifts

We know you're in a hurry, so we'll make this intro short. Whether you have postponed your shopping for lack of time, money, or inspiration, here are ideas to help you choose a timely gift in no time.

Grocery stores are wonderful places to shop for last-minute gifts.

- Fill a wok with oriental food favorites (don't forget the fortune cookies).

- Fill a sombrero with all the ingredients for a fiesta. Olé!

- Line a basket with a checkered cloth napkin and fill it with Italian specialties.

- Fill a decorative tin with holiday cookies from the grocery store's bakery.

- Give a cookie sheet with cookie cutters, a spatula, and a roll of cookie dough from the store's refrigerator case.

- Fill an ice chest with snacks, drinks, suntan lotion, magazines, and paperbacks for a day of relaxation on the beach.

Drugstores are filled with an array of merchandise for last-minute shoppers. Many are open 24 hours a day, providing one-stop shopping 'round the clock. Just look at the assortment of treasures you can find at the drugstore:

- Games, toys, and puzzles for recipients of all ages

- Electronic gadgets—personal stereos, electronic dictionaries, thesauruses, hand-held video systems and games

It's a Wrap!

To save time, keep an assortment of gift tags, greeting cards, and personal notecards with your wrapping supplies.

Last-minute Gifts

- Small appliances—Belgian waffle irons, popcorn poppers, ice cream freezers, telephones
- Cosmetics—makeup brushes, nail care accessories, fragrances
- Sports and exercise equipment—balls, bats, in-line skates, small weights, step exercisers
- Stationery and desk supplies
- Watches and clocks—alarm, radio, travel, shower
- Costume jewelry and fashion accessories
- Picture frames and photo albums
- A variety of flashlights—penlights, roadside, pocket
- Calculators—scientific, construction, big-buttoned
- Battery chargers and rechargeable batteries (perfect gifts for accompanying radios, recorders, toys, and games)
- Hair ribbons, barrettes, bows, and headbands
- Audio tapes, video tapes, and compact discs
- Holiday music, ornaments, tableware, linens

Like drugstores, bookstores offer a wide range of quick gifts for those of all ages:

- Sturdy picture books for infants and toddlers
- Counting, alphabet, fantasy, and rhyming books for pre-schoolers
- Humorous, adventure, and how-things-work books for grade schoolers
- Coffee table books for just about every interest from antique furniture to zoology

> ### Shopping Tip
> When time is of the essence, shop alone. Otherwise you may spend valuable time waiting for others or going to stores not on your list. If you enjoy shopping with a friend, do so when you have time to browse and relax.

Last-minute Gifts

> **Shopping Tip**
>
> In a hurry? Take advantage of in-store services such as personal shoppers, gift wrapping, delivery, and shipping.

- Leather- and fabric-covered blank books to serve as journals, phone directories, or note pads

- Large-print editions of favorite books for people with sight impairments

- Theme calendars for every interest

- Magazines—insert a note to mention that you have arranged for a gift subscription and then be sure to do so, or roll together several current magazines of interest to the recipient and tie them with a bow

- Gift certificates—a favorite for the bookworm

Don't overlook items around your house as gifts for last-minute giving.

- Give fruit, preserves, relishes, pickles, or homemade mustards or vinegars from your pantry.

- Pass on a piece of antique or heirloom jewelry to a daughter or granddaughter or give a piece of your costume jewelry to a niece or friend who has admired it.

- At Christmas time, share holiday greens from your yard—holly, pine boughs, pine cones, magnolia leaves.

- Write favorite recipes on pretty cards and share them with friends that have requested them.

- Repot a healthy house plant, "wrap" the pot in colorful fabric or paper, and tie it with a pretty bow.

- Put a school picture in a frame from your home and give it as a gift to grandparents or to an adoring aunt.

- Recycle baskets, vases, and accessories—assuming they are in good shape and in keeping with the recipient's taste and decor.

Last-minute Gifts • Men

- Give items from one of your collections: coins, stamps, baseball cards, books, records, quilts.

- And finally, what teenager, college student, or spouse could resist the use of your credit card for a purchase of his of her choice—with a specified limit, of course.

Men
SEE ALSO relevant interest categories

Many people have trouble selecting gifts for men because they simply forget that the only difference between men and boys is the price and size of their toys. With this in mind, selecting gifts for husbands, fathers, brothers, boyfriends, and male coworkers becomes child's play.

Crutchfield offers expert advice and discount prices on car stereo, home audio, video, and home theater products. Gift certificates are available. Phone: 800/955-3000.

Give the latest hand-held video game system with state-of-the-art big-boy programs and arcade games.

Survey Scoop! According to Debra Smith, Executive Director of the Professional Audio-video Retailer's Association, there is something for everyone in the stereo store. Boom boxes and personal stereo cassette players are favorites of the younger generation while home theater products are drawing back hobbyists lost to the computer rage. "Music is still very important to 35- to 45-year olds

Best/Worst

Best: My wife's permission to buy myself a hunting rifle

Worst: A musical car horn which I never even took out of the box

—MICHAEL W.

Men

It's a Wrap!

Tuck a small present or note in one of the following:

✔ His coat pocket

✔ His cereal box

✔ His desk drawer

✔ His running shoe

✔ Under his windshield wiper

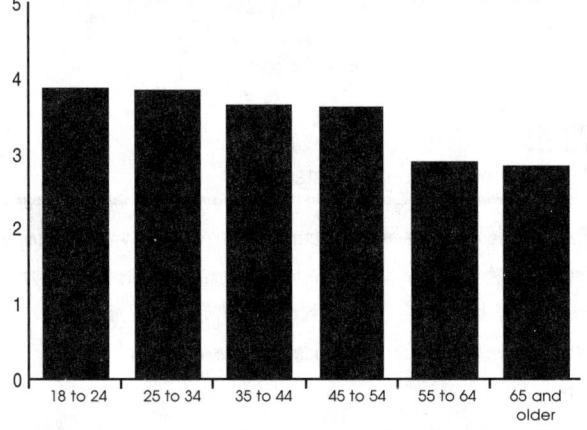

who wants gifts of
AUDIO/VIDEO?

Men's preferences for gifts of audio/video equipment, by age, on a scale of 1 being least preferred and 5 being most preferred.

Source: Discovery Research Group/Present Perfect Survey

for whom it was an intrinsic part of the culture 15 to 20 years ago, and they now have the money to buy the high-tech components they want," says Smith.

Give a prepaid membership in a gym, country club, civic organization, or another interest group.

The *Sharper Image* catalog is filled with big boy toys and great gifts for men. Phone: 800/344-4444.

Grown-up versions of a favorite toy may be just the perfect gift for the man on your gift list. Choose from remote-controlled airplanes, pint-sized pinball machines, electric train sets, and dart boards.

Men

Today's T-shirts are much more than fashion statements. From the amusing to the absurd, T-shirt slogans can express the political, educational, cultural, and social sentiments of the wearer. Since they can be customized to a specific recipient, and since—theoretically—one can never have too many of them, they make great gifts.

Give a mug, T-shirt, cap, key-ring, or another item with the logo of his favorite college or professional sports team.

Give him vanity license plates for his car. As a matter of fact, just about anything for his car would be well received. (See *Car Buffs*.)

Make a donation in his name to his high school or college athletics program, science club, music department, or fraternity.

Give him a season pass (two passes might be even better) to a cultural, sports, or lecture series of interest to him.

For audio, video, motoring, golf, photography, travel, and fitness gifts by mail, call for a *Herrington Catalog*. Phone: 800/622-5221.

To the craftsman, give precision tools or a gift certificate and catalog from Bridge City Tool Works. Phone: 800/253-3332.

Consider This

When giving gifts of clothing, consider the answers to these questions: Does he prefer to wear casual or tailored attire? What fabrics and colors does he favor? Where does he shop for clothing?

Best/Worst

Best: An ATV (all-terrain vehicle) when I was 12 years old

Worst: A belly dancer who performed for me at work

—Dana L.

Men

Give a framed picture of you to put on his desk or bedside table.

Flowers, For Men?

Oh, the glorious nineties! Our culture has reached new heights of political correctness, and male sensitivity is as chic as saving the rain forests. With this in mind, we decided to take a fresh look at flowers.

Steve Jenkins, a flower delivery person in Eugene, Oregon, has seen a wide range of reactions from men receiving flowers. Some take gifts of flowers in stride, others receive them in a profound state of shock. One perplexed male said, "I'll see you again at my funeral...this will probably be the last time I get flowers before I die."

"Pleasant, but bewildered" is how Steve describes the typical male response to blooming gifts. A full third of Steve's 1,000+ deliveries last year were to men. He's seen what works and what doesn't, and offers the following guidelines for giving flowers to men.

- ◆ Choose flowers that are masculine, not frilly. As a general rule, dark-colored and sturdy flowers are more apropos.

- ◆ Pay attention to packaging. Avoid delicate vases and containers. Opt for a sturdy mug, an earthenware pot, a fishing creel, or a sturdy wicker basket.

- ◆ Use a card to convey your sentiments! A few appropriate words can turn a fellow from confused to flattered.

- ◆ Consider plant alternatives. Nonflowering plants are popular gifts for men. Cactus gardens, although prickly, are especially well received.

Flower Power

When all is cut and dried, flowers are a progressive and dauntless gift for men. After all, what self-respecting male doesn't want to be sensitive? A gift of flowers and a card to this effect would make his day a memorable one.

Military Persons and Veterans

They're up at dawn, run ten miles in combat boots, eat in a mess, and have no permanent address. Whatever branch of the service they're in, military personnel lead Spartan lives so we can sleep peacefully at night. We salute United States Air Force First Lieutenant, Dirk Johnson, Coco Beach, Florida, and Private First Class, Michael Christensen, Utah Army National Guard, for their input for this section.

Pictures of the family, memoirs and letters from home, and homebaked treats were at the top of the list of gift requests from the single military persons with whom we spoke.

Hand-held video games are popular among crews on long flights or at sea. Game systems and game cartridges make fun gifts. Books and tapes are also good choices for filling long, empty hours.

Cameras, film, and mailers for developing the film all make appropriate gifts for service men and women.

To military personnel stationed abroad, send favorite food or personal items not available where they are located.

Give hobby supplies relevant to an interest of the recipient. Many enjoy woodworking, model building, and—yes—even needlework.

Packaging Checklist

✔ Rigid box with flaps intact

✔ Adequate cushioning material

✔ Items wrapped separately

✔ Strong tape designed for shipping

✔ No string or paper overwrap

✔ A clear, complete delivery address

✔ Single address label

✔ A clear, complete return address

✔ Duplicate label inside box

—Source: UPS

Military Persons and Veterans

From the Homefront

"When my husband was on an assignment in a remote area of Alaska, I sent care packages filled with items such as family pictures, musical recordings, oriental noodle soup, microwave popcorn, favorite razors and aftershave lotion, newsy letters, and writing paper with self-addressed, stamped envelopes (leaving him no excuse for not writing)."

—Karen H.

Although much of the service person's apparel is government-issued, gifts of casual clothing and accessories are generally appreciated.

Give an audio cassette player and then send audio tapes on a regular basis.

Give a subscription to a hometown paper or newsletter.

To commemorate a military retirement or another milestone, you can request to have an American flag fly atop the nation's Capitol. A letter indicating the date and occasion for which it was flown will be mailed with the flag to the recipient. Contact your state senator or representative for more information.

As a unique way of honoring and recognizing their service to our country, names of those that served honorably in the Navy, Marine Corps, Coast Guard, wartime Merchant Marine, or reserve components may be added to the computer log in the Navy Memorial Visitors Center in Washington, D.C. A $25 tax-deductible donation is requested for each log enrollment and a photo may be added to the log at any time. Phone: 800/821-8892.

Army Times, *Navy Times*, and *Air Force Times* are weekly independent newspapers for military professionals. They provide up-to-date news on a variety of issues including career advancement, pay, benefits, lifestyle, and the effects of the political administration on military policy. Phone: 800/368-5718.

Military Persons and Veterans • Money, Gifts of

Air Force members, veterans, and others interested in airpower and national defense might enjoy a subscription to *Air Force Magazine*. Write: Air Force Association, 1501 Lee Highway, Arlington, VA 22209.

The *Marine Corps Gazette* has been the professional journal of United States Marines since 1916. It is primarily written by and for Marines about all aspects of Marine Corps activity. Phone: 800/336-0291.

Money, Gifts of

We've got good news and bad news when it comes to gifts of cold hard cash. The bad news is that studies indicate giving money as a gift is more emotionally and socially complicated than it may appear. The good news—for those that prefer gifts of cash—is that monetary gifts are on the rise. Busy Americans are finding less and less time to shop for recipients whose wants have become more and more discriminating. Many relent with gifts of cash, assuming the recipients would prefer a gift of their own choosing. Critics of monetary gifts maintain money lacks intimacy and imagination, requiring the giver to devote little or no thought to what might please the recipient. Here are some ideas to consider.

Make gifts of money seem incidental to your wish for the recipient to have something she would really like. To do so, tuck a thoughtful note and the cash, or check, into an accessory item. Your token gift serves as a thoughtful reminder that you contributed to a major gift or event and would make receiving cash less awkward for the recipient who is sensitive to cash gifts.

◆ For your young grandson saving for his first set of wheels, put the cash in a bike helmet or water bottle

> **Special Presentations**
>
> Put hints about his present inside several balloons. Give the balloons (or have them delivered) one at a time at regular intervals throughout the day.

Money, Gifts of

> **No Cash, Please**
>
> Foreign currency— even in the form of commemorative coins— is prohibited by law in China and should never be offered as a gift.

with the note, "I heard you were saving for a hot new trail bike." For your older granddaughter, attach your gift to a key ring with the note, "I hope this will help toward the purchase of your first car."

◆ For the couple planning and saving for a honeymoon or anniversary cruise, stash the cash in a piece of luggage or a basket of cruise supplies—sunscreen, visors, beach sandals, sunglasses, and travel guides—with a note that reads, "Here's to a well-deserved voyage."

◆ To expectant parents, a contribution toward major baby needs may be a very appreciated gesture. Tuck your gift into a diaper bag or baby bottle with a note conveying your best wishes for the precious little one.

◆ Open a college savings account for your goddaughter to which you will make regular contributions. Present your gift with a small tree she can plant and a note that says, "Although money may not grow *on* trees, with proper attention, it does grow *as* trees. As this tree grows over the years, so will your education fund."

A variety of investment vehicles lend themselves to gift giving and can be tailored to the recipient's short-term, intermediate, and long-term financial needs. Givers can set up passbook savings accounts, certificates of deposit, or money-market deposit accounts in the name of a recipient, and can retain title to the investment if they are concerned about the recipient's ability to manage the money.

Stocks and mutual funds are good gifts choices for the more aggressive investor.

Money, Gifts of

Cash contributions to a recipient's charity interest are becoming popular gifts. Bing Edwards, Development Specialist for the National Wildlife Federation, considers each gift very singular. "Gifts from the heart, that's what they are," says Edwards. "They are really very sincere, very personal. You never know what's going to be in that letter." Edwards receives gifts from children sending donations in honor of their bar/bat mitzvah, gifts from grown children to their parents that have everything, and even gifts in honor of pets. She notes a trend for charitable donations in lieu of flowers for memorial gifts and says revenue in the Memorial Tribute Program has increased over the years.

Gifts of savings bonds have long been a favorite of grandparents, aunts, and uncles helping youngsters save for college.

Retailers and service providers have become willing intermediaries in the cash-for-gifts dilemma. Gift certificates are available for virtually every conceivable good or service, from auto detailing to landscaping, from a day at the spa to a week on a cattle drive. Although they don't conform to the convention that a recipient should never be apprised of the monetary value of a gift, the careful selection of a gift certificate from a store or service relating to the recipient's interest often conveys more sentiment and ingenuity than a gift of cash. (See *Gift Certificates*.)

Survey Scoop! Much to our surprise, gifts of money top the list in nearly every age, income, and education group in our national survey of gift preferences. Although they have long been considered in question-

What Gives?

How do you feel about giving and receiving gifts of cash? Do you know of a clever way to present gifts of money? Share your ideas with us. See page 277.

Money, Gifts of

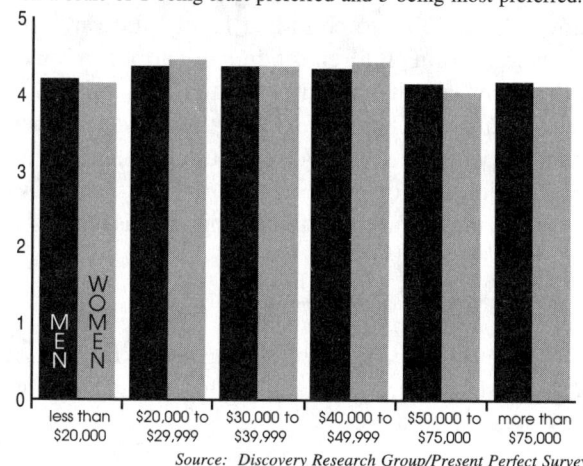

able taste by etiquette experts, gifts of money receive a top score (5 on a scale of 1 to 5) from sixty-seven percent of the survey respondents. Sixty-five percent of those with household incomes in excess of $75,000 per year give gifts of money a high five!

Does someone on your gift list wish money grew on trees? Give a potted tree with coins and bills attached to the branches.

Fill a large jar with coins and let children reach in to take all they can get in a handful. Sherri's uncles and mother do this and the grandchildren of all ages love it.

Best/Worst

Of all the people we have asked to name one of the best gifts they have ever received, not one has said "money." In light of the gift preferences survey results, we find this to be very interesting.

—SHERRI & LARRY

Mother's Day Presents

It's the Christmas of Momhood! And ever since President Woodrow Wilson's official proclamation of Mother's Day in 1914, nervous husbands and eager children have labored to find the perfect gift for Mom...with varying degrees of success. Yet, how can any gift acknowledge what our mothers mean to us? The truth is, it can't. Nevertheless, the tokens we choose for Mother's Day should reflect a sensitivity to her needs or concerns. Here are a few suggestions.

Present Mom with a collection of letters from you and your siblings telling her of the valuable influence she has had on your lives or describing a trait you admire in her.

Design and make (or have made) a quilt with blocks depicting accomplishments and events in her life.

Transfer your mother's old home movies to video tapes, or digitally transfer movies and photos to computer diskettes or compact discs (there are businesses to help you do this).

Plan a family dinner at which she is the guest of honor—arrange a special place for her to sit comfortably and visit while family members take turns with dinner preparations.

Arrange with the telephone company for a conference call to your mother from you and your long-distance siblings.

Best/Worst

Best: A watch and pearls from my 11- and 12-year-old sons that went without school lunch and saved their lunch money to buy them

Worst: A felt Santa toilet seat cover

—Anna G.

Mother's Day Presents

Present Danger!

In general, do not give Mom a vacuum cleaner (or anything like unto it). Utilitarian gifts—i.e., cleaning equipment—thrill Mom about as much as utilitarian gifts—i.e., garden hoses—thrill Dad. Besides, do you really want to be remembered by Mom every time she cleans up your messes? If you really want to lighten her workload, present her with a cleaning service. If you really want to give her a vacuum cleaner, go ahead. Just don't make a gift of it.

To some, an oh-so-comfortable hammock just may be the ultimate gift of total indulgence. Sherri has her eye on the Original Pawleys Island Rope Hammock. Request a copy of *The Legendary Low Country Catalogue* from the Original Hammock Shop in Pawleys Island, South Carolina. Phone: 800/332-3490. Fax: 803/237-9122.

Make a contribution in her name to an organization in which she has shown an interest.

Lighten her work load by taking over one of her tasks on a regular basis.

Organize a luncheon with friends she hasn't seen for a long time.

Make a date for a regular outing to her favorite restaurant, park, theater, or mall.

Pamper her with a maid-for-a-day service or a day at the salon.

Register her in a workshop on keeping a journal or assembling a personal history.

Record and transcribe conversations with your mother as you reminisce about her life. Present them to her in an attractive book.

Mother's Day Presents

What's Mom Getting for Mother's Day?

According to our research, Mom's presents for Mother's Day (from her grown children) may hinge on whether her children are men or women, how far they live from her, and how often she sees them.

Sons give twice as many gifts of candy, perfume, and kitchen gadgets. Daughters give twice as many gifts of clothing. Seventy percent of moms living 500 miles or more from the children receive long-distance calls. Mothers that see their children at least once a week receive four times as many gifts of perfume and clothing, and two times as many flowers as mothers that see their children once a year or less.

While 35 percent of mothers 45 years or older say they most like to receive visits or calls from their children, 25 percent of younger mothers most like to receive hugs and kisses, and peace and quiet.

Other survey highlights:

◆ Seventy-nine percent of American men and women convey Mother's Day sentiments with a card. Forty-seven percent pay tribute via a telephone call, and 45 percent say it with flowers.

◆ Thirty-five percent of those surveyed spend less than $25 on gifts for Mother's Day. Thirty-six percent spend between $25 and $49, and 25 percent spend $50 or more.

◆ Only five percent of mothers aged 55 or older expect to receive nothing for Mother's Day, while 22 percent of mothers under 35 expect to receive nothing.

SOURCE: DISCOVERY RESEARCH GROUP/PRESENT PERFECT SURVEY

The Little Things

It's fun to give Mom a little of something she would never buy for herself:

✔ A little gold chain

✔ A little bottle of her favorite perfume or cologne

✔ A little bit of handmade candy

✔ A little antique

✔ A little bouquet of exotic flowers

Music Lovers

Music Lovers
SEE ALSO *Arts Lovers*

Do you know someone whose heart, hands, and feet appear to be connected to his ears? From swaying and sashaying to toe tappin' and foot stompin', many music lovers are moved by their favorite tunes. Addressing the music lover's passions through your gift selections can be a great accompaniment to your relationship. We hope you'll find the following to be sound advice.

Give an autographed picture or poster of his favorite artist.

Season tickets to a concert series make great gifts for classical music lovers.

A trip to Branson, Missouri is sure to please the country music lover.

Hire a pianist, violinist, another instrumentalist, or small ensemble to perform a private concert or to provide background music for a dinner party or another gathering.

Give a subscription to *Down Beat* magazine. *Down Beat* covers the full spectrum of jazz and blues and delves into pop, R&B, funk, world music, and more. Phone: 800/535-7496. Fax: 708/941-3210.

To the serious music collector, give a subscription to *Fanfare,* which reviews about 500 classical, jazz, and soundtrack compact discs each issue. Write:

It's A Wrap!
Wrap concert tickets or other small gifts for the music lover in sheet music.

Music Lovers

Fanfare, P.O. Box 720, Tenafly, NJ 07670. Phone: 201/567-3908. Fax: 201/816-0125.

Give a tote bag, T-shirt, or other item bearing a musical message or motif.

For a truly extravagant present, give an antique instrument or an instrument played by an artist she favors.

Framed copies of antique sheet music or music composed by—or for—the recipient make nice additions to a music room or studio.

Give a new compact-disc player, boom box, stereo system, personal stereo, or headset.

If the music lover is also a computer buff, give a multimedia kit so she can play compact discs while in cyberspace. Or, give a software program for composing her own music.

Give a storage unit for his collection of record albums, cassette tapes, or compact discs.

To a professional musician, give a gig bag for hauling music or instruments to jobs.

To the instrumentalist, give sheet music, books of music, an instrument cleaning kit, or a gift certificate to a music supply store.

> **Celebrate!**
>
> Celebrate the anniversary of Wolfgang Amadeus Mozart's birth, March 27, by giving an appropriate recording to the classical music lover.

Music Lovers • New Neighbors

Shopping Tip

A trip with the recipient to a music store would give you a great deal of insight into his or her musical tastes and wishes.

Convert his treasured album collection to compact discs. (Some old hit albums are already available in compact-disc format.)

Pay dues to a professional music organization or fees for a music camp or series.

Make a splash with waterproof speakers installed in his bathroom. Caution: This may mean your music lover will never leave the bathroom!

New Neighbors

SEE ALSO *Homeowners* and *Housewarming Presents*

What do DINKS (Dual Income, No Kids), boomers, flower children, empty nesters, single parents, blended families, and couples with 2.3 children all have in common? The answer strikes close to home. Any of them can become your new neighbor. And, regardless of shape, size, or family status, each has some degree of Post-Moving Syndrome—a mixture of anticipation, exhaustion, and disorientation. So circle the welcome wagons and add your personal touches to the following ideas.

Organize a welcome-to-the-neighborhood party for new move-ins after they've settled in a bit.

Deliver a move-in survival kit to new neighbors. Include items such as paper plates and cups, plastic flatware, a can opener, a telephone book, a neighborhood directory, a map, a bottle of aspirin, and a flower arrangement. For families with small chil-

New Neighbors • New Year's Presents

dren, include crayons and coloring books to keep them busy while Mom and Dad unpack.

Arrange for a few weeks of seasonal yard services such as lawn mowing, leaf raking, and snow removal while the new neighbors are getting settled.

Give a town tour to show them the location of stores, schools, parks, and other services.

New Year's Presents

"Should auld acquaintance be forgot?" Not if you resolve now to be a better gift giver. Start the new year with a gift of one of the following.

Make arrangements for the recipient to celebrate New Years' Eve at Times Square in New York.

Give a gift in support of a New Years' resolution—but be sure it is the *recipient's* resolution and not a nagging hint from you. Here are some ideas:

◆ An electronic organizer to a busy friend resolved to make better use of her time

◆ A supply of paper to the writer determined to finish his book *this* year

◆ Season tickets to the symphony to the self-declared culturally challenged

◆ A stack of paper plates to the bachelor resolved to keep the sink free of dirty dishes

Celebrate!

Celebrate Good Neighbor Day (the fourth Sunday in September) in one of the following ways:

✔ Visit with someone who is lonely or ill.

✔ Invite someone to dinner.

✔ Run an errand for a busy neighbor.

✔ Take time for a troubled child or family.

✔ Donate magazines, books, and games to rest homes, youth centers, and correctional facilities.

✔ Organize families or other groups to fulfill larger needs in your community.

—SOURCE: GOOD NEIGHBOR DAY FOUNDATION

New Year's Presents

Try This

As a fun gift to many, host a prediction party for your friends. Follow up next year to see who was right.

- Lessons to one who has expressed an interest in learning to dance, ski, play a musical instrument, paint, sing, or sew
- Language tapes to one determined to learn a foreign language before his vacation
- Games, zoo passes, or amusement park tickets to the parent who wants to spend more time with the family
- A *Newsweek*, *Time*, or *Wall Street Journal* subscription to one who has resolved to be more informed about current events
- A book a month to one who has resolved to read the classics, every book on the best-seller list, or works of a favorite writer

---

A calendar marked with birthdays, anniversaries, graduations, weddings, and births for the upcoming year would make a great gift for busy people who like to be thoughtful.

Give a year's supply of birthday, holiday, and greeting cards.

Enroll the recipient in an item-of-the-month club—desserts, flowers, books, or fruit.

Give a journal or photo album in which to record events of the upcoming year.

Surprise him with tickets to a New Year's Day football bowl game or party.

Nurses

Whether at a hospital, vacation spot, children's camp, school, or workplace, chances are good that one of the 2.2 million registered nurses in the United States will touch your life, or the life of a loved one. You may wish to thank an especially attentive nurse or nursing staff with a gift.

Timesaving services make perfect gifts for nurses who work long shifts and tight schedules. Give a certificate for carry-out from her favorite restaurant, or pizza delivery on a night of her choice. Or, arrange and pay for housecleaning, lawn care, car washing, or auto detailing.

Stress relievers are thoughtful gifts to nurses that work in a tense environment. A day at a salon for hair styling, a manicure, a pedicure, or a professional massage may be welcome indulgences. Movie tickets, theater tickets, or a dinner out may be renewing. Membership to a spa or gym near the hospital or office would be a long-remembered gift.

A pen-on-a-rope for marking charts or a small notepad for keeping patient notes would make a useful gift. Perhaps you can find one with a nursing motif.

Give a tote bag for books, craft, or hobby supplies to be used in rare spare moments.

A car alarm, pepper spray, mini light on a key ring, self-defense course, or mobile phone would

> **It's a Wrap!**
>
> Hide a small gift in a huge bouquet of flowers, a jar of penny candy, a bucket of marbles, a box of chocolates, or a bag of popcorn.

Nurses

> **End on a Good Note**
>
> A note to a nurse expressing your sincerest appreciation for competent and sensitive care would make a treasured gift in itself.

show your concern for the personal safety of a home-care or night nurse.

There are several nice ways to thank an entire nursing staff:

- ◆ Arrange for a catered—but unobtrusive—breakfast, brunch, lunch, dinner, or midnight snack (depending on the shift). Individually-boxed meals may be the most convenient.

- ◆ Stock the nurses' pantry with instant soup mixes, crackers, and microwave popcorn, or fill the refrigerator with an assortment of juice drinks.

- ◆ Send a flower arrangement, potted plant, assortment of books, or magazine subscription for the nurses' station or lounge.

A reusable, insulated lunch bag or small cooler may be well received.

For comfort and convenience, a sweater or lightweight jacket with roomy pockets for surgical scissors, tape, pens, thermometers, and nursing miscellany may be nice. A fanny pack is also great for keeping items accessible.

To military nurses stationed in sick bays aboard navy ships or in tents at remote locations around the globe, send care packages filled with the following: paperback books, magazines, newspapers, nonperishable food, powdered drink mixes, spices, cosmetics, holiday decorations and music, camera equipment, film, and a long-distance calling card.

Nursing Home Residents

Many people feel isolated and confined when moving to a nursing home. Treasured personal possessions are often left behind due to space limitations. Self-reliance and independence yield to managed care. Your thoughtful gestures, meaningful gifts, and sensitive concern can make a significant difference to those that experience this dramatic shift in lifestyle.

Arrange and pay for regular hair styling, pedicure, or manicure services.

A supply of stationery, cards, and postage, along with your assistance in writing notes and letters, would make a very thoughtful gift.

Food favorites, as permitted, make welcome additions to institutional fare. (Be sure there is a place and staff available to store special foods.)

If his health permits, arrange an outing for lunch, the theater, visiting friends, or a pleasant stroll.

Give a subscription to her hometown newspaper or city magazine.

Engage him in conversation about past memories, family traditions, vacations, homes, employment, and friends. Write a personal history from your conversations with the recipient and other family members, or hire someone to do so.

> **It's a Wrap!**
>
> To design your own gift wrapping paper, spatter-paint, rag-roll, sponge, or stencil sheets or rolls of plain-colored paper.

Nursing Home Residents

Give a tote bag that can be easily attached to a walker or wheelchair.

Regular letters, cards, and visits from loved ones are among the very best gifts for nursing home residents.

Audio/video equipment, where there is room for it, would make a nice gift. Give a television set, a VCR, a radio, a cassette recorder, a compact-disc player, and favorite tapes, compact discs, and movies. (Be sure to teach him how to use the equipment.)

Hang a bulletin board in her room and arrange pictures and cards from family and friends on it. Or, organize the pictures, cards, and letters in a photo album. Be sure to include pictures she remembers from her past as well as current snapshots of her family and friends.

Give a new pair of comfortable slippers.

Arrange with a florist to deliver fresh flowers on a regular basis or for special occasions such as her birthday or wedding anniversary.

Most nursing home facilities supply residents with personal items such as shampoo, soap, and toothpaste. However, some residents prefer brands other than those provided. If so, these items make much-appreciated gifts.

Outdoor Cooks

SEE ALSO *Cooks* and *Hosts and Hostesses*

You can find them serving up hot guts (spicy link sausage) ranch-side in Texas, barbecuing lobster and clams seaside in New England, and grilling vegetables poolside in California. They assemble en masse in heated competition and smoldering debates at the Lovelady Lovefest, the Hog Happenin', and the Big Pig Jig. Masters of the grill are a diverse bunch—each with his or her own ideas about the perfect sauces, aromatic woods, meats, and seasonings. We've cooked up the following hot gift ideas for the outdoor cook on your gift list.

The first thing outdoor cooks disagree on is the proper grill. Investigate the recipient's preference for gas or charcoal grills and the requisite bells and whistles. Other basic equipment gift ideas include a portable grill, hibachi, or camp stove for outdoor cooks on the go; a water smoker for cooking large cuts of meat; dutch ovens and accessories for cooking 'round the campfire; or an indoor electric griller or stove-top grill for when the weather moves the cookout indoors.

A plethora of gizmos and gadgets are available for outdoor cooks. Here are just a few: steak and poultry buttons, a grill thermometer, kabob racks and skewers, heat- and flame-resistant barbecue gloves, scissor tongs, a gas match, a tool and sauce holder, grill maintenance accessories, grilling grids and baskets (for fish, hamburgers, chicken, vegetables), a chimney starter (charcoal lighting tool), telescoping roasting rods, or a wireless intercom system or telephone for direct communication with central command (the kitchen).

Barbecuing is an easy and fun way to entertain. Give gifts that add flair and style to outdoor en-

Celebrate!

The Barbecue Industry Association estimates there are over 66 million barbecuers across the country and that men *and* women are firing up the grill every day of the week. Gift a griller to commemorate National Barbecue Month and National Hamburger Month—both in May.

Outdoor Cooks • Party Favors

All Fired Up!

Gifts for the grill—or the griller—are a great way to thank a host, welcome a new neighbor, or congratulate a new home owner. The type of grill or other cooking method used, such as open fire, pit, or dutch oven, are important cues when selecting gifts for outdoor cooks.

tertaining: a steak knife set, steak platters, sturdy dinnerware, glassware, flatware, a condiment caddy, a serving cart, an apron or chef's hat emblazoned with the appropriate sentiment or nickname, table cloths and clips, lanterns, or a picnic table and benches.

Great tasting food is the number one reason for grilling outdoors, according to a survey by the Barbecue Industry Association. Gifts of great taste include choice steaks or seafood from the local market or a specialty mail-order catalog, a collection or cookbook of favorite outdoor recipes, an assortment of sauces and marinades, smoking woods, and herbs and herb rubs blended for seafood, poultry, or beef.

Many of the gifts listed above as well as other great gifts for the outdoor cook can be found in the *Grill Lover's Catalog*. Phone: 800/241-8981.

Party Favors

Humans have been throwing parties for millennia. And though nobody knows what favors were given out at the first parties, sharp sticks and rocks were likely among them. Today's hosts and hostesses still seek tokens of remembrance to distribute among departing guests. So whether you throw your bash in a cave, casa, or condo, consider the following party favors.

Cluster potted plants or flowers to form a centerpiece or foyer decoration. As guests leave, give each of them a "piece" of the arrangement.

Party Favors

Wrap individual presents—picture frames, books, candles, key chains, mugs, or candy—to put at each place at the dinner table, the gift tag doubling as a place card. Packages can be unwrapped at any time suggested by the hostess, or taken home by guests to unwrap later.

Theme parties and dinner menus often suggest suitable party favors. Give one of the following:

- Small ginger jars filled with fortune cookies for a Chinese New Year's party
- Miniature flags for a Fourth of July celebration
- Small nutcrackers for a Christmas luncheon
- Candle holders with a heart motif for a Valentine's dinner
- Jars of your special recipe barbecue sauce for a Texas-style barbecue
- Decorated tins filled with your best-loved homemade cookies for just about any occasion

---

Children's party themes also suggest appropriate gifts for guests. Give flashlights for sleep-overs, water pistols for water parties, beach accessories (sunglasses, pails, shovels, beach balls) for beach parties, or the latest action figures or posters for hero parties.

Loot bags for guests at children's birthday parties are the custom in many areas. Bags may be filled with candies, magic tricks, piggy banks, coin purses, crayons, markers, puzzles, hair clips, ribbons, costume jewelry, dominoes, bubbles, sidewalk chalk, noise makers, miniature vehicles, and other small trinkets.

Best/Worst

Best: A surprise dinner and birthday party given to my wife from our children

Worst: Men's cologne

—Brent B.

Photographers

Photographers

They say a picture is worth a thousand words. But, if you think Leicaflex is a sportswear fabric, that an f-stop is where you get off the bus to go to the mall, or that a glycerin sandwich is a high-energy lunch food, you may do well to let the photographer worry about the vocabulary while you focus on one of the following gift ideas. Perhaps the shutterbug on the receiving end will use some of those 1,000 words to express appreciation.

Arrange to send the recipient on a weekend getaway to a scenic spot, or on a photography hunt, safari, or another adventure. A travel agent can help you with the details.

For a gift that will make him say "cheese!," turn a spare closet or basement room into a darkroom.

Register the shutterbug on your gift list in a photography class or arrange for one-on-one instruction with a professional photographer.

In a camera bag, assemble items such as film, lenses, a tripod, shutter cable, neck straps, and other picture-perfect odds and ends.

Arrange to have her work displayed at a public library, restaurant, or gallery.

Give one of the many books or magazines on photography. Check the local newsstand or bookstore for the current offerings.

Celebrate!

May is National Photo Month. Surprise the photographer with an assortment of picture frames and photo albums.

Photographers • Photographs, Gifts of

Give a gift certificate to a photography supply store or catalog.

Photographs, Gifts of

Fuzzy or focused, colorful or in shades of gray, photographs capture life's treasured moments. Create a lasting impression with the gift of a photograph or portrait. Picture yourself giving one of the following gifts.

Assemble an album, a scrapbook or a collage of pictures from fun or memorable times with the recipient. Or, create a video scrapbook with the help of a business that does film-to-video transfer service (look in *The Yellow Pages* under "video"). For fun, add background music to create a music video.

Give a framed portrait for placement on a bedside table, office credenza, or library bookshelf. Or, give several miniature photos in coordinating frames.

Give a candid picture of the recipient, his family members, or his friends.

Enlarged photos of the recipient's current or previous house make thoughtful gifts.

Dress up photos with pre-cut photo mats. Add interest with double matting, French matting (mats embellished with marbleized paper) and mats cut in a variety of designs. These are available at drug stores, photo retail stores, and framing centers.

Photo Op

"My neighbor Scott 'stole' all the neighborhood children one afternoon and took their pictures at a nearby park. After enlarging and mounting the photos, they were given to pleasantly-surprised parents as Christmas gifts."

—MARY ANN G.

Photographs, Gifts of • Physical Disabilities, People with

If you feel a little daring, consider a makeover and a fashion or glamour portrait for your significant other. Or, how about a mural-sized color print of you?

Physical Disabilities, People with

When giving gifts, the rules are the same for every recipient: give something that makes the person feel valued and unique. Choose items that relate to the person's interests, hobbies, and abilities rather than those that call attention to his or her disabilities.

The American Toy Institute has published a guide to help you find toys for children with visual impairments. Write: American Toy Institute, c/o TMA, 200 Fifth Avenue, Room 740, New York, NY 10010.

The Toys 'R' Us *Toy Guide for Differently-Abled KIDS!* features symbols to identify which toys promote social skills, gross motor skills, language development, creativity, and self-esteem.

Plan an evening at the theater, ballet, or another event. Don't forget to make arrangements in advance for special seating or other accommodations.

Is your friend who has a hearing impairment also a video buff or couch potato? If so, give a personal television amplifier.

To the cook, give pepper mills, can openers, peelers, and cutlery designed for persons with limited grip, strength, or mobility.

Notable Quotables

"The richest gifts we can bestow are the least marketable."

—Henry D. Thoreau

Physical Disabilities, People with

To the game lover, give jumbo-design and magnetic playing cards, card holders and shufflers, a checkers game redesigned for individuals with visual impairments, or a Scrabble board with a gridded and recessed surface on a turntable for greater accessibility for all players.

To the gardener, give easy-grip gardening tools, knee rests, and rolling seats.

To the person who enjoys crafts, give a floor-lamp magnifier for detailed handiwork.

Give a subscription to *Accent on Living*, a quarterly magazine for people with physical disabilities (paraplegics and quadriplegics). It features inspirational stories, travel and vacation reviews, and product information. Phone: 800/787-8444.

Blindskills, Inc., a nonprofit corporation based in Salem, Oregon, publishes two magazines for people that are blind or have difficulty seeing.

- *Dialogue* features articles on mobility, employment, independence, guide dogs, arts, crafts, health, technology, cuisine, and gardening.

- *Lifeprints* is a career, sports, and leisure information magazine composed of first-person articles authored by role models that are visually impaired.

Both magazines are published quarterly in three formats: braille, large print, and 4-track cassette tape recordings. Write: Blindskills, Inc., P.O. Box 5181, Salem, OR 97304-0181. Phone: 503/581-4224. Fax: 503/581-0178.

What Gives?

Do you have any great gift suggestions for people with disabilities? If so, we would love to hear from you. See page 277.

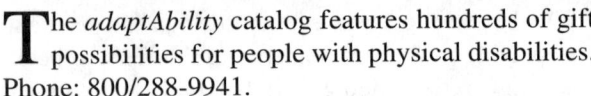

Shopping Tip

Shop by phone, when possible. This is particularly helpful if you're looking for a specific item. Have brand names, model numbers, sizes, colors, and descriptions ready for the salesperson.

The *adaptAbility* catalog features hundreds of gift possibilities for people with physical disabilities. Phone: 800/288-9941.

The *SHHH Journal* is a bimonthly magazine for people that are hearing impaired. The magazine features practical and useful information to help cope with hearing loss and the latest information on products, services, research, and technology in the hearing health care field. Write: *SHHH*, 7910 Woodmont Avenue, Suite 1200, Bethesda, MD 20814. Phone: 301/657-2248 (Voice) or 301/657-2249 (TDD).

Retirement Presents/Retirees
SEE ALSO relevant interest categories

Those that retire are honored and envied by their colleagues, but many retirees miss the routine and camaraderie of the workplace. For better or for worse, retirement is a major life transition. To convey your congratulations and support, consider the following gifts.

Give a supply of business cards reflecting the retiree's new status: fisherman, golfer, consultant, traveler, beach bum.

Host a dinner or reception in the retiree's honor.

Give a book of coupons for discounts on travel, accommodations, dining, and shopping. Many are sold through community groups and schools to raise funds for various causes.

Retirement Presents/Retirees • Romantic Presents

Depict the retiree's accomplishments in a painting, quilt, needlepoint pillow, or cross-stitched plaque.

Give an address book filled with addresses of coworkers and associates.

Clocks, watches, luggage, books, custom artwork, and travel are typical retirement gifts.

Romantic Presents
SEE ALSO *Valentine's Day Presents*

"I'm not the romantic type," you say. "All that mushy stuff just isn't my style." Relax. Woo your sweetheart with your own inimitable style—the style that bedazzled him or her in the first place.

Be yourself. Be creative. Be irresistible. Here are a few ideas to get your creative juices flowing:

- ◆ **Be attentive:** Give her something you know she wants, but might never buy for herself—something she considers too extravagant, expensive, or excessive.

- ◆ **Be mysterious:** Use a series of clues to lead him to a private rendezvous.

- ◆ **Be witty:** Send him a bottle of steak sauce with a note that says, "Let's sizzle." Plan a scintillating steak dinner for two.

- ◆ **Be sincere:** Simply tell her how much you love her. It's a gift she'll never get tired of receiving.

- ◆ **Be unabashed:** Scrawl a glaring declaration of your love across a billboard she passes regularly.

> **Consider This**
>
> Don't forget that romantic gifts often come in small packages, or no package at all. Often it's the little things wrapped in love that turn day-to-day living into day-to-day loving.

Romantic Presents

> **Special Presentations**
>
> Organize a treasure hunt with the final clue leading to the present. Sherri once did this for Larry. The clues were written in verse, and when all were found, they composed a poem—about him.

- **Be spontaneous:** Whisk him away to a romantic retreat.

- **Be nostalgic:** Give her a tape recording of the songs you fell in love to. Dance the night away.

- **Be clever:** Insert your own impassioned predictions and affirmations in fortune cookies.

- **Be gentle:** Tuck a tender note in a drawer, briefcase, or pocket.

- **Be sensitive:** Stroll along a moonlit beach while you listen attentively to what she is saying.

- **Be outrageous:** Give him skydiving lessons for two with a note inviting him to *fall* in love again.

Want to spend more time with your sweetheart? Give a gift you'll enjoy together:

- A tandem bicycle

- Two place settings of china, crystal, and silver to be reserved for use on special occasions

- Enrollment in a dance class

- A picnic basket equipped for two—include a book of romantic poetry, a pair of candle holders for picnics under the stars, or rowboat rental certificates

- Registration for two in a class relating to the recipient's interest

---

If it's true that the way to a man's heart is through his stomach, a romantic repast may be just the perfect present. Setting the proper mood and keeping the menu simple are keys to seductive dining.

- Create an exquisite setting. Whether you prefer chic or whimsical, elegant or understated, carry it

Romantic Presents

out with style. Fresh flowers, crisp linen napkins, sparkling crystal, and silver add a special touch to an intimate breakfast in bed or candlelight dinner for two.

♦ Keep the food simple to enable both of you to enjoy the occasion. Consider catered and carry-out options as well as foods that can be prepared in advance. Or, make the preparation part of the romance. Many couples enjoy spending time together in the kitchen.

> **Best/Worst**
>
> Best: Flowers from my husband—just because he loves me
>
> Worst: A sewing machine—I had two at the time
>
> —JANE E.

Are repetition and predictability producing boredom in your romantic rendezvousing? Want to add a little intrigue and anticipation to your next evening out for two? Looking for a tryst with a twist? Celebrate Romance offers romantic adventure kits, complete with preprinted cards, intriguing props, and step-by-step guidebooks. Phone: 800/368-7978 or 714/459-7621.

An original poem makes a wonderfully romantic present. But if writing poetry is not your forté, take some cues from the masters. Delve into Tennyson, Browning, or Shakespeare and you too could soon be thinking in rhyming couplets. With heart in hand, composing an original verse may be as simple as writing new words to fit the meter and rhyme scheme of a poem you like. You may be no match for Tennyson, but a little awkwardness may add warmth and charm to your prose.

Emulating the poetic style of another can be an easy way to spark your own creativity. But if you just can't get your rhyme in time, the following thought may be helpful. Henry Wadsworth Longfellow said, "Next to being a great poet, is the power of under-

Romantic Presents

Love in Bloom

"Back in the 1940s, my grandfather, a hard-working and fairly unemotional farmer, gathered some wildflowers, put them in an old bottle, and left them on the kitchen table for my grandmother with a note that read: 'My love for you is as wild as these flowers.' Fifty years later, my grandmother, now in her nineties, still remembers that gift."

—Kent B.

standing one." Find a poet whose style and words best express what's in your heart and share that poet's poetry with your sweetheart. Thousands of love poems have been written, and one that strikes your lyrical fancy is likely among them.

Research shows that both men *and* women think time spent together is the most romantic gift they can give. For a romantic gift that is sure to please, make arrangements for a getaway.

◆ Escape to a bed-and-breakfast or quaint country inn.

◆ Arrange with friends for use of their mountain cabin, lakeside condo, or beach-front bungalow. Or, exchange residences for the weekend—your city townhouse for their country farmhouse.

◆ Go to dinner and the theater out of town. Some airlines offer "fun fare" packages with discounts on hotel accommodations, theater tickets, or other entertainment. Check with your travel agent.

◆ For a quick getaway close to home, check into a nearby hotel or resort. Many offer romantic weekend packages—some include breakfast in bed or a candlelight dinner for two.

◆ Surprise him with a return trip to the place where you met, or fell in love, or honeymooned.

◆ Spend the night or weekend at home—just the two of you. Arrange for the children to be cared for by friends or relatives and take the phone off the hook. Enjoy a quiet dinner, share a warm bath, and relax in front of a cozy fire.

◆ Sleep in the guest room. Make the bed with your company-best linens and put out your most luxurious bath towels and accessories. Fill the room with flowers and candlelight.

Romantic Presents • Runners and Walkers

Give a framed dinner menu, theater stagebill, movie poster, admission ticket stub, or another memento from your first date.

Give a personalized custom song. The people at Songs-4-U will write a song from information you provide and put it on a cassette tape for your special someone to play over and over. Phone: 800/447-3708.

> **Celebrate!**
>
> February is Creative Romance Month. Present your better half with the most creative, romantic gifts you can think of.

Runners and Walkers
SEE ALSO *Fitness Buffs*

It's simple. It's natural. It can be done just about anywhere, by just about anyone, at just about any time. Running—and walking—is a great way to relieve stress, stay in shape, and enjoy the scenery. One can scarcely walk down the street without tripping over gift possibilities for those whose passions range from leisurely strolls to marathons. However, to keep your presents from running amuck, choose clothing, equipment, and accessories carefully.

An optical measuring instrument or pedometer would help the enthusiast keep track of the miles she covers.

Give a personal stereo or compact-disc player with a headset and a supply of tapes or compact discs.

The folks at Road Runner Sports can help you find the perfect shoe for the runner or walker on your gift list—whether she be a supinator or pronator, on- or off-roader, fitness walker or training racer. Phone: 800/551-5558.

Runners and Walkers • Self, Gifts of

> **Getting an Earful**
>
> "I love the personal stereo cassette player my husband gave me to take the tedium out of my long walks. He even gave me a fanny pack in which to carry it."
>
> —CLAUDIA K.

Gifts of apparel include running shorts, singlets, T-shirts, spandex tights, sweat bands, and moisture-wicking socks. When the weather turns chilly, add warm-up suits, gloves, jackets, caps, and cold-weather masks.

Give a subscription to *Runner's World*, a magazine for recreational and competitive runners. *Runner's World* offers training advice, shoe and clothing reviews, information on nutrition, reports on races, and articles that inspire and entertain. Phone: 800/666-2828.

The Baby Jogger lets the mom or dad on the run take the little one along. Several models are available. Phone: 800/241-1848.

Give snowshoes to the active winter runner or walker. Redfeather boasts snowshoes that have revolutionized the sport. Call them for a brochure. Phone: 800/525-0081.

Self, Gifts of

When it really is the thought that counts, it might be more relevant and appreciated to give a portion of yourself than to spend hours shopping for a present. Gifts of self can provide the ultimate match of a giver's talents to the wants or needs of the recipient. Bestow your gift of self with charm, whimsy, or elegance. Write a clever poem or riddle alluding to the gift or give a token toy, trinket, or photograph depicting the thought or intent of the present.

Self, Gifts of

Share your expertise in the following:

- Architecture, landscaping, or interior design
- Computing
- Woodworking, furniture refinishing, upholstering
- Flower arranging
- Sailing, cycling, driving
- Sports (tennis, golf, swimming, team sports)
- Tax accounting (advice or preparation)
- Estate planning, accounting

Provide one of the following services:

- Wardrobe or color consulting
- Tutoring, coaching
- Document design, word processing
- "Maid service" for a day, for a special occasion, or a specified time
- Nursing care
- Hair cutting or styling
- Transportation
- Child care
- Shopping, errand running
- Holiday gift wrapping
- Auto repair, painting, maintenance, or cleaning
- House-sitting or pet-sitting

It's a Wrap!

Create a signature wrap that reflects your personal style. Perhaps you prefer the elegance of white satin ribbon on white embossed paper, or the casual simplicity of raffia tyings on brown packaging paper. Maybe the flair of layering colorful cellophane tied with Mylar ribbon is more your style. Experiment with various combinations of paper and tyings until you find one that says "YOU!" Then use that combination as your own signature wrap for all of your gifts.

Self, Gifts of

> ### Well Versed
>
> **"I have a friend who is a poet. He writes me poems for special occasions. My friend is also an attorney. Fortunately, he doesn't gift me with incomprehensible legal documents."**
>
> —GREGORY H.

Share one of the following talents:

- Cooking—Issue dessert-of-the-month certificates, prepare a special meal, or share a secret recipe.
- Music—Provide entertainment for a party or reception, or give a tape recording of your music.
- Dressmaking—Sew a prom dress, wedding gown, costume, or another outfit.
- Calligraphy—Address wedding announcements or copy and frame a favorite verse, quotation, or scriptural reference.
- Quilting, knitting, embroidery—Donate your handiwork for a fund-raising crafts fair or bazaar.
- Painting—Give a custom work of art of the recipient's choice.

Help with a project:

- Plan and prepare for a party.
- Wallpaper a room.
- Refinish a piece of furniture.
- Organize a collection.
- Decorate a friend's house for the holidays.
- Construct a treehouse, go-cart, or a model.
- Plant or harvest a garden.
- Build or paint a fence.
- Clean out a garage, barn, or storage shed.
- Help restore a boat, car, or bicycle.

> ### Best/Worst
>
> Best: A clean kitchen—and boy, was it dirty!
>
> Worst: Earrings someone else didn't want
>
> —RANAE T.

Self, Gifts of

Give companionship:

- Attend a class, lecture, concert, or sports event with the recipient.
- Read to a person who is sight impaired.
- Take a child on a boat ride, a hayride, or to a zoo, museum, festival, or amusement park.
- Visit a person who is confined to bed in the hospital, in a care center, or at home.

Emerson wrote, "The only gift is a portion of thyself," but many people feel they lack the time or creative talent to give of themselves. However, with just a little imagination and effort on your part, you can put a portion of yourself in every gift you give.

- Appliqué your own design on an apron, sweater, or kitchen linens.
- "Monogram" gifts to children—a lunch box, a backpack, a flashlight, an article of clothing—with marking pens and paints.
- Pass on a note about a gift's origin or significance when giving something unique or uncommon, or when passing down a family heirloom.
- Giving a cookie jar? Fill it to the brim with your best homemade cookies.
- Include a bouquet of flowers from your garden with the gift of a vase.
- When giving a journal, record a memory of an experience with the recipient.
- Include a photograph with the gift of an album or a picture frame.

> ### Notable Quotables
>
> "Rings and other jewels are not gifts, but apologies for gifts. The only gift is a portion of thyself. Thou must bleed for me. Therefore the poet brings his poem; the shepherd, his lamb; the farmer, corn; the miner, a gem; the sailor, coral and shells; the painter, his picture; the girl, a handkerchief of her own sewing."
>
> —RALPH WALDO EMERSON

- ◆ Compose an original poem for the inside cover of a book of poetry.
- ◆ Prepare and freeze a meal, side dish, or dessert to include with your gift of bakeware, a crock pot, or a microwave.

Seniors

Oh, the privileges of having finally arrived—discounted air fare, theater tickets, and car rentals; reserved parking spaces; access to retirement funds; once-in-a-lifetime capital gains exemptions; specially-formulated vitamins. Many seniors are capitalizing on these and other privileges, trading in their rocking chairs for running shoes, and happily spending their children's inheritance. Gifts relevant to new passions and old are sure to please them.

To one who has always had a passion for quilting, give a book on the history or art of quilting. Better yet, assemble a scrapbook with pictures of quilts she has made for others over the years accompanied with their notes of appreciation.

Has gardening been his life's passion? Take him to a garden show, give him a comfortable bench on which to sit and admire his beautiful garden, or give him one of the many wonderful gardening books or magazines.

Does she still love the ballet? Many are now available on video tape.

Seniors

Arrange a conference call or video teleconference with faraway friends or relatives.

Host a luncheon, tea, or another get-together in his or her honor.

Sign him up to take a community art, photography, exercise, or another class in which he has an interest. If possible, offer to drive him to class. Better yet, take the class with him.

With the video camera or tape recorder rolling, reminisce about his life's memories. Transcribe the tape to compile a life history book.

Have old family photos restored and organize them in an album.

Video tape family reunions and other special gatherings to give to loved ones that are unable to travel.

Give a remote-controlled television, compact-disc player, or radio. Be sure to set it up and teach the recipient how to operate the remote control as well as the machine itself.

The gift of a new lap quilt or blanket would provide warmth and comfort, and brighten a bedroom or living room.

> **Show Stopper**
>
> "In recent years, my aging parents stopped going into the city to enjoy the theater because of the inconvenience of driving and parking. For our gift to them last Christmas, my siblings and I made arrangements for them to be driven—by limo—to dinner and the theater. They loved it!"
>
> —MaryAnn G.

Seniors

Consider This

Wants and needs vary from physical and expressed to emotional and unexpressed. The need to be pampered, to feel attractive, to develop outside interests, to know one is cared about, or to feel appreciated can all be addressed through sensitive gift giving.

A cordless telephone and regular calls from you make a great gift for a senior who desires frequent contact with friends or family. Preprogramming frequently-called numbers into the phone is an extra nice touch.

The gift of an answering machine or messaging service would permit her to take calls at her convenience and save special greetings to be played again and again.

Front door intercoms, garage door openers, and motion-sensor lights make nice gifts to seniors.

A room makeover with a fresh coat of paint and new window coverings would provide a change of scenery for a homebound person.

A bird feeder, birdbath, wind chimes, or patio planter box would enhance a favorite outdoor space.

To a senior who likes to entertain or have friends drop by, give an assortment of nuts, candies, dried fruits, smoked meats, or gourmet cheese to share with guests.

Hire a reliable teenager or handyman to shovel snow, rake leaves, paint fences, clean gutters, or perform other chores around the house and yard. Or, provide these services yourself. If the senior enjoys puttering around the yard, give a labor-saving tool—a leaf vacuum, snowblower, or riding mower.

Seniors • Snow Sporters

Prepare a supply of freezer-to-oven (or microwave) meals. Attach a label indicating the contents, heating instructions, and date the meal was prepared.

Where there is a financial need, it may be nice to send a monthly check or make an annual bank deposit to help with living expenses. This should be done tactfully and without strings attached. Or, you could arrange to have telephone, utility or other bills sent directly to you.

> **Best/Worst**
>
> Best: Family genealogy
>
> Worst: A handmade doll and basket fashioned from pins and beads
>
> —Lin C.

Snow Sporters

Snow sporters come to life when the rest of nature sleeps. By the thousands, they converge on snow-covered terrain with skis, boots, boards, mobiles, toboggans, and sleds. When it's time for your snow sporter to hit the slopes, consider the following gift ideas.

Arrange for a weekend getaway to her favorite resort or to a new resort at which she has always wanted to stay.

Give a daily, weekly, or season lift pass to his favorite ski slope.

Give a thermos with an assortment of gourmet hot-drink mixes.

Arrange for him to take skiing or snowboarding lessons from a pro, or give him an instructional skiing or snowboarding video.

Snow Sporters • Sports Fans

Give snow clothes and accessories or comfortable clothing for lounging around the fire after a day on the slopes.

Assemble a snow-emergency kit to keep in his car. Include warm blankets, flares, tire chains, a shovel, a lock de-icer, and a windshield scraper or two.

To the outgoing and adventurous skier, give a subscription to *Powder: The Skier's Magazine*, which features award-winning photography. Phone: 800/289-8983.

To the snowboarder, give a subscription to *Snowboarder* magazine. *Snowboarder* is geared to people ages 12-30 and incorporates progressive action photography and design. Phone: 800/955-9120.

> **Present Danger!**
>
> Do not give seasonal gifts out of season. Snow skis in March or water skis in October do not have the impact of snow skis in October or water skis in March. If you purchase something at an "end of season" sale, stash it away to give at a more appropriate time (unless you're sure the recipient wants it right away!)

Sports Fans

Armchair athletes display tremendous agility while juggling a beverage can, a bowl of popcorn, and a foot-long pastrami sub (with extra mayo, hold the onions). They also exhibit profound understanding of the human condition ("That ref is blind *and* crazy!"). It's hard to imagine a more lovable creature. Here's how to make a sports fan happy.

Give a program from the first pro football game he attended back in 1958. Or, give a 1946 copy of *Sport Magazine* featuring Joe DiMaggio on the cover. For these and other sports collectibles such as World Series, All Star, Super Bowl, and College Bowl game-day and special-event tickets dating from the

Sports Fans

1890s, call Lou Madden's Concord Collectibles. Phone: 800/345-7474.

Gifts for baseball enthusiasts are abundant. Nostalgic and current baseball caps, audio/video tapes, books, games, clothing (sweats, jackets, jerseys, and T-shirts), collectibles, and many more gifts for baseball fans can be found at the local sports shop or ordered from the Baseball Hall of Fame. Write: Baseball Gifts, P.O. Box 590A, Cooperstown, NY 13326. Phone: 607/547-2445.

Survey Scoop! As expected, men show a strong preference for gifts of sports equipment. With advances in monitoring devices, performance, and aesthetics, state-of-the-art sports equipment makes a

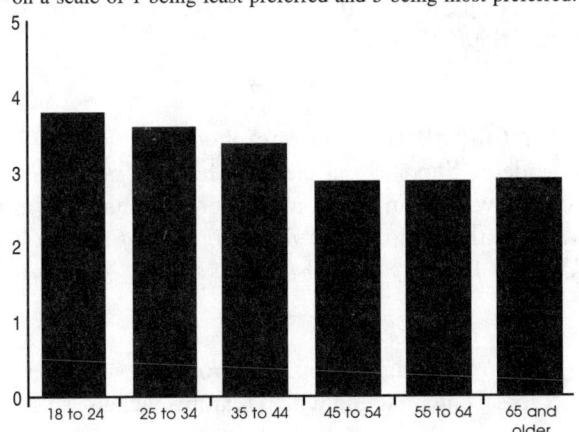

who wants gifts of
SPORTS GEAR?
Men's preferences for gifts of sports equipment, by age, on a scale of 1 being least preferred and 5 being most preferred.

Source: Discovery Research Group/Present Perfect Survey

Grass Roots Support

What do you give the sports fan who has everything? How about a piece of the action? To prepare for the NFL's Super Bowl XXX, Arizona groundskeepers removed the old sod and put in a new playing surface. The sod was sold in relatively small amounts, offering fans a new way to show grass roots support. (This was an especially timely gift for University of Nebraska fans whose team had won the national championship on the field just a few weeks earlier.)

Sports Fans

welcome gift for sports fans of all ages—especially young men. However, gift preference scores for sports equipment decline with income and age. According to Sebastian DiCasoli, Director of Marketing Services for the Sporting Goods Manufacturers Association, "The mature enthusiasts tend to be more discriminating and demanding." DiCasoli says, "With the wide range of options available, many prefer to choose their own equipment instead of receiving it as gifts." In spite of generally high appeal, gifts of sports equipment are not for all men. Twenty percent of men give sports equipment a score of 1 on the scale of 1 to 5.

If you know an enthusiast's favorite football, baseball, basketball, soccer, or hockey team, you won't have to look far for a sure-to-please present. If one can wear it, eat off it, drink out of it, sit on it, sleep under it, or put it on one's head, chances are good that it can be found emblazoned with the name and logo of your sports fan's favorite team.

Athletic Supply of Dallas, Inc.'s catalog is filled with apparel and sports gift ideas and boasts "one stop shopping for all your [sports] video needs." Phone: 800/635-4438.

For football fans, autographed footballs, NFL videos, Super Bowl plaques, holiday ornaments, clothing with team logos, and other paraphernalia are available through the *Pro Football Hall of Fame Gift Catalog*. Phone: 800/869-8207.

NCAA fans might enjoy a gift from the NCAA Visitors Center catalog which features jackets, sweat-

Celebrate!

February 6 is the anniversary of Babe Ruth's birthday. Authentic, fitted caps from the Sultan of Swat's team, the New York Yankees, are available from the Baseball Hall of Fame. Contact them for a catalog and ordering information. Write: P.O. Box 590A, Cooperstown, NY 13326. Phone: 607/547-2445.

Sports Fans

ers, shirts, caps, mugs, pennants, lapel pins, and souvenir programs. Phone: 800/859-5049.

Make arrangements for a sports fan to take a trip to a sports hall of fame.

Tickets to a sporting event, zoom binoculars, stadium blankets, coolers, portable folding chairs, and combination stadium seat covers/tote packs are winning gifts for sports fans.

Start or add to a collection of items from her favorite team or sport. Trading cards, caps, and jerseys are popular collectors' items.

Give a subscription to one—or more—of the following magazines which feature player profiles, action photos, official rosters, schedules, scouting reports, humor, and crossword puzzle quizzes. Write to the following magazines at the Post Office boxes listed. All are in Mt. Morris, IL 61054:

- ◆ *Baseball Digest*, P.O. Box 360
- ◆ *Basketball Digest*, P.O. Box 238
- ◆ *Football Digest*, P.O. Box 571
- ◆ *Hockey Digest*, P.O. Box 572
- ◆ *Soccer Digest*, P.O. Box 349

Obtain an autograph of his or her favorite sports hero.

> **Special Delivery**
>
> Compose a poem, song, or riddle about a gift that will be delivered at a later date.

Sports Fans • St. Patrick's Day Presents

Give a split-screen television so she can watch two sports events at once.

Give a subscription to online sports information via the Internet.

Make arrangements for the young sports enthusiast to attend a summer sports camp. Many are hosted by colleges and universities.

Give a gift from the United States Olympic Spirit catalog and support America's Olympic movement at the same time. Choose from apparel, sports bags, fanny packs, caps, key chains, mugs, beach towels, and pennants. Phone: 800/231-1996.

St. Patrick's Day Presents

You needn't catch a leprechaun or have the luck of the Irish to choose a fitting gift for St. Patrick's Day. Just think green, or choose one of the following.

Emeralds are green and come beautifully arranged in necklaces, bracelets, rings, pins, cuff links, and tie tacks.

While thinking green, think jade. How about a jade vase, paperweight, or other ornament?

Give a charm bracelet to which you may add new charms each year.

St. Patrick's Day Presents • Star Gazers

To a person of Irish descent, give a book, a map, or various souvenirs from Ireland.

Give a food treat: Key lime pie, shamrock-shaped cookies or cakes, Lucky Charm cereal, kiwis, lime drinks, green M&Ms, or other green candy.

Give a cassette or compact-disc recording of Irish music.

Make a shamrock, horseshoe, or lucky-charm decoration or door wreath.

Fill a basket with green bath items: bath oil beads, Irish Spring bath bars, green shampoo, a green bath mitt or sponge, and green towels.

> ### The Gift of Gab
>
> The Blarney stone is said to endow the gift of eloquence and flattery to those that kiss it. Legend has it that smooth talking once saved the Blarney Castle in Ireland from attack. Hence the power of the stone, which is built into the southern wall of the castle.

Star Gazers

Under cover of darkness, they gaze upon heavenly bodies. With night lenses and telescopes, they peer in shameless awe while calling out such names as Venus, Miranda, and Seven Sisters. Whether in the name of love or of science, star gazers have a passion for things celestial. The following ideas will put you light years ahead in your gift-giving endeavors.

Install a bedroom skylight for a view of the night sky.

Give a cozy hammock or other comfortable outdoor furniture for night-sky observation.

Star Gazers

> **What Gives?**
>
> Does your family, culture, or religion observe any fun or unique gift-giving traditions? Are you aware of any interesting gift customs anywhere in the world? See page 277.

Give special lenses and other gear for photographing celestial phenomena.

Give a gift membership or make a donation in the recipient's name to the Astronomical Society of the Pacific (ASP). Membership includes a subscription to *Mercury* magazine, monthly *Sky Calendar* and *Star Map* publications, access to the ASP Astronomy News Hotline, a 10% discount on ASP catalog purchases, and more. Call for information. Phone: 800/335-2624. Fax: 415/337-5205.

Tapes of the Night Sky audio cassettes, celestial globes, computerized solar system simulators, posters of the cosmos, placemats, rugs, books, silk ties, and other stellar items for gift giving are available from the Astronomical Society of the Pacific's catalog. Phone: 800/335-2624. Fax: 415/337-5205.

Give her a telescope, star charts, a blanket, and a picnic basket outfitted for a starlight repast.

Enroll the star gazer on your gift list in an astronomy class at a college, university, or adult-education program.

Have a star named after him. For information, call the Ministry of Federal Star Registration (800/528-7827) or the International Star Registry (800/282-3333).

Arrange for membership in an astronomy club or association.

Students

SEE ALSO *Apartment Dwellers* and *Graduation Presents*

Are you looking for a gift to kick off the new semester, banish the midterm blues, or inspire the bored of education? For high marks in gift giving, take note of the following.

Send school supplies "wrapped" in a backpack or portable file box. Include notebooks, pens, a calculator, computer diskettes, a stapler, paper clips, a tape dispenser, and other desk accessories.

Order a pizza delivered at some time during the finals-week cramming session or another busy time during the semester.

Give tickets to a basketball, baseball, football, or other such game. If your gift budget can handle it, season tickets would also be nice.

Give tickets to a campus concert or theater series. Prepaid movie tickets to a theater on or near campus, or books of video rental coupons also make great gifts.

Laundry, linen, dry-cleaning, and housekeeping services would make much-appreciated gifts.

Give a gift certificate to the university bookstore where, in addition to textbooks, students can choose from an array of clothing, household, and entertainment items.

Best/Worst

Best: A car during my senior year of college—it was a combined birthday, graduation, and Christmas present

Worst: A set of white monogrammed handkerchiefs for the sixth year in a row

—Bill C.

Students

Round-trip airfare home—or to another destination—for the holidays, spring break, or summer vacation would make a fantastic gift.

To a dorm dweller, give a microwave oven or mini-refrigerator.

Give a sturdy safe for storing personal items and valuables—jewelry, diaries, letters, medical records, prescription medications.

Set up a credit card account in the student's name—with a predetermined limit and other ground rules, of course. (The real gift here is the tremendous amount of trust you demonstrate in the student. Many happy returns!)

Arrange for an internship or introduce the student to a professional in her field of study.

Where they are allowed on campus, give a bicycle, a moped, a skateboard, or in-line skates to help the student get around campus in a hurry.

Give an oversized poster of his favorite ad, television or movie celebrity, sports interest, or vacation spot to hang in his dorm room or apartment. Be sure to choose a poster that will not be offensive to his roommates. Sherri remembers a picture of a male centerfold her roommate hung over the kitchen table. Although mild by today's standards, she thought it was in poor taste.

Best/Worst

Best: A small pocket-watch with an alarm

Worst: Gadgets that wear out after a couple of weeks

—Richard T.

Teachers

Sherri can still recite Polonius' advice to Laertes, sense Albert Schweitzer's dedication to his humanitarian beliefs, and recall in graphic detail her first—and last—taste of dried squid. Miss Nellie Castle had a way of making learning come alive for a class of inquisitive Southern California sixth-graders. Through investigation, she taught them to think. Through example, she taught them to care. Through firsthand experiences, she exposed them to culture. These were her invaluable gifts to them. When it's time to give back to a teacher, the following gift ideas get high marks.

Teachers in many school districts spend their own money on visual aids, math manipulatives, bulletin board materials, stickers, certificates, awards, and other classroom supplies. Donations of these materials or a gift certificate from a teachers' supply store or a bookstore would make great gifts for teachers.

To teachers that loan books from their private libraries, give personalized bookplates or an embossing stamp. Additions to their libraries would be appreciated gifts also.

Give a roomy tote bag or folding cart for lugging supplies. After all, have you ever seen a teacher with his hands free?

A project smock or lab apron would be a useful gift for a teacher who likes to get her hands (but not her clothes) dirty on the job.

Pardon Us

"My son's fifth-grade teacher once gave a welcome gift to each of her students. It was a coupon that read 'Good for one free homework assignment'."

—Marcia J.

Teachers

Teacher's Pet

"I like the idea of gifts to teachers that allow them to make things better for the students. Telling stories, sharing a hobby or collection, or coming in to spend one-on-one time with the children are great gifts from parents. Books, plants, tapes, and music for classroom use are also nice."

—Val Bleazard,
Third-Grade Teacher

Give books about subjects such as holiday customs around the world, science or math concepts made easy, or indoor play activities.

Write a sincere letter of appreciation to a teacher who is doing a great job or who has been especially helpful or sensitive. Send copies to the teacher's principal, the school superintendent, and the school board.

Nominate an exceptional teacher for a Teacher of the Year Award or other recognition.

Instead of the standard gifts of food, perfume, and bric-a-brac, try some of these suggestions from the National PTA:

◆ Provide teachers (that would like to attend) with tickets to a lecture or workshop at a local college.

◆ Create a resource file of parents with special talents and experiences to provide teachers with a co-instructor for special projects and activities.

◆ Help teachers spend more quality time on the important aspects of their jobs by volunteering to do one (or more) of the following: locate and reproduce copies of work sheets for the classroom, design and construct classroom and hallway bulletin boards, prepare and possibly instruct art or holiday class projects, help the teacher organize paperwork for the students, or work with the teacher to produce a weekly parent newsletter to send home with students.

◆ Have a flower arrangement or plant delivered to the classroom.

Teens

Ask teenagers what they want for Christmas (or any other holiday or occasion) and more often than not, the answer will be MONEY! Wanting to please, you respond with gifts of cash only to discover that the money runs through their fingers like water, with no residual value or remembrance of you—the giver—or the occasion for which your gift was given. What do you do the next time you want to give a gift? For starters, remember that there is a vast difference between what most of us would like to give to teenagers and what they would like to receive. Keep in mind that most teens enjoy music, driving, sports, parties, junk food, clothes, makeup, and friends. Here are a few gift ideas you might try. (As this was written, our teenage son was asking, "Why don't I get all those cool gifts?" In his wisdom, he then added, "Never give them clothes!")

Give tickets to a concert, play, or movie the teen would like to attend. You might also want to throw in some cash for concessions and souvenirs.

Prepaid video rentals and a bushel of snacks make a great gift the teen can share with friends.

Give a party at a favorite teen spot.

Assemble a car-care kit by filling a durable cleaning bucket with sponges, car cleaner, wax, chamois cloths, window cleaner, squeegees, dash cleaner, and car freshener. Give it to a teenager who has just received his driver's license or has recently purchased a new car.

Teens

Consider This

Rent a jukebox or pinball machine for a teen's birthday party or other get-together.

Order personalized license plates from the Department of Motor Vehicles.

Arrange for the services of a disc jockey or other entertainment (magician, comedian, caricaturist, instrumentalist, vocalist, gorilla, or strolling musicians) for a sweet sixteen, bar/bat mitzvah, or another party.

Give a magazine subscription. *Mad* magazine is popular among teens. Other favorites include: *Seventeen, Teen, Sports Illustrated*, or one of the many fanzines. Pick one up at the bookstore or newsstand, mail in the subscription form, and give the magazine with a note mentioning the forthcoming issues.

Rent a limo (or loan your car) for a special event—homecoming, an awards banquet, prom night, graduation.

Give all the fixin's for the ultimate ice cream sundae. Assemble assorted sauces (fudge, butterscotch, caramel), marshmallow creme, nuts, and candy toppings in a basket. Add an ice cream scoop and a coupon for ice cream or frozen yogurt. Top it off with a can of whipped cream and a jar of maraschino cherries for a gift of total indulgence.

If driver's education classes are not offered at the teen's high school, arrange and pay for driving lessons for the teen approaching driver's license age. Present a gift certificate for the lessons along with a key chain or car accessory—customized floor mats, console drink holder, dashboard sun shield, steering-wheel wrap, seat covers.

Teens

Give passes to an amusement park, miniature golf course, water slide, or another popular teen spot.

Pass on a family heirloom with a note about its origin and significance.

Give a television, video-cassette recorder, compact-disc player, boom box, or personal stereo.

Install a telephone—perhaps with a private line?—in the teen's room. (This could prove to be a nice little gift to yourself, as well.)

Arrange for a makeover, color analysis, hair styling, contact lenses, or ear piercing to give the teen a new look.

Extend the teen's curfew for a special event or weekend night. Present this "gift" in the form of "coupons" good for one-hour curfew extensions.

Teenagers love their privacy! Give a locking diary, safe, or box for storing private items.

If you decide to give a gift of cash, what teenager wouldn't love his or her own credit card or checking account (with a predetermined limit, of course)?

A final word about gifts of money to teenagers. If you know the teen is saving for a specific item—a stereo, a car, a college education—and you wish to

---

Best/Worst

Best: A journal

Worst: Jewelry I didn't like

—Denise E.

Teens • Tennis Buffs

make a contribution toward that item, by all means do so. But remember, once a gift is given, the giver has no control over what the recipient does with it. Even if you suspect that the funds have been misappropriated, don't ask!

Tennis Buffs

They say that love means nothing. But tennis buffs are generally an easy bunch to court—so just play along. After all, it's only a game. And when it's your turn to serve up a gift, give them something they won't return.

Give a customized or personalized racquet cover.

Give tickets to a tennis tournament he would like to attend.

Make arrangements and pay to have her tennis racket restrung.

Arrange for a trip to the International Tennis Hall of Fame Museum in Newport, Rhode Island. Or, order a gift from the museum gift shop's catalog. Choose from apparel, accessories, books, videos, posters, and more. Phone: 800/457-1144.

Give a gift membership in the United States Tennis Association. Write: United States Tennis Association, P.O. Box 1726, Hicksville, NY 11802.

Consider This

A word of caution: giving gifts directly related to a hobby or interest can be tricky. The devoted enthusiast may have very specific preferences.

Tennis Buffs

When Love Means Nothing

"The only time love means nothing is on a tennis court," says our friend, Fred McNair, former French Open and Masters doubles champion. However, it is with much love that McNair embraces the game of tennis, which he refers to as his father's greatest gift to him. And it is the six-time title of National Father and Son Doubles Champion he shares with his father, Frederick V. McNair, III, that brings him the most joy and satisfaction.

"My father introduced me to all facets of the world of tennis—from its competitive elements to its gentlemanly side," McNair said. The benefits he's gained within the tennis environment are abundant. "I have maintained a high degree of health, developed enduring friendships, gained an understanding of competitive sportsmanship, traveled the world, and enjoyed financial success through tennis," he said. "Tennis even paid for my college education via a scholarship."

But these benefits have not come without a price. "Hours of hitting a tennis ball against a cement wall taught me the work ethic—that there is a price to pay for every reward," McNair said. It was during those hours of repetitive exercise that he processed the dream of participating in tennis at the professional level.

One of McNair's all-time favorite gifts is an on/off court all-season warm-up suit from his wife, Linda. "She knows I could live in a warm-up suit," he said. "She put a lot of thought and time into choosing the colors and style I like."

Here are a few of Fred McNair's favorite gifts for tennis aficionados:

Father to Son

"I have...traveled the world...through tennis, my father's greatest gift to me."

—Fred McNair

Tennis Buffs • Travelers

> **Celebrate!**
>
> June is National Tennis Month.

- White tennis shirts with city, club, or charity logos to serve as fun reminders of events attended or participated in
- A tennis calendar depicting the beautiful settings of tennis clubs and resorts all over the world
- Reprints or note cards of LeRoy Neiman's art portraying sports action (McNair favors these for their impressionistic style and colorful ambiance)
- A subscription to a tennis magazine
- A series of lessons from a favorite tennis pro (tennis clubs can help choreograph a schedule for early-bird, lunch-time, or after-work sessions)
- A certificate for a group clinic at a pro tennis club
- Paid-in-advance court time

Travelers

Whether the recipient is leaving town for a cross-country adventure, or leaving the country to embark on a world tour, your gift says, "Have a pleasant journey." Presents for travelers should take into account the who, what, when, where, why, and how of travel. The next time you need a gift to wish a friend bon voyage, to send off your favorite business traveler, or to bid farewell to neighbors embarking on a cross-country motor tour, consider giving one of the following.

Fill a tote bag with an assortment of hangers and clothespins, a portable clothes line, a travel iron or clothes steamer, a roll-up ironing pad, and a voltage converter.

Travelers

Give a new camera bag filled with assorted photo albums, a good supply of film, a tripod, and other camera accessories.

To those that make their journey by motorhome, give accessories and furnishings for their house on wheels. Comfy throw pillows, luxurious or whimsical linens (for bath, bed, and table), and fun kitchen and tableware make motoring more enjoyable.

Maps and guidebooks are welcome gifts for domestic as well as foreign travelers. If you are familiar with the accommodations or sites at the traveler's destination, you might arrange and pay for a stay at a bed-and-breakfast you fancy, dinner at a favorite restaurant, or tickets to an attraction, event, or tour they would enjoy.

To the European traveler—or would-be traveler—give videos from the *Museum City Videos* series. Subtitled *The Cities of the World Seen Through the Eyes of Their Artists, Architects and Poets*, the series explores timeless treasures in cities that have become living museums. Featured are: *Florence: Cradle of the Renaissance*; *Venice: Queen of the Adriatic*; *London: City of Majesty*; *Rome: The Eternal City*; *Barcelona: Archive of Courtesy*; *Seville: Jewel of Andalusia*; *Vatican City: Art & Glory*; *Paris: City of Lights*; and *Jerusalem: City of Gold*. These and other travel videos are available from V.I.E.W. Video. Phone: 800/843-9843. Fax: 212/979-0266.

To the family setting out on a road trip, give a cooler filled with goodies such as seedless grapes, un-

> **It's A Wrap!**
> Wrap bon voyage presents in maps of the recipient's destination.

Travelers

Gifts to Go

There are many ways to creatively present a gift of travel:

✔ Record details of travel arrangements on a cassette tape (perhaps with music and fanfare).

✔ Give an atlas, travel brochures, or maps along with details of any arrangements you've made for transportation, accommodations, and restaurants.

✔ Give a basket of food specialties from the region or country the recipient will visit.

✔ Give airline tickets with foreign language tapes or a book of phrases.

✔ "Pack" a travel itinerary in a piece of luggage.

✔ Attach a note to a toy airplane, boat, or train.

---

salted snacks (peanuts, pretzels, popcorn, nuts), vegetable sticks, cheese (bite-size chunks, wrapped single slices, string cheese), and small cans or boxes of juice. Also include wash-and-dry towelettes, reclosable bags, disposable tableware, and a water jug.

To keep the children occupied while on the road, give travel editions of popular games or packages containing a selection of the following items according to their ages and interests: sugar-free chewing gum, project supplies (pencils, construction paper, staplers, string, tape), books, hand puppets, travel journals, and maps.

Give a nice map on which to mark routes and destinations to someone planning on extensive travel.

Give a cellular telephone for keeping in touch while en route.

Arrange to have flowers in her hotel room when she arrives at her destination.

To the business traveler, give a pocket-sized computer for recording travel, meal, and entertaining expenses.

For the convenience of those that travel the highways and byways by car, give a car-top carrier, a luggage rack, a lock de-icer, an opisometer (map meter, distance wheel), an auto compass, a folding emergency shovel, custom car mats with a logo or monogram, a travel compact-disc holder, a mini car vacuum, a travel

Travelers

thermos, a car organizer, seat pockets, a folding bicycle, a suction-mounted travel mirror, or a magnifying glass for reading maps and directions.

For driving comfort, give deerskin driving gloves, a driving posture cushion, car sunshields, or an inflatable travel neck pillow.

For safety on the road, give a car emergency kit or roadside hazard lights. For safety in the hotel, give a portable door jam.

To foreign travelers, give a world-time clock radio, a currency converter, a foreign language dictionary, electronic word translator, a traveling stereo sound system with language or instructional tapes, a leather-bound world atlas, a lead-lined film box (protects film against security X-rays), a travel journal, a leather passport portfolio, a portable water filter, a voltage converter/adapter kit, or international appliances (hair dryer, electric razor, radio).

Luggage pieces and accessories make great gifts for people on the go. Give a leather duffle bag, a sports carry-on, a tote bag, a garment bag, an over-the-shoulder traveler's wallet, a money belt, luggage combination locks, luggage tags, a leather tie carrier, or organizers for cosmetics, lingerie, and jewelry. Many luggage pieces now come with wheels to make them easier to maneuver through busy airport terminals and train stations.

Survey Scoop! Whether it's a weekend getaway or a trip around the world, men and women agree

Best/Worst

Best: A stay at a bed-and-breakfast from our children

Worst: A huge, used tablecloth for a wedding present —it's been used for 27 years as a picnic-table cover

—Marion D.

Travelers

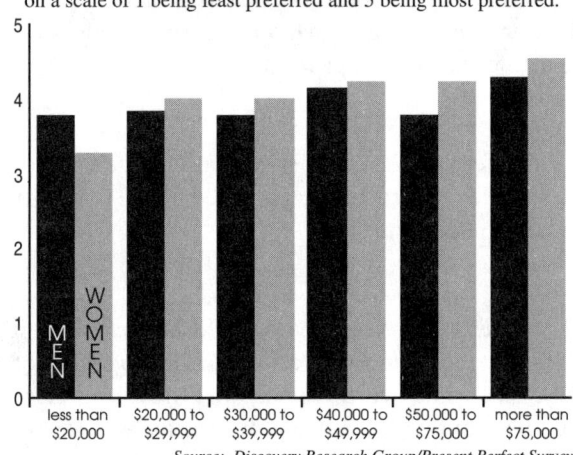

who wants gifts of TRAVEL?
Preferences for gifts of travel, by income, on a scale of 1 being least preferred and 5 being most preferred.

Source: Discovery Research Group/Present Perfect Survey

A Gift of Love

Along with his brothers and sisters, David Love arranged a cruise to the Bahamas as a fortieth wedding anniversary gift to his parents. "The travel agent prepared a package of colorful brochures and daily itineraries for us to present our gift," Love said. The gift was such a hit that Love and his siblings are saving to give another gift of travel for their parent's fiftieth wedding anniversary.

that travel makes a great gift. Preference is high in all age, income, and education groups, but it increases with education and income. David Love, editor of the American Society of Travel Agents newsletter, *ASTA Notes*, says giving a travel gift is very easy, and he should know (see sidebar). In addition to planning and booking travel arrangements, travel agents can arrange for special touches such as a fruit basket in the recipients' cabin or a bouquet of flowers to welcome them home.

To the well-groomed traveler, give a shaving kit, compact manicure kit, shoe-shine kit, sewing kit, pocket clothes brush, or compact folding umbrella.

Valentine's Day Presents
SEE ALSO *Romantic Presents*

It's amazing that Valentine's Day ever catches anyone by surprise. Most people smell it coming a good three weeks away—the combined odors of flowers, perfume, and innumerable confections forming an unmistakable olfactory warning. So, once you know it's coming, the trick is to find a Valentine's Day present as unique as your love itself.

Addressing the passions of gift recipients is one of the best ways to convey your sentiments. When choosing Valentine's presents this year, consider your first love's second loves.

- ❤ To the love with a green thumb, the gift of a garden shed poignantly says, "I support your interest."

- ❤ To the couch potato, the gift of a cozy afghan gently whispers, "I love you just the way you are."

- ❤ To the dog lover, the gift of a new dog cushion says, "I'll keep you and your dog." (Hey, in our house, this would be a loving communiqué.)

For additional gift ideas, look under relevant interest categories.

Does he have a passion for the arts? Send him a ticket to a romantic ballet, concert, or play. Attach an intriguing note. When he arrives, he'll find you waiting in the next seat.

Is her second love baseball? Give her a pair of season tickets. Show her what a good sport you are by attending—and enjoying—the games with her.

Valentine's Day Presents

> **It's A Wrap!**
>
> A bag of potpourri inside a package makes a sensory treat.

Take him on a romantic sleigh ride or carriage ride in the moonlight.

Express your feelings in an audio or video love letter.

Compose a collection of love notes, letters, or poems. Place them in a keepsake letter box or tie them together with a ribbon and give them to her on Valentine's Day. Add to the collection each year for a gift that is sure to become a personal treasure.

Send the lyrics of a favorite love song or the verses of a romantic poem via fax, e-mail, special delivery, or singing telegram. Your own composition may be especially romantic.

Order and pay for a private (hot!) line and voice mail service for your messages exclusively.

Send an anonymous gift of balloons or flowers to him at his office or home. For added intrigue, compose a riddle or message to accompany the delivery.

To keep your love a secret, conceal your identity with a postmark from one of the following towns. Mail a stamped, addressed card or envelope and a note with your request to the attention of the postmaster:

- ✔ Loveland, CO 80537-9998
- ✔ Loving, NM 88256-9998
- ✔ Valentine, NE 69201-9998
- ✔ Valentine, AZ 86437-9998

Valentine's Day Presents

If you can't be with your love on Valentine's Day, arrange with a caterer to deliver breakfast. Instruct the caterer to include the bed tray, fresh-cut flowers, and the morning newspaper.

To the long-distance Valentine, give a telephone and calling certificates or a debit card to remind him to call often. Program the phone with your home, office, and cellular telephone numbers.

Classy items for Valentine's giving are available from the Metropolitan Museum of Art (800/468-7386), the Winterthur Museum (800/767-0500), and Williams-Sonoma (800/541-2233).

- ♥ Tinned-steel heart-shaped tart pans for making berry-and-custard tarts, fruit tartlets, big brownies, or chocolate-chip cookies. (Williams-Sonoma)
- ♥ Heart-shaped earthenware molds for making crème brûlée. (Williams-Sonoma)
- ♥ Hand-molded transparent red glass heart paperweights. (Winterthur)
- ♥ Handmade and hand-painted ceramic lattice heart dishes resembling a woven Victorian wicker basket. (Winterthur)
- ♥ Cast-pewter valentine frames inspired by a paper Valentine. (The Metropolitan Museum of Art)
- ♥ Stoneware reproductions of a white salt-glaze Staffordshire dish (circa 1740-1760). (The Metropolitan Museum of Art)
- ♥ Heart waffle iron, with recipes. (Williams-Sonoma)
- ♥ Glazed heart-shaped porcelain dessert plates with four different berry patterns. (Williams-Sonoma)

Hotlines

"One Valentine's Day when I was traveling, my wife wrote me a wonderfully intimate, romantic poem that she read to me over the telephone. It's a great poem! But, there's no way I'll let it be printed in this book!"

—Anonymous

Water Sports Enthusiasts

Water Sports Enthusiasts
SEE ALSO *Boaters*

You can surf, ski, and sail on it; swim, splash, and soak in it; and submerge, scuba, and snorkel under it. Indeed there are divers (make that diverse) ways to play on, in, or under the water. To make a splash with those that have water on their recreational brains, choose one of the following gifts.

What do air chairs, water darts, ski discs, kneeboards, sea sleds, and skiboards have in common? They are all conveyances to be towed behind a power boat, and they make great gifts for people with power boats.

Give aqua shoes, floating sports goggles, life vests, wet suits, dry suits, and waterproof watches to outfit the waterbaby.

Bart's Watersports catalog is full of great gift items for the water sports enthusiast. Call for a catalog. Phone: 800/348-5016.

Reserve a water park and host a party for the water sport enthusiast.

Give a remote control boat. They are fun to play with at the beach, on the lake, or in the pool.

Give an assortment of skin care products: sunblock, lip balm, aloe gel, lotions.

Shopping Tip

When comparing prices, be sure that you are comparing apples to apples, i.e., brand name, model number, and options. Scan newspaper ads, catalogs, television commercials, and direct-mail ads for comparative pricing information.

Water Sports Enthusiasts • Wedding Presents

For a diver, arrange a diving adventure through a PADI (Professional Association of Diving Instructors) Dive Center or by calling 800/729-7234.

To a surfer, give a subscription to *Surfer* magazine which features incredible surfing photos and worldwide travel stories. Phone: 800/289-0636.

To a sailboarder, give a gift certificate from Sailboard Warehouse. Phone: 800/992-7245.

Wedding Presents

Weddings have been a symbolic and literal basis for political, commercial, cultural, and family alliances throughout human history. They are also cause for celebration. Although specific practices and protocols vary with culture and circumstance, the giving of gifts to the newly wedded is universal. If you want your gifts to make a lasting impression, engage yourself in giving one of the following.

Family heirlooms or treasures are often passed on as wedding presents. These are especially meaningful when accompanied by a description of the item's significance or history.

If you have a relevant talent, offer your services to:

◆ Make the bride's gown

◆ Make dresses for the bridesmaids, flower girl, or bride's or groom's mother

◆ Take pictures or make a video tape of the reception

Around the World

Gifts of money are customary for Japanese weddings. Monetary gifts are given at the wedding hall in special envelopes that are available at Japanese stationery stores. Gifts of silver, china, and crystal are also fitting.

Wedding Presents

> **Around the World**
>
> In Germany, gifts of money are not considered appropriate wedding presents from non-family members.

- Make the wedding cake or prepare other food for the reception
- Make centerpieces, backdrops, or other decorations for the reception or wedding
- Address the wedding invitations

Wedding Presents Remembered

Years after the thank-you notes are written, the duplicate gifts are exchanged, and the hideous gifts are stored out of sight, which wedding presents continue to make an impression? Is it the intrinsic or the monetary value of a gift that makes it memorable? Is it the message borne or the bearer that speaks to the recipient? Is it the practicality or the extravagance of a gift that remains unforgettable? It all depends on whom you ask.

- **Heirloom Bound.** Home on a short leave during World War II, Lynn proposed to Beverly on Tuesday and married her on Saturday. There was no time for a wedding reception, but friends pooled their limited resources to give the newlyweds a satin quilt that Beverly says, "grew up and faded with our children." A heart-shaped patch covers the nail-polish remover spill acquired when their daughter took the quilt to college. Lynn and Beverly's granddaughter now lays claim to the 51-year-old quilt—an heirloom, patch and all.

- **A Promise Kept.** As a young girl, Arlene wistfully admired a figurine from her Aunt Edna's curio collection and was promised the piece as a wedding gift. When Arlene married, she was surprised to receive the figurine—or any gift—from her aunt who had died 12 years before Arlene's wedding. Prior to her death, the aunt informed a family member of the promised gift. It continues to be a

Wedding Presents

treasured possession 29 years after Arlene's wedding.

- **Better With Age?** The true value of a gift may not be discovered until years after the wedding. Thirty-seven years ago, Carolyn thought she would never use the huge glass bowl she received as a wedding gift. Her mother encouraged her to keep the bowl, which she told Carolyn she would treasure someday. For 20 years it was used to store tennis balls on a back hall table. Then, suddenly, the tennis balls gave way to a beautiful floral arrangement when Carolyn discovered it was a Waterford crystal bowl. It now graces the dining room table, and—to Carolyn—has become the treasure her mother promised it would.

- **A Perfect Match.** The message borne by a gift is often of much greater significance than the object by which it is symbolized. Sheryl remembers a case of tennis balls she and her husband, Dale, received from her old boyfriend. "The gift was special because it said that he was thinking about Dale and me, and something we enjoyed doing together," Sheryl said. She added that the gift was "different, useful, and very personal."

- **Belle of the Ball.** Dale, on the other hand, remembers a basketball emerging from the pile of wedding gifts. "It was the only practical thing in there," he recalls. And, it was also the most sentimental. The gift was from a buddy who helped Dale through a tough time and with whom he formed a mutual bond—on the basketball court.

- **Out Of Sight....** Often-used gifts are constant reminders of the givers. The beautiful silver trays and bowls Ludene and Kent received for their wedding remain in the cabinet awaiting special occasions. It's the everyday items—the Farberware cookware; the big, brown, glazed bean pot; the

Clean Sweep

"At my wedding shower, one of the best gifts I got was also the most practical. A friend filled a sturdy bucket with all kinds of cleaning supplies, sponges, and a mop. It was just what we needed to start housekeeping on our own!"

—Kristen B.

Wedding Presents

Memories

"Among our most memorable wedding presents were graduate school tuition, dinner at our honeymoon destination, and a handmade quilt."

—SHERRI & LARRY

hand-cranked ice cream freezer—and their givers that Ludene and Kent remember most. Each turn of the crank evokes memories of the roommates that gave them the ice cream freezer 28 years ago, and family members are often remembered when the cookware (which Ludene says "has been through everything") is used.

◆ **Light the Candles.** Some gifts serve as reminders of other gifts. Ann's wedding dress has been in mothballs for 17 years, but she remembers the dear friend who made the dress every time she uses the elegant crystal candlesticks the dressmaker gave her for a wedding present.

◆ **Enough is Enough.** Gifts are sometimes remembered because of the sheer number received. When Jack and Reva married 44 years ago, they received enough melamine dish sets to stock their own cupboards and those of several others to whom they gave their remaining bounty as subsequent wedding gifts.

Answers to Frequently-Asked Questions

Ethnic, religious, familial, and regional customs greatly influence wedding gift customs. In our community, for example, wedding receptions tend to be informal, neighborly affairs, most of the guests having known each other for years. Presents received prior to the wedding are often displayed at—and many guests bring gifts to—the reception. In other circles, receptions are catered affairs with assigned seating, to which one would never think of bringing a gift (having sent it to the bride-to-be months previous when the invitation was received). There are, however, some general questions we are often asked.

Wedding Presents

♦ **Question:** Is everyone that receives a wedding announcement or invitation obligated to send a gift?

Answer: No. Gifts are never mandatory, although if you care enough about the wedding couple to attend the wedding reception, you will want to send a gift.

♦ **Question:** If I haven't received a thank-you note for a gift I sent to a wedding couple, should I call them to see if the gift was received?

Answer: No. You should call the delivery service through which you arranged delivery—the store from which you purchased the gift or the post office, for example.

♦ **Question:** How long after a wedding may a wedding gift be sent?

Answer: Some etiquette experts say up to one year, but we can't imagine a gift being refused after the "deadline."

♦ **Question:** Is it proper to print "No gifts, please," or "In lieu of gifts, please send a donation to..." on a wedding announcement?

Answer: Since gifts are not compulsory, it would be presumptuous to dictate your preferences in this manner. However, family members and friends may spread the word by sharing your wishes with those that ask. You can always donate any cash gifts you receive to your favorite charity. In any event, be prepared to graciously receive gifts from those that still wish to give them.

♦ **Question:** How can we let others know we prefer gifts of money?

Answer: Ditto.

Around the World

It is a popular German custom for friends of the bride and groom to smash old pottery at the door or under the window of the bride's house on the eve of the wedding. The custom is called Polterabend and it is thought that the loud noise will avert bad luck. Those invited to Polterabend bring presents for the bride and groom. Other wedding gifts are delivered to the house while the family is at the church ceremony.

Wedding Presents

> **Yours, Mine, Ours?**
>
> Spouses may be "given in marriage," but some property is not. Even in community property states, gifts given to individuals are not considered jointly-held assets.

◆ **Question:** How soon after a wedding should thank-you notes for gifts be sent?

Answer: Handwritten thank-you notes should be sent as soon as possible—but no later than two weeks—after a gift is received. If you will be going on an extended honeymoon, arrange to have cards sent to acknowledge the receipt of gifts and send your handwritten notes as soon as you return.

◆ **Question:** What can we do with wedding gifts that do not reflect our taste or lifestyle?

Answer: Write a sincere note to thank the sender for his or her thoughtfulness and then—depending on the value you place on the relationship versus that which you place on the gift—exchange it, discard it, give it away, or store it for easy retrieval in the event of a visit by the donor.

◆ **Question:** Our marriage was annulled shortly after the wedding. What is the proper thing to do with the wedding presents?

Answer: As in the case of a cancelled wedding, each of you is responsible for returning presents sent by your own friends and family along with a brief note of explanation.

◆ **Question:** Is there an easy and inexpensive way to keep track of wedding presents and thank-you notes?

Answer: Yes. Simply record the following information on a 3x5 index card: the giver's name, address, and telephone number; the item and date it was received; and the date your handwritten thank-you note was sent. The cards are easy to sort as needed and serve as a directory for friends and relatives after the wedding.

Wedding Shower Theme Gifts

Lingerie, kitchen, and linen showers for the bride are giving way to travel, hardware, and electronics showers for the bride and the groom. The next time you're invited to a wedding shower, it just may be a shower for two. The savvy hostess (or host) plans the party according to the couple's lifestyle, possessions, and needs. To aid guests in choosing appropriate gifts, a theme may be chosen to suggest the type of gifts to be given. So instead of working yourself into a lather the next time you host a shower for two, consider these fun themes and gift ideas.

Start a home library for the couple by hosting a "Book Bash." Give a dictionary, a medical handbook, coffee-table books, cookbooks, home repair manuals, audio books, a reading lamp, bookends, and bookplates. (See *Bookworms*.)

Give a "Grill Lover's Gala." Gift possibilities include a favorite outdoor recipe with all the ingredients and equipment needed to prepare it, a barbecue cookbook, grilling accessories (grids and baskets, steak and poultry buttons, kabob skewers, gas match), a portable grill, a hibachi, and a camp stove. (See *Outdoor Cooks*.)

Host a "Home Improvement Happening," with gifts of painting supplies, hand tools, power tools, ladders, a wheelbarrow, a shop vac, sand paper, and a wallpaper stripper. (See *Homeowners*.)

Bid farewell to the traveling duo with a "Bon Voyage Send Off." Pool your resources for a con-

What Gives?

Have you been to any great wedding showers lately? Have you heard of any creative or unusual shower themes? Please write to tell us about them. See page 277.

Wedding Shower Theme Gifts

Shower Power

"I had been in my own apartment seven years before I married and I had all the basic kitchenware. Friends gave me a hostess shower with gifts for entertaining."

—Kalei K.

tribution to the travel fund, or give luggage, a voltage converter, travel guides, luggage tags, a travel iron, a money belt, an electronic word translator, a travel journal, an opisometer (map meter, distance wheel), or a portable water filter. (See *Travelers*.)

Throw a "Home Office Party," with gifts of file folders, organizers, desk lamps, accessories (stapler, hole punch, letter opener, paper weight, tape dispenser), and telephone directories. (See *Home Office Dwellers*.)

Focus on fitness with a "Fitness Fest." Gift ideas include a pedometer, a personal stereo, a fitness magazine subscription, exercise equipment, a club/pool/spa membership, exercise videos, and motivational tapes. (See *Fitness Buffs* and *Runners and Walkers*.)

Have a "Happy Camper" shower. Give such gifts as a two-person tent, a sleeping bag for two, a camp stove, a portable shower, a folding table and chairs, a hammock, back packs, and bug repellent. (See *Campers*.)

Throw a "Tree Trimming" shower. Gift possibilities include Christmas tree lights, a tree stand, a tree skirt, ornaments, a tree topper, garland, beads, and other trimmings. (See *Christmas Presents*.)

Give a "Green Thumbs Up" shower with gifts of house plants, plant containers, a watering can, outdoor shrubs and trees, seeds, bulbs, gardening

Wedding Shower Theme Gifts • Wedding Registries

equipment, landscaping and gardening books, a garden bench, patio furniture, a hose reel, and gardening hats and gloves. (See *Gardeners*.)

Schedule a "Sights and Sounds" shower. Give compact discs, videos, cassette holders, cleaning and maintenance supplies, and gift certificates from an audio/video store or to a movie, concert, or the theater.

Wedding Registries

How do prospective brides and grooms communicate their gift preferences and needs without seeming crass or solicitous? How does a giver avoid errors in taste or duplication when selecting wedding gifts? With just enough distance between giver and recipient, the wedding registry does both. It is an easy and effective way to match the wants and needs of the new couple with a giver's desire to please the recipients.

Traditionally, brides-to-be registered at department stores for china, crystal, silver, and linens. Today, couples register for chain saws and lawn mowers at hardware stores, compact discs and video cassettes at music stores, backpacks and bicycles at sporting goods stores, even limited-edition prints and art books at museum shops. And why not? Today's bride and groom are older and more sophisticated than their counterparts of yesteryear. Some are postponing marriage to complete educations, travel, or pursue careers. Others are going at marriage the second time around. Many have already furnished their homes and set up housekeeping. They know what they want and need—and it may not necessarily be linens and tableware.

House, Farm, and Garden

"In the quiet little valley where we live, engaged couples register at the local implement store. Cash contributions by neighboring townsfolk are used to purchase sundry items for use around the house and farm."

—EMILY B.

Wedding Registries

Where to Register

- ✔ Hardware stores
- ✔ Music stores
- ✔ Travel agencies
- ✔ Sporting goods stores
- ✔ Book stores
- ✔ Computer stores
- ✔ Audio/video stores
- ✔ Camera stores
- ✔ Museums
- ✔ Art galleries
- ✔ Office stores
- ✔ Cookware stores
- ✔ Furniture stores

Some couples consider the exercise of selecting and listing preferences a valuable one. Although she doesn't expect to receive all of the items she and her fiancé listed, one bride-to-be said, "It made us think about the things we needed to set up our new home." She added, "It was also fun to talk about our different tastes and see how things will blend." For example, on the issue of cookware—she prefers Farberware, he prefers Revereware—she conceded to him. "After all," she said, "he will do more cooking than I, at least in the beginning."

Getting the word out on where a couple is registered can be a delicate matter. If more people had been aware that one recent groom and his bride were registered at a local department store, the newlyweds may have received more of what he refers to as the "normal stuff we registered for" rather than the ten crystal serving trays and other "things we won't use until we're 35." Short of printing where a couple is registered on the wedding announcement (a definite no-no) how are friends and family informed? Generally, by word of mouth. When asked, the couple's families and the wedding attendants may pass on this information. In addition, a hostess may make note of the registry on a shower invitation. However, this information is provided only to assist the prospective donors, not to suggest that gifts must be selected from the registry.

The registry makes easy work of giving gifts guaranteed to please the newlyweds. For the giver's convenience, gifts may be ordered over the telephone or purchased in the store. After obtaining a registry list (most of these are now computer printouts), the giver is able to peruse the store to inspect patterns, color schemes, and styles chosen by the couple.

Wedding Registries • Wedding Attendants, Presents to

Opponents of the registry service feel that a list of pre-selected items limits givers in their gift choices and allows the recipients to know the exact amount spent on a gift. A wise couple would list a variety of items in a range of prices. Although china and silver patterns are usually designated by the couple, other selections allow for some discretion by the giver. For example, a giver might select a tablecloth or centerpiece to complement the couple's choice of tableware.

Personal touches in wrapping and embellishing the gift and a thoughtful note reflecting the giver's sentiments can make a gift—even one pre-selected by the bride and groom—memorable and meaningful.

Wedding Attendants, Presents to

The gifts you choose for your wedding attendants should be lasting mementos of your appreciation and friendship. Ideally, each would reflect something special about your relationship to the recipient. Such gifts are usually given to each individual at a convenient time before the wedding, or by the groom at his bachelor dinner and the bride at a luncheon or party for her attendants.

Gift possibilities for the bridesmaids and flower girls include:

- ◆ A piece of jewelry (locket, bracelet, pendant, earrings, pin) engraved with the wedding couple's initials and the date of the wedding

- ◆ A jewelry box, picture frame, photo album, silver compact, bud vase, or hair accessories

- ◆ A framed picture of the wedding party or of the bride and the recipient

Wedding Attendants, Presents To • White Elephant Gifts

Spouse to Spouse

A couple's gifts to each other can range from whimsical to traditional.

✔ Whimsical: a pair of pajamas to share

✔ Romantic: a song composed for your wedding day

✔ Sentimental: a framed picture of your first date

✔ Traditional: an heirloom strand of pearls, a watch, cuff links, a bracelet, or a locket

◆ An engraved silver tray, bowl, trivet, or set of coasters

◆ An item made by the bride—a needlepoint pillow, cross-stitched sampler, watercolor picture, pottery jar or bowl, or leaded glass ornament

Gift possibilities for the groomsmen and ring bearer include:

◆ A piece of jewelry (watch, tie tack, cuff links) engraved with the wedding couple's initials and the date of the wedding

◆ A dresser-top organizer

◆ A framed picture of the wedding party or of the groom and the recipient

◆ Desk accessories, bookends, a pen and pencil set, or a key chain

◆ Sports equipment relevant to the recipient's interests

White Elephant Gifts

Have you been invited to a party at which "white elephant" gifts are to be exchanged? We assume you have no elephants of any color, and are wondering about proper alternative gifts. You've come to the right place.

White elephant gifts are household objects—generally of limited value—you no longer want. This might include the trout-shaped vase your fishing buddy gave you for your wedding, the ceramic paperweight your niece brought you from her last trip abroad, and a previously-read romance novel, but does

White Elephant Gifts

not include unwelcome houseguests or obstreperous house pets.

Unwanted audio or video cassettes, old record albums, and 45s make sound white elephant gifts.

You'll be cookin' with gifts such as unused crockpots, gelatin molds, french fryers, salad spinners, and other kitchen gizmos and gadgets.

Ransack the basement, the attic, or the garage. You're sure to turn up such white elephants as baskets, lawn ornaments, pottery, art work, small furnishings, home accessories, jewelry and fashion accessories, sports equipment, potted plants, books, and magazines.

Here are instructions for a game we have played at several parties where white elephant gifts were exchanged:

- Guests are seated in a circle around a coffee table upon which the wrapped gifts have been placed.

- One of the guests selects and opens a gift and shows it to the rest of the guests.

- Each person, in turn, is given the option of "stealing" any already-opened gift or opening a gift selected from those on the table.

- If a gift is "stolen," the person from whom it is taken opens another gift and the next person in the circle takes a turn until all gifts have been opened.

It sounds harmless enough, but there is inevitably a gift or two everyone wants.

> ### Contents Under Pressure
>
> "What am I supposed to do with junk—like Christmas-tree-shaped candy servers and "decorator" popcorn tins when the goodies are gone? I mean, these are hardly keepsake quality, but I feel that the givers intend for me to keep them."
>
> —GEORGIA G.

Women

Women

"Coming up in this half hour," announced the morning show host, "what every woman wants for Christmas." That got Sherri's attention. But first, the news...the weather...the celebrity interview. Finally, the gifts-every-woman-wants-for-Christmas expert was speaking. For several minutes, she presented a dazzling array of designer silk scarves, luxurious cashmere sweaters, quality costume jewelry, shiny patent leather handbags, and perfumed bath products. Segment over. Coming up next.... That was it?! The host promised gifts *every* woman wanted. Sherri wanted none of them. Where were the state-of-the-art walking shoes, the latest desktop publishing software, and the Mozart compact disc? Missing were the pewter candlestick holders, the garden bench, and the *Wall Street Journal* subscription. She felt as if she had opened someone else's present. How many men had seen the program and been misled into thinking that a shiny purse or gaudy jewelry was just what his significant other needed to complement her Land's End wardrobe? We can tell you precisely how many. Too many! Fortunately for Sherri, Larry was pouring over financial reports at his office when the segment aired.

Give her shares of stock in a company in which she has an interest—a phone company, a department store chain, a cosmetic company, an automobile manufacturer.

In spite of advertising and advice to the contrary, the latest contrivance by the designer of the month is not categorically the perfect gift for every woman.

You might be surprised at how many women tell us they don't care for gifts of flowers. Some regret the money wasted on impermanence. (Try giving an arrangement of dried flowers or a potted flower or

Women

plant.) Others are frustrated by insensitive choices—"Doesn't he know I'm allergic to gladiolas? that I loathe purple?" (Be attentive to her preferences.) Still others are underwhelmed by haphazardly assembled grocery store bouquets. (Give flowers according to their meanings. [See *Flowers and Plants, Gifts of.*])

> ### Present Tense
>
> "Whatever I get her, she's going to bring in experts from all over the country to analyze it."
>
> —JERRY SEINFELD
> ON THE TV SHOW *SEINFELD*

Intimate apparel and other highly personal items—even when relationship-appropriate—should not be given in public gatherings!

Survey Scoop! Women prefer gifts of clothing over jewelry and flowers or plants. According to Gregory Blow, fashion merchandise director for Sears, articles that function as wardrobe extenders make wonderful gifts. Gifts of clothing and accessories a woman may not be able to justify treating herself to

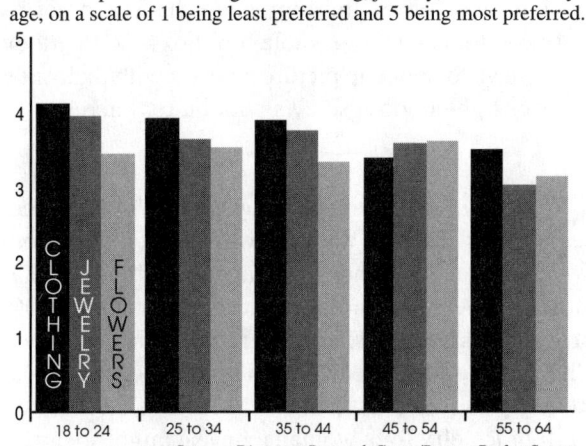

who wants gifts of CLOTHING?

Women's preferences for gifts of clothing, jewelry, and flowers, by age, on a scale of 1 being least preferred and 5 being most preferred.

Source: Discovery Research Group/Present Perfect Survey

Women

It's A Wrap!

Tuck a small present or note in one of the following:

✔ Her pillow case

✔ Her jewelry box

✔ Her handbag

✔ Her gym bag

✔ Her dinner napkin

---

are excellent ways to indulge a recipient. "There are a lot of great items that are just so beautiful or so terrific, people may have guilt pangs about buying them for themselves," says Blow. If hand-knit sweaters and leather coats are not in the gift-giving budget, Blow suggests moderately-priced fashion and costume jewelry, leather gloves, or a knit cap and muffler set as great wardrobe-boosting gifts.

Gifts of fragrance are risky unless you are sure about the recipient's preferences. If perfume is out of your budget, try a soap, lotion, powder, splash, or shampoo in her preferred fragrance. (Hint: The perfume bottles in the medicine cabinet are not always reliable clues. Some may have been there for years...unused.)

For a scent-imental gift, give potpourri or candles in seasonal fragrances. Choose pine or bayberry for Christmas, spice for Thanksgiving, and florals for spring.

Some women might appreciate their own set of basic tools—in a lockable tool box—so that they won't have to pound in picture hangers with their shoe heels or tighten loose screws with butter knives.

Survey Scoop! Diamonds may be a girl's best friend, but the friendship wanes as women get older. From sweet-sixteen diamonds to engagement rings and diamond anniversary bands, gifts account for at least 80% of jewelry store sales, according to Michael Roman, Chairman of the Board for Jewelers of America. Roman points out that a man will spend a lot more on a gift of jewelry for a woman than she might spend on herself. He attributes an increase in sales of low- and

Women

who wants gifts of
JEWELRY?

Women's preferences for gifts of jewelry, by age, on a scale of 1 being least preferred and 5 being most preferred.

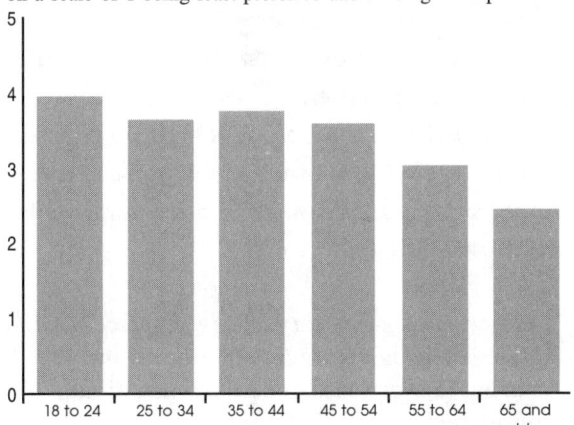

Source: Discovery Research Group/Present Perfect Survey

moderately-priced silver jewelry to the escalating prices of flowers and candy. "People are realizing that for the same money, they can give a gift of jewelry that will last forever," says Roman.

Enroll her in a class she's always wanted to take. Better yet, sign up to take the class with her.

Arrange to have her car washed, waxed, and vacuumed. Some businesses that provide this service will even go to her home or office to do the work.

An AAA membership or a cellular telephone would make a great gift for a woman who commutes to work or chauffeurs children on a regular basis.

Gift with a Bang!

A woman attending one of our seminars said she was probably the only one there to ever receive a gun as a gift from her mate. Her husband liked to hunt. The gift was his way of inviting her along. On their first hunting trip, she shot a deer! After three days of crying, she gave the gun back to her husband, and to this day refuses to accompany him on his hunting trips. (By the way, two other women in the seminar had also received guns as gifts from their husbands!)

Workplace Gift Exchanges

Workplace Gift Exchanges
SEE ALSO *Business Gifts* and *Employee Gifts*

Although many enjoy the exchange of gifts in the workplace, others approach the prospect with apprehension—if not outright dread. In the absence of a well-defined company gift policy, coworkers are left to muddle through gift exchanges year after year or to initiate informal guidelines on their own. To alleviate undue stress, those that wish to participate in gift exchanges in the workplace should decide in advance how they will handle gifts for birthdays, weddings, new babies, hospitalized coworkers, job transfers, promotions, retirements, and various holidays.

Since circumstances vary from workplace to workplace, there is no single solution to the gift dilemma, but in every case, the following points should be considered:

♦ **Participation.** Attitudes on gift exchanges in the workplace vary widely—from those that wish to acknowledge every minor event in their own lives as well as in the lives of others to those that wish to celebrate milestones in their own social circles rather than in work settings. Some may not feel inclined to participate in office gift giving. Others may be happy to contribute to the birthday or wedding gifts of workmates, but wish not have their own birthdays acknowledged. Respect these preferences.

♦ **Contributions.** Determine whether coworkers will be expected to contribute on a monthly, quarterly, semiannual, or annual basis. Or will collections be made as occasions and events arise?

♦ **Administration.** Agree on who will be in charge of collecting and administering the funds. Discuss whether transactions will be handled on a cash basis or if a separate checking account will be set up.

Be Happy

"My sister-in-law has her own way of dealing with the awkwardness of giving gifts to coworkers with whose tastes she is not familiar. She simply tells them that she hopes they will be happy with the gift—and if that means giving it to someone else or putting it in the trash, so be it. And she really means it!"

—SANDI W.

Workplace Gift Exchanges

- **Budget.** Determine how much money will be allocated for each gift or type of gift.

- **Gift Selection.** Decide whether the same predictable gift will be given for each occasion—i.e., flowers for a hospitalized coworker, balloon bouquets for birthday celebrants—or if an effort will be made to customize presents. Will one person be responsible for selecting all gifts, or will gifts be chosen by the coworker(s) who best knows a specific recipient?

The exchange of small presents among coworkers during the holidays is a common practice. However, constraints of time and money leave many wondering how to express good wishes without exhausting holiday resources. Consider these options.

- Draw names and specify a price range for gifts exchanged among coworkers. Many clever and appropriate gifts—scented candles, small boxes of candy, puzzles, picture frames, magazines, and key chains—can be found for under $5.

- Collectively give the *office* a gift—a microwave oven, an espresso maker, a clock, a plant, an accessory for the reception area or another common area. Note: Determine how much each member of the staff is willing to contribute before deciding what to buy.

- As a group, contribute your time or make a donation to a charitable cause or appropriate organization.

- Exchange token gifts (home-baked cookies, tree ornaments, candles) with immediate coworkers.

- Ban all gift exchanges in the office—a drastic, but sometimes warranted measure.

Up The Ladder

"Congratulations!" "You've earned it!" "Welcome to the top." Organizations often reward the newly promoted with higher pay, a corner office, and a key to the executive washroom. You may find the following ideas useful in communicating your best wishes to the rising star.

✔ Give "money-to-burn" fire starters with a note that reads, "With a raise in pay, you'll now have money to burn."

✔ If the recipient wants a new look for the new job, arrange for a makeover or hair styling.

✔ A consultation with a wardrobe or image consultant may also be appropriate.

Workplace Gift Exchanges

How Embarrassing

Giving highly personal, very extravagant, or off-colored gifts in the presence of others may put the recipient in an uncomfortable spot.

Although it is generally not necessary for employees to give gifts to their bosses, there may be circumstances when at least a token gift is warranted. If you work closely with your boss, have worked a long time for him or her, or have become friends with his or her family, you may want to give a gift at Christmas time or for a special birthday. Such gifts should not be too expensive or too personal. Give something for her favorite pet, goodies from your kitchen or garden, or a book relating to one of her interests. If you want to give a gift that would really be appreciated, do your job honestly and well.

Appendix

Personalized Gift Bio Forms

PERSONALIZED GIFT BIO

Name _____
Birthday _____ Birthstone _____ Flower _____
Other Special Dates _____

FAVORITES

Artists/Composers _____
Books/Authors _____
Celebrities _____
Colors _____
Fabrics _____
Fashion Accessories _____
Flowers/Plants _____
Foods/Drinks _____
Fragrances _____
Games _____
Jewelry _____
Magazines/Newspapers _____
Movies/Stars _____
Music/Performers _____
Pets/Animals _____
Places/Vacations _____
Sports/Teams _____
Other _____

SIZES

Women
  Dress _____
  Blouse _____
  Skirt _____
  Jacket _____
  Lingerie _____

Men
  Suit _____
  Shirt _____
  Pants _____

Accessories
  Shoe/Sock _____
  Sweater _____
  Hat _____
  Ring _____
  Belt _____

AFFILIATIONS

Alma Mater/Other Schools _____
Religious/Cultural/Ethnic _____
Civic/Business/Professional _____
Clubs/Teams _____

Personalized Gift Bio (Continued)

PREFERENCES

Prefers Practical or Extravagant Gifts? _____
Clothing Styles _____
Hobbies or Interests _____
Collections _____
Home Furnishings _____

OTHER CONSIDERATIONS

Wants/Needs _____
Dislikes _____
Transitions _____
Restrictions _____
Major Purchases _____

GIFT IDEAS

_____
_____
_____
_____
_____

RECORD OF GIFTS GIVEN

Date	Occasion	Gift	Comments
____	_____	____	_____
____	_____	____	_____
____	_____	____	_____
____	_____	____	_____
____	_____	____	_____

PERSONALIZED GIFT BIO

Name _____
Birthday _____ Birthstone _____ Flower _____
Other Special Dates _____

FAVORITES

Artists/Composers _____
Books/Authors _____
Celebrities _____
Colors _____
Fabrics _____
Fashion Accessories _____
Flowers/Plants _____
Foods/Drinks _____
Fragrances _____
Games _____
Jewelry _____
Magazines/Newspapers _____
Movies/Stars _____
Music/Performers _____
Pets/Animals _____
Places/Vacations _____
Sports/Teams _____
Other _____

SIZES

Women
  Dress _____
  Blouse _____
  Skirt _____
  Jacket _____
  Lingerie _____

Men
  Suit _____
  Shirt _____
  Pants _____

Accessories
  Shoe/Sock _____
  Sweater _____
  Hat _____
  Ring _____
  Belt _____

AFFILIATIONS

Alma Mater/Other Schools _____
Religious/Cultural/Ethnic _____
Civic/Business/Professional _____
Clubs/Teams _____

Personalized Gift Bio (Continued)
PREFERENCES

Prefers Practical or Extravagant Gifts? _____
Clothing Styles _____
Hobbies or Interests _____
Collections _____
Home Furnishings _____

OTHER CONSIDERATIONS

Wants/Needs _____
Dislikes _____
Transitions _____
Restrictions _____
Major Purchases _____

GIFT IDEAS

_____
_____
_____
_____
_____

RECORD OF GIFTS GIVEN

Date	Occasion	Gift	Comments
____	_____	____	_____
____	_____	____	_____
____	_____	____	_____
____	_____	____	_____
____	_____	____	_____

PERSONALIZED GIFT BIO

Name _____
Birthday _____ Birthstone _____ Flower _____
Other Special Dates _____

FAVORITES

Artists/Composers _____
Books/Authors _____
Celebrities _____
Colors _____
Fabrics _____
Fashion Accessories _____
Flowers/Plants _____
Foods/Drinks _____
Fragrances _____
Games _____
Jewelry _____
Magazines/Newspapers _____
Movies/Stars _____
Music/Performers _____
Pets/Animals _____
Places/Vacations _____
Sports/Teams _____
Other _____

SIZES

Women
   Dress _____
   Blouse _____
   Skirt _____
   Jacket _____
   Lingerie _____

Men
   Suit _____
   Shirt _____
   Pants _____

Accessories
   Shoe/Sock _____
   Sweater _____
   Hat _____
   Ring _____
   Belt _____

AFFILIATIONS

Alma Mater/Other Schools _____
Religious/Cultural/Ethnic _____
Civic/Business/Professional _____
Clubs/Teams _____

Personalized Gift Bio (Continued)
PREFERENCES

Prefers Practical or Extravagant Gifts? _____
Clothing Styles _____
Hobbies or Interests _____
Collections _____
Home Furnishings _____

OTHER CONSIDERATIONS

Wants/Needs _____
Dislikes _____
Transitions _____
Restrictions _____
Major Purchases _____

GIFT IDEAS

_____
_____
_____
_____
_____
_____

RECORD OF GIFTS GIVEN

Date	Occasion	Gift	Comments
____	_____	____	_____
____	_____	____	_____
____	_____	____	_____
____	_____	____	_____
____	_____	____	_____

PERSONALIZED GIFT BIO

Name _____
Birthday _____ Birthstone _____ Flower _____
Other Special Dates _____

FAVORITES

Artists/Composers _____
Books/Authors _____
Celebrities _____
Colors _____
Fabrics _____
Fashion Accessories _____
Flowers/Plants _____
Foods/Drinks _____
Fragrances _____
Games _____
Jewelry _____
Magazines/Newspapers _____
Movies/Stars _____
Music/Performers _____
Pets/Animals _____
Places/Vacations _____
Sports/Teams _____
Other _____

SIZES

Women
  Dress _____
  Blouse _____
  Skirt _____
  Jacket _____
  Lingerie _____

Men
  Suit _____
  Shirt _____
  Pants _____

Accessories
  Shoe/Sock _____
  Sweater _____
  Hat _____
  Ring _____
  Belt _____

AFFILIATIONS

Alma Mater/Other Schools _____
Religious/Cultural/Ethnic _____
Civic/Business/Professional _____
Clubs/Teams _____

Present Perfect: The Essential Guide to Gift Giving

Personalized Gift Bio (Continued)
PREFERENCES

Prefers Practical or Extravagant Gifts? _____
Clothing Styles _____
Hobbies or Interests _____
Collections _____
Home Furnishings _____

OTHER CONSIDERATIONS

Wants/Needs _____
Dislikes _____
Transitions _____
Restrictions _____
Major Purchases _____

GIFT IDEAS

_____
_____
_____
_____
_____

RECORD OF GIFTS GIVEN

Date	Occasion	Gift	Comments

PERSONALIZED GIFT BIO

Name _____
Birthday _____ Birthstone _____ Flower _____
Other Special Dates _____

FAVORITES

Artists/Composers _____
Books/Authors _____
Celebrities _____
Colors _____
Fabrics _____
Fashion Accessories _____
Flowers/Plants _____
Foods/Drinks _____
Fragrances _____
Games _____
Jewelry _____
Magazines/Newspapers _____
Movies/Stars _____
Music/Performers _____
Pets/Animals _____
Places/Vacations _____
Sports/Teams _____
Other _____

SIZES

Women
   Dress _____
   Blouse _____
   Skirt _____
   Jacket _____
   Lingerie _____

Men
   Suit _____
   Shirt _____
   Pants _____

Accessories
   Shoe/Sock _____
   Sweater _____
   Hat _____
   Ring _____
   Belt _____

AFFILIATIONS

Alma Mater/Other Schools _____
Religious/Cultural/Ethnic _____
Civic/Business/Professional _____
Clubs/Teams _____

Personalized Gift Bio (Continued)

PREFERENCES

Prefers Practical or Extravagant Gifts? _____
Clothing Styles _____
Hobbies or Interests _____
Collections _____
Home Furnishings _____

OTHER CONSIDERATIONS

Wants/Needs _____
Dislikes _____
Transitions _____
Restrictions _____
Major Purchases _____

GIFT IDEAS

_____
_____
_____
_____
_____

RECORD OF GIFTS GIVEN

Date	Occasion	Gift	Comments

What Gives?

We look forward to your comments about *Present Perfect* and your suggestions for future editions. If you are the first to send an idea used in a future edition of *Present Perfect*, we will send you a free copy of the book. Here are some ideas to get the wheels turning.

◆ Describe your most embarrassing or awkward gift-giving situation.

◆ Share an interesting, romantic, cherished, or memorable gift experience.

◆ Write about interesting gift-giving customs or traditions you practice or of which you are aware.

◆ Send suggestions for interest categories to be included in future editions.

◆ Give your definition of the "perfect gift."

◆ Share an anecdote about how this book helped you find a great gift.

◆ Tell us how you've creatively used the book (other than as a doorstop, as a paperweight, for propping up a projector, or a cure for insomnia.)

Mail correspondence to:

Present Perfect Gift Consultants
P.O. Box 356
Hyde Park, UT 84318

Leave a message and your address on our voice mail at:

801/755-7747

E-mail us at:

athay@cachenet.com

Look for us on the Internet at:

http://www.vpp.com/gift

The Perfect Gift!

Present Perfect makes a great gift. For each copy you would like, send $12.95 (Utah residents add $0.79 per book for sales tax) plus $3.00 shipping and handling to

Mobius Press
P.O. Box 8
Hyde Park, UT 84318

For a one-year subscription to *Gift Rap!*, the bimonthly newsletter of creative giving, send $10 to

Present Perfect Gift Consultants
P.O. Box 356
Hyde Park, UT 84318

For both the book and the newsletter subscription, send $19.95 (Utah residents add $0.79 per order for sales tax) plus $3.00 shipping and handling to Present Perfect Gift Consultants at the above address.

About the Authors

The Athays (Athay rhymes with Kathy) are not your typical book authors. Ironically, each was voted many years ago—at schools over 2,000 miles apart—as "Most Unlikely to Write a Book on Gift Giving." Sherri has spent much of the past decade searching *Forthcoming Books In Print*, half hoping and half fearing that someone else would write the quintessential guide to gift giving. This is not to say the Athays don't take the subject of gift giving seriously, it's just that gift giving can be so much fun, and writing so much work. They attribute their sometimes-quirky prose to sleep deprivation, brain(storm) seizures, and a diet high in who-has-time-to-eat?

Through seminars, consulting, and media, the Athays have addressed the gift concerns of individuals and businesses for the past 12 years. They have researched gift giving from many perspectives: communications, psychology, economics, marketing, sociology, even anthropology. This extensive research includes nationwide polls conducted exclusively for their company, Present Perfect Gift Consultants.

Sherri is founder of Present Perfect Gift Consultants and editor and publisher of *Gift Rap!*, the bimonthly newsletter of creative giving. To the delight of her family (and perhaps a few million other readers), Sherri's articles about gift giving have appeared in magazines, trade publications, and newspapers across the country. Dozens have been distributed by the Los Angeles Times Syndicate. Sherri has also shared gift-giving tips on the radio and television.

Larry has an MBA, with an emphasis in Finance, and a B.A. in Economics—neither of which has anything to do with writing a book about gift giving, but which come in handy in his capacity as consulting director and business manager for Present Perfect Gift Consultants. He also has a Masters of Cliché which is put to good (and bad) use throughout *Present Perfect: The Essential Guide to Gift Giving*. Call it coincidence, call it fate, but the common thread connecting this book to Larry's professional experience in business consulting, management, financial analysis, and real estate development is that business consultants, managers, financial analysts, and developers all give and receive gifts!

The Athays have been married since 1978 and have three children—David, Michael, and Lauren—and a sheepdog named Oreo.